Praise for Mailman

"A coming-of-age (at middle age) story . . . *Mailman* more than delivers."
—*Booklist* (starred review)

"Warm and oddly patriotic . . . [this] perceptive book kept me turning the pages. . . . A working-class hero is something to be."
—Dwight Garner, *The New York Times*

"I needed this reminder that Americans can commit to the greater good, that public servants can be heroes, and that our crazy-quilt culture is a strength, not a weakness. Thank you, Mr. Mailman."
—A.J. Jacobs,
New York Times bestselling author of
The Year of Living Constitutionally

"A highly personal, utterly charming tribute to this American treasure."
—David Von Drehle, *The Washington Post*

"Heartfelt . . . *Mailman* paints a canny portrait of Appalachia, with its insularity, spectral natural beauty, and the flinty resilience that defines its culture."
—*The Atlanta Journal-Constitution*

"A love letter to the Blue Ridge Mountains . . . an indictment of government austerity, and a witness statement attesting to the remarkable and at times ruthless efficiency of one of our oldest federal bureaucracies. Not least, *Mailman* is a lament for the decline of service as an American ideal. . . . [Grant] proves to be a compelling and empathetic guide, observing his country and its citizens, not just himself, with open and unjaded eyes."
—Tyler Austin Harper, *The Atlantic*

"*Mailman* takes readers on a wild ride . . . as Grant pulls back the curtain on the US Postal Service, revealing its foibles and idiosyncrasies alongside its stalwart heart."

—*Southern Review of Books*

"If you've ever fantasized about ditching your corporate job for a quieter life in the country, *Mailman* could be the memoir for you . . . Grant's honesty and humor . . . have me hooked."

—*Garden & Gun*

"An entertaining and illuminating read. . . . Grant is a great storyteller and a wonderful writer—lyrical, descriptive, and honest. He's fervent in his belief that the US Postal Service is necessary, impartial, and downright patriotic."

—Laurie Hertzel, *The Washington Post*

"I loved the swagger of the author's unique, debut voice . . ."

—Lindsay Powers, Amazon;
Amazon Editors' Pick and bestseller

"A charming book that's guaranteed to make you think differently about the USPS."

—*Kirkus Reviews* (starred review)

"*Mailman* pulses with humor and the beauty of simple, everyday courage. In the heart of a small mountain town, Steve Grant's route as a rural mail carrier becomes a journey of personal redemption, of finding purpose and dignity."

—Jonathan Safran Foer,
New York Times bestselling author of
Everything Is Illuminated

“In this good-natured memoir . . . Grant illustrates how the work helped him feel useful to a town he’d left behind and reignited his sense of vitality. This has charm to spare.”

—*Publishers Weekly*

“Funny, honest, and deeply human . . . *Mailman* is a terrific book that offers a revealing perspective on the Postal Service and on whom we are as a nation, examining what we have in common and why it’s so important that we keep talking to one another—not past one another.”

—Michael Smerconish, CNN

Berthe
NEW

MAILMAN

My Wild Ride Delivering the Mail in Appalachia and Finally Finding Home

STEPHEN STARRING GRANT

SIMON & SCHUSTER PAPERBACKS
New York Amsterdam/Antwerp London
Toronto Sydney/Melbourne New Delhi

Simon & Schuster
1230 Avenue of the Americas
New York, NY 10020

Some names and identifying characteristics have been changed and some dialogue has been re-created.

First Simon & Schuster trade paperback edition April 2026

SIMON & SCHUSTER Paperbacks and colophon are registered trademarks of Simon & Schuster, LLC

Interior design by Wendy Blum
Illustrations on pages vi and viii–ix by Mathilda Grant

Manufactured in the United States of America

10 9 8 7 6 5 4 3

Library of Congress Cataloging-in-Publication Data has been applied for.

ISBN 978-1-6680-1804-0
ISBN 978-1-6680-1805-7 (pbk)
ISBN 978-1-6680-1806-4 (ebook)

For Alicia, and all our elusive dreams and schemes

Bertha's Clams

AUTHOR'S NOTE

THIS IS A MEMOIR. A WORK OF MEMORY.

The events and personalities in this story are real, as near as I can remember. I have changed the names of some people because it is not my intention to get anyone in trouble at work. These are my memories and my thoughts. I am not a spokesman for the United States Postal Service, and this manuscript was not reviewed by any representative of that organization, so I cannot and do not speak for them in any official capacity. I was about as far down the chain of command as you can get in the USPS, Rural Carrier Associate, so please accept my views from the limited perspective that they offer.

My job was to deliver the mail, and I did it the best I could. When I didn't follow regulations, I always followed what I believed to be the spirit of the job and of my oath of office. If it was possible, given my very limited abilities as a letter carrier, I delivered every letter, every flat, every parcel, every day. My charge was to protect the sanctity and security of the mail, and I did that. My official duty was to provide universal service to the citizens on my route, and to the best of my ability and judgment, that's what I did.

So, with my imperfect memory, biases, the warpage of personality, my confabulatory writer's memory, and a healthy dose of hot air from the Starring side of my family, that's what I'm going to try to do here: tell the story of my time as a mailman in Blacksburg, Virginia, and tell it as best I can.

Contents may have settled during shipping.

CONTENTS

MAILMAN

OVERTURE

Your Tax Dollars at Work

I'M BLASTING MY WAY UP THE HOLLOW, HAULING ASS up the dry dirt road past the sign that reads END STATE MAINTENANCE, driving a 2001 Ford Explorer from the right-hand seat, left leg stretched across the space where the center console was torn out to allow easy access to the pedals, left arm ape-hanging across to the steering wheel with its sloppy, slippery linkage, the leaking power-steering fluid smelling like industrial aromatherapy. Here, on the northern side of the draw, it is a land of permanent shade. All the trees are scrub pine, the road narrow enough that I can reach out and feel my fingertips get whipped by the needles as I'm driving past.

This isn't some purpose-built vehicle. I'm driving a Plain Jane, bone-stock, factory-basic, left-hand-drive car. But for slinging mail on backroads, it is hard to beat the Explorer. "Ford tough," this rusty beast has survived long beyond the planned obsolescence built into it by the engineers in Detroit because this thing has got a soul, man, Made-in-America magic that is still pulsing through it nineteen hard years after it rolled off the assembly line in Louisville, Kentucky.

I'm driving as fast as this old crate will stick to the road, slipping in and out of the coefficient of friction and adjusting my trajectory with a little Kentucky windage at the steering wheel because I am behind schedule and this route is almost sixty miles long, and besides, this is where Google Girl says I need to be, headed toward the destination of the next parcel, and I would follow Google Girl's voice to the gates of hell like she was Satan's sweetheart because all summer long I've either been following her, the river, or the passage of the sun across the sky because without something to follow in this time-warp wilderness I'm just lost. Not spatially lost. Geographically, I know exactly where I am. I'm where I grew up, in the hardwood, sedimentary Blue Ridge Mountains, the heart of the Appalachians, the place I thought was home. What I'm feeling is a spiritual disorientation, lost in the sense that I don't know what I'm doing, lost in confronting the reality of being back in my hometown at fifty years of age, delivering the mail. When you're delivering the mail as a functionary of the US government during a pandemic, the countryside and the nation itself become something alien and distant. It's all bandit country. Down here at the level of individual mailboxes, time works differently, flattening a finite number of letters and packages and stretching them out over hours, months, and years, spreading the time thinner and thinner, approaching limit zero like a calculus problem, or, as my granny used to say, "too much bread and not enough butter." What time is it? What day is it? It's parcel time, the only kind of time that matters anymore, and I've got a delivery to make, one that I've been waiting on since I left the post office that morning.

In the back is a long cardboard box, over three feet long and about six inches deep. The return address reads "MUSASHI KATANA, LITTLE ROCK, AR."

I didn't watch Kurosawa films over and over when I was a kid to not know what those words mean. There is a goddamned sword in that box. And the weird sisters of the United States Postal Service have sent me here to deliver it.

In a clearing at the end of the dirt driveway was a single-wide trailer with a small deck out front. I unassed the Explorer and was carrying the box toward the trailer with both hands, supporting it from beneath, like the guy with a sword on a pillow processing up to the queen in Westminster Abbey.

Through the sliding-glass front door of the trailer, I could see into the living room, a space dominated by a TV so big that it partially blocked the hallway into the bedroom in back. The man who lived here had to lift his hands up over his head and slide crabwise through the gap, a move he must have made dozens of times a day, which I suppose says a lot about the kind of trade-offs people are willing to make for picture quality in a TV set. In a world of compromise, there are some things you just don't sacrifice.

The guy pulled open the sliding-glass door and jogged out. He was lean, in a baggy blue T-shirt, shorts, and flip-flops, with long, crow-black hair. A Buck folding knife in a leather snap sheath on his belt. Another guy like me who never quite feels dressed in the morning without a belt and a knife.

When he saw the box I was carrying, he stopped.

"Oh, goddamn."

Sometimes you get the feeling that you have been brought somewhere to do a thing by powers larger than yourself.

"Hey, man, I think this is your sword," I said. I could feel myself smiling.

Now he started to smile.

"Oh, goddamn!"

"What did you get? A Katana? A Nodashi?" I asked.

That got me an appreciating look. His tone became serious.

"No, man, nothing Japanese. European. Two-handed sword. I got that second pandemic check and I knew I was finally going to get the motherfucker. You want to see it?"

"Hell yes, I want to see it!" Because I could feel it now too.

He took the box from my arms and laid it in the grass, as gently as if it were a sleeping child.

Have you ever been there when someone has gotten exactly what they want? Something that they have wanted for as long as they could remember? Something maybe useless and yet charged with mythic power, an idea that had been carried around for years and was now landing in reality as three long feet of tempered steel?

He had his pocketknife out in a flash and cut through the packing tape. Pulled back the thin layer of interior foam. Resting in a cardboard cradle was a two-handed sword in a black leather scabbard. He took the sword's grip in his right hand, the scabbard in his left, and in a single smooth stroke loosed the blade, which, as if someone had dubbed in a sound effect, rang like singing silver in the afternoon sun.

"Whoo! Yeah! This is Anduril, Flame of the West!"

"Reforged from the shards of Narsil by the elves of Rivendell."

We looked at each other.

"Yeah, man. The blade that smote Sauron."

It was one of the most intimate moments I've ever had with a stranger. We weren't up a hollow deep in the Blue Ridge Mountains, lost in the radio hole at the center of one of the longest rural routes in the Blacksburg, Virginia, post office. We were in the middle of a myth, a molten dream of a place where great deeds, brave words, and the right sword in the right hand could make a broken world whole again.

Honestly, I don't think I've ever seen my tax dollars put to better use.

I want to clarify an important point. Your tax dollars did not pay for the USPS to deliver this sword. The retailer did, or maybe the customer if he was charged an extra thirty dollars for shipping. The USPS does not take a dime of taxpayer money. Stamps cover most of the operating expenses, along with pricier shipping services like Priority Mail and Registered Mail. Congress pays the USPS about $50 million a year to cover free voting by mail for US citizens living abroad, and free mailing privileges for blind Americans. But those are payments; the Congress is just another customer. The USPS is a universal service, the largest postal system on the planet, invisible infrastructure like the Federal Aviation Administration's air traffic control system or the Food and Drug Administration's food safety programs. Except that the United States Postal Service pays for itself.

The US Treasury paid for the sword.

Twenty twenty was a weird time to be working for the federal government in rural Virginia. I was alive in a place where the possibilities of a job taken in desperation played out against a wild, mutating, horrific, chaotic, insulting, stultifying, dangerous, edifying, and sometimes transcendent experience of dealing with my fellow Americans during a national emergency. There were days I felt like I was part of a public service announcement, where the simple appearance of someone with the mail, at the right time and in the right place, was evidence that the American people had not been abandoned, that help was coming, and that at the end of the last mile that great machine that is the US government was me, here in your yard, with your medications, your Social Security check, or a letter from a loved one.

I got to be there, to put a sword in this man's hand at this particular moment in time—the lockdown, a contested election, an attack on the US Capitol that was half insurrection, half comic-book convention, a day-trader takedown of Wall Street, and a web of conspiracy theories around germ warfare and Russian intelligence operations—a time of bare grocery store shelves and day drinking and delivered-to-your-door marijuana and sex toys, all of it unspooling in a media environment that fed on itself like a snake eating its own tail, shrouded in magical thinking and dread. In the crabgrass and broken-glass front lawn of this single-wide aluminum-sided trailer, a perfect stranger and I reenacted the moment where Elrond calls on Aragon to stop dicking around, put aside the Ranger, and become the man he was meant to be.

I get it. We all want a sense of purpose. I could blow a bunch of smoke up my own ass about how I was there out of a sense of civic duty, that I was doing the Lord's work, placed here by the hand of providence, by Whitmanian democratic impulse, by the manifest will of the American people, by the authority of the postmaster general. And I can say with a straight face that all those things were true. I can also say I was often miserable during the year I spent delivering the mail, and at times in grave danger to my physical and mental health, and coping nearly every day with tedium that could break the strongest among us. But I would be lying if I didn't confess that I perversely enjoyed the endurance-sport aspect of it, the voluntary suffering. And a lot of the time it was just fucking fun. It was like being back in the Scouts again. Doing a good turn daily. It was the deepest trip into the heart of the American experience that I have ever had the grace to take. It expanded my soul.

This is a story about carrying the mail at a time I was carrying a lot more than just the mail. A story about how the year I spent as a rural-route mail carrier saved my life, taught me who I was, and educated me deeply about a country I had lost touch with.

I fell back in love with America during that year. I feared for her and prayed for her, even though prior to carrying the mail, I did not spend much time in prayer. But here in my hometown, where I grew up, in midlife I found myself working a different kind of job, and I became a different kind of person.

I was the guy with the goods, and I carried the candy and the respirators and the dog food and the lube and the heirloom tomato seeds, the hot rod magazines, the handwritten pleas from incarcerated uncles, the scientific journals, tabloid-size book reviews, model train sets, illustrated children's Bibles, the hand-painted postcards from artistic cousins and estranged girlfriends. The story I told myself was this: I had joined a brotherhood that stretches back to Benjamin Franklin, to men on horseback and in biplanes. I had become a flag-wearing, sworn federal officer in a position of trust, the duly appointed agent of the United States government in a time of national crisis, the dedicated and beloved civil servant of the people.

I was the goddamned mailman.

Chapter One

FUCK CITY

I WAS LAID OFF FROM MY CONSULTING GIG. THAT'S how my pandemic began.

It was early March in 2020. I was in the Charlotte, North Carolina, airport, rushing to make my flight up to New York City, where the agency I worked for was headquartered out of SoHo. Plan Z was a boutique marketing consultancy—one part startup, one part ad agency, and the rest a sort of experimental decentralized phantom equity holding company. If you think that's tough to get your head wrapped around, the market agreed.

I was head of strategy and I was flying up because we were kicking off a big project with a new client, a somewhat secretive law firm that specialized in getting rich people their money back when the counterparty (corporations, foreign governments, other rich people) was hiding overseas. The client wanted a marketing plan to become the go-to firm for helping the ultrarich, only the ultrarich.

It was possible to make it from Blacksburg, a tiny college town in the Blue Ridge Mountains of western Virginia, to New York for a same-day meeting, but doing so was an obscure Olympic sport similar to the pentathlon. The consultant's version involved a pickup truck, sprinting, flying, and a cab ride. If you caught the earliest plane out of Roanoke to

Charlotte and made the connection to New York's LaGuardia Airport, you could wake up in the cold, foggy, blue-black of predawn Appalachia and find yourself sitting in a glass conference room with a view of anonymous office buildings in midtown Manhattan by late morning.

This morning, my pentathlon was canceled midrace. In Charlotte, I got a call that the meeting was off, postponed indefinitely. The work was on hold because the law firm was "buttoning up." The client had a number of ex-military folks working for them, and "buttoning up" is army slang for dropping down into an armored vehicle, like a tank, and closing the hatches behind you. They were going into a defensive posture because of what the gate agent called "this virus thing." "Everybody is turning around and flying home, hon."

Waiting for my flight back in a couple of hours' time, I noticed the business lounge nearly empty. The whole place was library quiet. It was a weird, haunted-house feeling, like I was in the establishing shot of a science fiction film.

That was when I got the whim whams. A deep, animal sensation—full body, with my frontal lobes racing to catch up. It was a feeling I would come to recognize intimately over the year to come. The ground moving under my feet, the train switching tracks from one timeline to another, the world moving from normal to flat-out fucking weird. You didn't need to be an epidemiologist or government contingency planner to know that we were all going someplace new, probably bad.

It is easy to forget sometimes how afraid everyone was in that moment. Nobody had any faith that our government or the world's governments would be able to coordinate a response. So Big Business did the only sensible thing—it turtled. Across the business world, leadership teams cut spending and stockpiled cash while their firms developed a response. This had all the predictable second-order effects. Any business on thin margins, not just my experimental ad agency but neighborhood restaurants, art house movie theaters, bookstores—they all choked to death.

I was still waiting for my flight home when the call from my boss came. "Steve," he said, "we're both adults, so I don't need to belabor this."

He was a gentleman and a pro about it, like he always was. I'd had the pleasure of working with him for years, and now that was over.

At four that morning, I had been employed. Now I was not.

The central concourse of the Charlotte airport is acoustically hot, typically 90 decibels of ADHD torture chamber. When I sat down in one of the airport's signature white rocking chairs that line the big glass wall overlooking the tarmac, it was so quiet I could have been on the front porch of a remote mountain cabin.

I knew I needed to tell my wife, Alicia, that I'd been laid off but I didn't see the point of sharing this over the phone. I wanted to savor this in-between time, when I was the only one in my family who knew I'd been let go again. I walked over to the Burger King counter, bought a Whopper and onion rings, and ate the food slowly while I rocked in a wooden chair next to the people-mover belt. For years I would eat a Big Mac after a successful job interview to seal in the good luck. Or as a ritual sacrifice to ward off evil after a layoff. Stuck with a Whopper, it felt like some cosmic signal that my luck had truly run out.

My work in the two decades before the pandemic had a bunch of names—Brand Strategist, Marketing Consultant, Consumer Psychologist, the sort of psychologist that, instead of helping you feel better about yourself, helps corporations feel better about how to sell you things. In late capitalism, we call this "creating demand." It was not a skill set that was widely recognized and not particularly practical outside of a very narrow context.

I wasn't a cardiologist or a plumber with a concrete, certified set of skills. I did not hold an honorific like doctor or professor. No rank like captain or major. I was the grease in the global capitalist machine. Because the worst-kept secret in corporate America is that the black arts of marketing work. I had been a strategist for some of the biggest corporations in the world, helping the glass-tower crowd understand how "regular people" make the wheels on the bus go round and round, which is good-paying work as long as corporate America is buying. But marketing is notorious for being the canary in the coal mine of corporate spending. Just a few years earlier, my behavioral economics lab at Prudential was shut down during a corporate reorg. It had taken months to get a new job, and that was with a party-time economy. Sitting in that rocking chair in the neutron-bomb-empty airport, I could see how much worse this situation was. Getting a new marketing job was going to be a near impossibility for the foreseeable future. It was certainly never going to happen before my health insurance ran out in a couple of weeks.

Which was a problem. Because I had cancer.

I had only known about the cancer for a couple of months. My father had survived prostate cancer, and his brother, my uncle Rich, had survived it as well. So I hadn't been too worried, honestly. At least that was the story I was telling myself. My urologist told me the malignancy was contained inside the prostate. The tissues uncovered in the biopsy were submillimetric, too small for the MRI to detect. My Gleason value, a scoring system for classifying the aggression and danger of the cancer, was low. My cancer was as benign as cancer gets. But what had seemed manageable—treatable—now loomed as an existential issue. I was about to become one of the undoctored in America while I knowingly carried a disease that could kill me. The world was going someplace weird. And I was sitting in a white rocking chair in an abandoned airport, eating a Whopper with a biological time bomb strapped to my nuts.

I was a husband and a father of two teenage girls, and everybody in our big modernist house up on Brush Mountain in Blacksburg was counting on me to keep them in the upper middle class because I lived in a house full of artists, deep feelers, and dreamers who I couldn't bear realizing how precarious our situation had become. Up there on Brush Mountain, our glass-walled house with the art on the walls and the piano in the library was a bubble where people painted, played music, studied, and wrote. Where people felt their feelings. A gentle place where people kept journals, knit sweaters, and ate home-cooked meals.

But I knew where I was right now, and it was not that gentle place.

My old man had a name for it. Fuck City.

Fuck City is that in-between place, between where I was supposed to go and where I actually was. In between jobs. In between knowing what was going on and having no idea at all. Having wandered into a career and gotten used to a version of myself—not my "authentic self," whoever the fuck that is, but a version of myself I could live with—and now wondering, if I didn't have this job, who was I? (My intrusive thoughts were very quick to supply an answer: "You're an unemployed loser, that's who.") Of suddenly knowing with cast-iron certainty that the world was about to go batshit crazy, that the order of the things that came before was just a set of norms, a consensual illusion, a bunch of made-up shit. That the "real world" is as arbitrary as a playground game because that's all late capitalism ever was, just a game, a game that I'd played pretty well until I was told to take my toys and go home. Yeah, yeah, the VUCA world—volatile, uncertain, complex, and ambiguous. It's one thing to use that term in a PowerPoint presentation about consumer attitudes, but something else to be feeling it down in your guts.

The whole world was now Fuck City.

What the fuck was I going to do?

Chapter Two

TWO FOUR ZERO SIX ZERO

THE UNITED STATES POSTAL SERVICE SEES BLACKSburg as zip code 24060, operating out of the Main Post Office or MPO, on University Boulevard, with subsidiary post offices downtown on Main Street and in McCoy. When I was a kid, the downtown branch was the only one, built in 1935 as part of the New Deal, a humble but proud brick building with high arched windows that evoked the architecture of Colonial Williamsburg. The zip code is composed of thirty-one carrier routes, covering 23,645 delivery addresses—homes, apartment blocks, businesses, and laboratories. Schools and doctors' offices. Churches, taxidermists, farms, machine shops, rock quarries, a country club, and an airport with a single 5,500-foot-long runway they've been expanding for years to make it long enough to accommodate a 737 and spare the football team the forty-five-minute drive to Roanoke. Hokie football, the state religion of southwestern Virginia.

When old high school classmates saw on LinkedIn I had moved back in 2011, they all wrote the same thing: "A real job and living in Blacksburg! That's the dream." There is something dreamlike about it, that's for sure, a departure from the usual professor's-kid narrative of going off to college in a big city and never coming back. But leaving had always been my dream. I went to college in North Carolina, graduated, and moved to Los Angeles and then London and then New York. I liked having the land mass of North America—maybe even an ocean—between home and me. And then, around forty, I'd started longing for those mountains.

Blacksburg is "The Cambridge of Appalachians"—a college town of 44,000 of whom over 25,000 are students. It's a company town, and the company is the Virginia Polytechnic Institute and State University, but nobody calls it that. Everyone calls it Virginia Tech. Even the university now calls itself Virginia Tech in official communications. Its mascot is the "Hokie," a wild turkey. It's a big university in a small place, an R1 research institution whose primary product is highly educated skilled labor, a STEM powerhouse that is often ranked with Stanford and MIT. It's forty minutes from the West Virginia border, tucked down in the southwestern corner of the state, far from DC and Richmond, far from everything, really.

Except the mountains. Mountains that shimmer from an almost radiant hardwood green in the noonday sun to a purple-blue as dusk comes on. The range is the Appalachians, the spine of the East Coast. Our specific geology is Valley and Ridge, long limestone-bedded valleys with rich bottomland and rugged sandstone ridgelines, where sometimes the trails weaving between the trees will pool out into beach sand because that's what these mountaintops are. Beach sand from three hundred million years ago. The mountains are not distinct peaks, but long ridges that can span multiple counties, punctuated with knolls and saddles. Brush Mountain, where I live, sprawls some twenty miles from the upper branch of Craig Creek in the northeast down to where Poverty Creek cuts off the southwestern end of the mountain at Poverty Gap. Blacksburg is hemmed in by this geology on all sides. I've seen the Alps, the Sierras, the Rockies, the Chugach, and the Sangre de Cristos, but to me the Appalachians of Virginia are the most beautiful mountains in the world. These mountains are old. Their formation began half a billion years ago, the first mountains of a young and angry Earth, now worn down by weather and time. They have a stillness to them, and if you can pause and feel it, you can share in some of that peace.

Blacksburg feels like a mountain town. You can be fly-fishing in twenty minutes on water that folks book vacations to fish. You can wear fleece and boots to the office, and nobody cares, because that's what everyone is wearing. The mountains bring mountain weather—a temperate climate, all four seasons. Summers are cool by southern standards. Winters can be searingly cold, but it's been years since the town's gotten the blizzards I remember from my childhood.

I've always considered myself a son of Blacksburg. I still carry a pocketknife, just like I have since I was eight years old. If given the chance, I'll dress more like I'm about to go fishing than to head into the office. But I'm not a native. I wasn't born here. I was born in New Orleans, where my mother's family is from. My dad, a biomedical engineer, is from West Virginia, where the Grants moved from Scotland in 1780 to make window glass. He escaped to Louisiana by volunteering to help build an amines production plant for Union Carbide. After medical school at Tulane and a stint with Dupont, Dad started as a professor at Tech in Engineering Science and Mechanics, teaching statics and dynamics, the fundamental physics of all engineering. It had been his dream to teach, but also to return to the mountains. Once I admitted it to myself, I realized that was my dream too. It surprised me at first, having been so grateful to escape this place as a young man. But the Grants had lived in these mountains for over two hundred and fifty years. Why wouldn't I long to go home?

As a kid, we were taught to think of Blacksburg as the far western outpost of the Commonwealth of Virginia (never a mere state), to take pride in our civilizing role on the eastern edge of the mountains. To take pride in Virginia, too, "The First Colony," "the Mother of Presidents," and *Primus*

Inter Pares, the first among equals of the original thirteen. This Virginian self-regard—what Thomas Jefferson called "a mountain of conceit," still strong after four hundred years—drives my North Carolinian wife crazy. But like me, my daughters have been brought up on it as mother's milk from the bare-breasted Amazon on the Commonwealth's flag.

Blacksburg is not immune to history or tragedy. It has layers of human geology and change. The college campus is built on land once owned by William Preston, who served in the Confederate congress. And the campus has two different memorials to two different massacres—one by Shawnee Indians, one by a school shooter—separated by about a third of a mile and 252 years. But my memory of Blacksburg when I'd think about moving back was like a Norman Rockwell town, with a drugstore and movie theaters, arcades and outdoor supply stores, a town hall, dentist and doctors' offices, and the rest of the model train set of an American Main Street. "Downtown," was where the three arcades, the donut shop, and the used bookstores were. I could ride my bike off the mountain or hitch and spend the day there with my friends. After school I would walk from Blacksburg Middle School to Newman Library on campus, where I was supposed to be doing homework, but mostly just read books at random or watched videos in the A/V lab. Then I'd walk over to Dad's office in Norris Hall and get a ride back up the mountain.

I wanted that kind of childhood for my girls, Mathilda and Walker, then five and three. Alicia and I talked it over at the kitchen table in our apartment in Fort Greene, Brooklyn. I was making the most money I had ever brought in, and it still wasn't enough to buy a home in New York City. We could become homeowners if we moved. Every dollar went further in Blacksburg. We could buy cars, drive to the grocery store. Our kids could play in the woods and a yard and go to some of the best schools in the country, paid for by our taxes. Blacksburg has been rated the most "economically equal" town in Virginia. The rich aren't too rich, because if you had real money you'd live someplace else. And the poor aren't too poor, because the influx of outside cash provides too many good jobs (facilities at Tech, advanced manufacturing in the industrial park). It's as middle-class a place as there is left in America, and we wanted to give the girls a picture of what a more equitable country might look like.

And my parents still lived in town. My girls could get to know, really know, their grandparents. My mother's mother, Granny, had lived with us until she passed my senior year of high school, and her love was foundational in my life. Sometimes she would say out of the blue, "Stephen, you are a fine fellow and I love you so much." Without her open, unconditional love, I would have been a very different person, harder and colder. I wanted that love for the girls.

When we first moved back to Blacksburg, most people would ask me, "What department are you with?" instead of "What do you do for a living?" I had to explain that I was a marketing consultant, working remotely before that was a thing. Still, I did eventually teach consumer behavior at the business school. It was something I used to dream about when I was in undergrad, Dad and I teaching together. Not the same course, but just professors at the same time, same place. I had imagined a feature in the *Roanoke Times. Look at this,* people would say. *They must be so close, the family business. Maybe they share an office*?

When I brought it up to him, how wild that we were both professors at Tech, he didn't seem too impressed. "I'm an emeritus teaching statics, and you're just an adjunct. Not even a real professor."

"Well," I said, "I thought it was cool."

Mom had been a scientist, too, a microbiologist. I'm the oldest of three brothers, and Mom's theory was that what was "wrong" with David and me is that our uterine environments were based on New Orleans tapwater. "New Orleans is downstream of everything," she'd say. "It's like the nation's drain. Anything they dumped into that river wound up in that drinking water. And it was fluoridated." She would share this idea every single time the subject of drinking water came up. Mom's job was in testing drinking water quality, so it came up a lot more frequently than you might think.

She put John, our youngest brother, in a different category. John's uterine environment was composed of Connecticut well water, from Dad's stint working in the Dupont labs there. The water was incredibly pure, deposited into a limestone aquifer during the last ice age. Dave and I are redheaded and hot-tempered. John runs cooler, is about six feet six, and has worked in the nonprofit sector for the last couple of decades.

So that was one reason the reality of going home didn't live up to the fantasy. Mom and Dad were wonderful grandparents, with reserves of patience, love, and fun they rarely displayed when I was growing up. Dad fixed broken toys and made up voices for the deer in the yard. Mom was always cooking breakfast, picking the girls up from school, sneaking them off to McDonald's. But my hopes of closing the distance with Dad, the big Appalachian mystery in the heart of the Valley and Ridge? That Mom and I might arrive at some new mutual understanding? No. That had never entered any conscious calculation on my part.

And twenty-five years had changed Blacksburg too. To touring parents from New Jersey, it must still look quaint—small brick homes, horse pasture, no Whole Foods, no Trader Joe's. But real estate conglomerates have bought up the downtown's commercial and residential property, replacing one of a kind restaurants with generic bars and sub shops, and erecting massive student apartment complexes that were torn down and rebuilt every fifteen years, with each rebuild growing ever higher, ever closer to the highway. Blacksburg was once so rural that in the 1980s, the vice principal of Blacksburg High would issue dire threats over absenteeism during the first week of open season for deer, and yet when November rolled around, more than half of the male student population would evaporate into the hills. Since then, the gap between Townies and Gownies has grown into the respective groups seeming to inhabit totally separate realities. The school board has become a flashpoint for culture war. After Trump's 2016 election, there were suddenly Confederate flags everywhere, something I'd never seen shown openly as a kid. Blacksburg was experiencing the same tensions as the rest of the country, except that the Blue and the Red were living right next to each other. And rather than seeing the place as a living laboratory of how the political divide might be bridged, it was as if we were all better off if we just pretended the other side didn't exist.

So while I'd bought a home, the fact was that I didn't feel at home here. I slipped into the mountains like an old pair of boots, but the town was something else, a formerly familiar place where I now felt like a stranger. But there was a living laboratory in Blacksburg, one where a real experiment in us actually living together was happening every day. I just needed to lose my job in order to find it.

Chapter Three

MOTIVATED REASONING

RURAL CARRIER ASSOCIATE—
USPS Cave Spring, VA. Rural Carrier Associate (RCA)

In this role you deliver and collect packages along routes in rural areas during weekdays, weekends, and holidays. Only one day a week is guaranteed. You also provide a variety of services to customers along your assigned route. You may be required to use a personal vehicle if a postal vehicle is not provided. As an RCA you are eligible to receive health benefits and promotion to a career opportunity. This position is ideal for candidates who enjoy staying active and working independently outdoors with occasional customer service interactions.

TO GET MY PANDEMIC BENEFITS CHECK, I HAD TO apply for unemployment. Every week I would get on the Virginia Employment Commission website, find anything I was even remotely qualified for, apply, and then get my check. I can tell you that those checks made a big difference in our lives. Which is good, because the jobs I'd find myself picking were almost all in Northern Virginia, with the rest in Richmond, and there was never a snowball's chance of me getting any of them. They all seemed to be defense industry work, with opaque titles like *Configuration Matrix Controller III*. Locally, there was nothing. Except for the letter carrier job—and it came with health care on day one.

The pay cut was eye-watering. I hadn't worked a job at that wage level since my early twenties. But in other respects, the RCA role seemed perfect. It had health care and the position was only guaranteed for one day a week, like the Postal Service National Guard, so I could use the rest of the time to find something better. I had my truck and would definitely enjoy working outdoors for a change—and independently. Cave Spring was a little over forty minutes away on the outskirts of Roanoke, which wasn't great. But one day a week? How bad could it be?

The thing about the internet is that it shortens the distance between impulse and action, which may not be the best thing for someone with impulse control issues. Before I knew it, I was filling in my name and address and something like my CV and being told I was going to be given some aptitude and psychological testing right then and there. I would later learn that this was the infamous USPS 474 Virtual Entry Assessment. On the r/USPS subreddit there were scores of entries about people who had applied but flunked this test. I could see why.

You see a coworker. They are struggling with a task. You are on your way to complete something, and your supervisor has told you it needs to be done immediately. The coworker is crying and very upset. What do you do?

A. Stop what you are doing and assist the coworker.
B. Ignore the coworker and carry on with your task.
C. Bring in other coworkers to assist, then continue with your task.
D. Tell the coworker that they should see the supervisor.

I chose D.

The question seemed like a hypothetical. But it wasn't. Yes, there is a lot of crying at the post office.

Alicia has always been something of a strange fit for Blacksburg. Petite and sophisticated with cosmopolitan style, she not only gave off a "not from around here" vibe, but something more like "not from America." Her striking features are right at home in Spain or France. When we've been in Europe, everyone wonders *What is this beautiful woman of ours doing with that giant, pale Yank*?

Alicia and I have the habit of doing our family strategy sessions walking by the fire road that runs along the ridge of Brush Mountain, the boundary between private property to the south and the 1.8 million acres of the Jefferson National Forest to the north. For private, adult-to-adult discussion, our home's open floor plan is a disaster. There are only two options: talk sitting in the bathtub or take the conversation outside.

"So I think I found a job that offers health care, with the Postal Service," I said.

"The Postal Service is hiring marketing people?"

"No."

"Then who are they hiring?"

"Letter carriers." I assured her that since it was just one day a week, I would keep looking for other jobs the rest of the time.

"What does it make?" she asked.

"Eighteen fifty an hour."

"That's nothing!"

"We need health care in two weeks. Let's address the immediate problem."

Alicia was thinking.

"It's one day a week," I said again.

"This sounds like a hobby. We need real income." Alicia had worked as a film producer and graphic designer, but for the last few years I was the primary breadwinner.

"I know that. Believe me, I know that. There is just nothing out there. Nothing." I felt like I was apologizing for Blacksburg, for all of southwestern Virginia, for there being not one local job, skilled or unskilled out here that paid a living wage, at least one I was qualified for and who was hiring right now. I had spoken with the head of the Marketing department at Tech's business school, but there was a hiring freeze. Nothing would be possible for a year. Maybe people like us just weren't meant to live here. Moving here had always been a gamble, and now I seemed to have lost the bet. I was working hard to hide my desperation, to sound positive.

Silence. She was crunching numbers in her head.

"Listen, I don't want to be dramatic, but I think we have to consider how bad things might get."

"Don't pitch me," she said.

Alicia was right to be wary. My mother's side of the family, the Starrings, had made their way in the world as wildly gifted salesmen. They had made mountains of money selling cars, x-ray machines, horses, and gas pipeline equipment. I was lucky enough to have caught just a fraction of this ability. But of all the people I was good at selling ideas to, my best prospect was always Steve. The wilder the scheme, the more dubious the idea, the murkier the risks, the better I became at selling myself. It wasn't rational, it was motivated reasoning, and my motivations were the danger. Curiosity, escape from boredom, spite, the imp of the perverse. These had reliably gotten me in trouble over the years. This was how I once wound up sixty feet underwater using homemade dive equipment or moving us back to the sticks.

"I think this pandemic thing, it could go on for a long time," I said. "The normal economy might collapse. Being attached to the federal government might not be a bad thing."

"What are you not telling me?" Alicia asked.

"I'm telling you everything I know!"

"It's just that you are really excited about this. You've got that look. Is this job safe? Be honest."

"We get two weeks of training, and it's supposed to be a safe job." The truth was I had no idea how safe the job was. In fact, as I would learn on the job, in God's good time, it was the most dangerous job I had ever worked.

"This is one of your quests," Alicia said. As usual, she saw through me like she was reading my source code. I had visions of smiling people greeting me at their doors while I wore a US-government-issued gas mask and some deep sense that this might be . . . fun? Strange? Hard? I just knew that I wanted it.

"My quests?" I asked.

"Like when you drove around LA, finding lost dogs." Which, yes, is how I had spent the six months I was unemployed in my early thirties. It was the first of the three times I've been laid off over my career.

"Do you get the health care right away?"

"Yes. This is a holding action. I work one day a week and use the other six days a week to put together something better."

More numbers were moving inside her mental spreadsheet. In our household division of labor, I was on the revenue side of things. Alicia ran operations.

"If you got health care right away, we wouldn't need COBRA. I think that would stretch our savings out at least nine months, maybe as much as a year," she said.

As we were walking, I could see Alicia leaning forward, leaning into a wind I couldn't see. She was following her nose, her intuition, crunching all the variables by some calculus I would never know. Then she shrugged. "We need the runway. We need to keep the house, so just do it. Survive and advance, like Coach Valvano."

Jim Valvano, who had lead the NC State Wolfpack basketball team to a national championship in 1983, was a modern saint in North Carolina, and a personal hero of Alicia's. If she was quoting Coach V, she was in deadly earnest.

"Yeah, babe, that sounds good. Survive and advance."

It takes a grown-up woman with a lot of confidence in her own judgment and reason to go along with something like this, because she is blessing her idiot partner to go do something that, if not necessarily stupid, is at the very least a hard swerve. This wasn't a career plan. We needed a salary to replace my income, and this didn't even come close. And she was absolutely right; there were a number of things I knowingly and unknowingly omitted. I had not mentioned the fact that I might need to supply my own vehicle. Or that the first ninety working days were probationary. I had taken at face value that "one day a week" was a fact, when the reality was almost always going to be six or seven days a week, week after week, a fact that three minutes of research on the r/USPS subreddit would have revealed. But I was already deep in the waking dream of becoming a postapocalyptic mailman, which is one thing as a daydream and another as a cosplay fantasy while your family is counting on you.

Now she was nodding her head, to herself, not me. "You are going to do this. Something is going to come out of this." It was a statement, not a question.

Our friend Todd had lived with us and the girls since we had moved to Virginia. We had worked together in our twenties in an independent film collective in North Carolina and California, and now he was working on his fantasy epic; we had lured him down with the promise of cheap rent and cheaper living in the guest room of our giant house. If Todd was disappointed that after a decade of trying to make it in Hollywood, I had walked away from film to become a career man and raise a family, he'd never shown it. Our families were close, and we were friends with not just Todd, but his sister Melody and his father, whom even I called Mr. Flinchum. When he told Melody that I was becoming a letter carrier, she said, "Todd, I just got a chill. Steve is supposed to do this. He's going to be there for something important." Now, that could have been crazy talk of any American flavor—California Cosmic, Northeastern Hunch, Baptist Received Wisdom. The Flinchums had a long history of access to channels of information that regular folk simply didn't have the equipment to receive. I was not in the habit of ignoring these intuitions from the Flinchums, and Alicia had given me clearance to move ahead.

I got an email that afternoon informing me that I had passed the test.

Chapter Four

TWO KINDS OF PEOPLE

ONCE I HAD PASSED MY TEST, HAD BEEN FINGERprinted, and had gotten my background check done I reported for training at the Roanoke Postal Academy for two weeks of training at the Roanoke Processing and Distribution Center, which everyone called the "P and DC," but it always sounded like "PNDC." The Postal Academy was only a small part of a very large, multistory, mostly windowless building. Institutionally, the Post Office had a thing against windows, for the security and privacy of the mail. The Roanoke P&DC was the kind of place that seemed to be all back and no front. It was hard even to figure out where I was supposed to enter. Finally I found the door by looking for loitering smokers. In the small, institutional, Formica-floored entrance beyond was a sign that read "Why come to work? Numerous studies have shown personal and financial benefits to those who show up to work as scheduled."

For these two weeks, my friend and classmate was Jackie. The first time I met her, she asked if there was toilet paper in the building. It wasn't an insane question, as there had been national shortages since the start of the lockdown just a couple of weeks earlier. Jackie could have been fifty and she could have been seventy. She was tiny, didn't weigh more than one hundred pounds, wore rose gold wire-frame glasses, and had a full set of braces on her teeth. Her haircut was almost a flattop. She was alert, hyperalert, the way a bird reacts to every nearby sound.

"Like, in this building?" I asked, more white professional male asshole tone than I care to admit leaking through. The tone of "You mean in this massive federal facility? Of course there's toilet paper here. The last people to have toilet paper in America will be using the flush toilets in NORAD."

"Yeah. I brought some if you need it." Here I was judging, and she was sharing.

She showed me the inside of her purse, which was closer to the size of a USMC gunny sack than anything from Michael Kors. Inside were three rolls of toilet paper, a full-sized aluminum-bodied Maglite, and what was almost certainly a J-framed Smith & Wesson .38 Special, the sidearm equivalent of Virginia Slims, the classic "lady gun" of the South.

"I've practically got a store in my basement. I buy it all at Dollar General when it goes on sale. All these shortages haven't meant shit to me. But I have to lock it up because my no-good sister comes over and tries to steal it."

Why I qualified for the paper and her sister didn't was a question of sorting people into two categories—the folks pulling their weight and the freeloaders who didn't. I don't think this is unique to folks from Appalachia. But people here do this sorting fast and hard. Solid or shiftless. Show up or no-count. Here I was, looking for work like her. Maybe I wasn't pulling my weight right now, but I was trying. Over our time together at the Academy, she was always generous with me.

Our first day of training was nothing but PowerPoint presentations and videos on the mission of the USPS. At the start of the morning, the material was the usual haze of mission statements and corporate culture bullshit that I'd been subjected to since I was a bag boy at Kroger in my teens.

The first clue that the USPS was different was an entire module on how the USPS was a self-funding agency, complete with talking points we could share with customers. Leadership wanted people to know we did not take any taxpayer money.

The tone of these presentations changed. We were shown a film called *Ghost Town*, an animated thriller about a letter carrier who was given a parcel to deliver to an abandoned house. The new carrier was drawn as pretty, blonde, and distinctively curvy. As she turned onto the street leading through the "bad part" of her route, the background shifted to homes with cars up on blocks in the front yard and overgrown lawns. The plot got rolling when the next parcel she was to deliver was to an abandoned home. Loitering on the front porch was a cigarette-smoking character named "Moth," racially indeterminate but tattooed and wearing wraparound sunglasses that made him look like he was visiting from *The Matrix*. He was hanging out with a very ethnically representative gang, one part cyberpunk, one part "Say No To Drugs" PSA. The blonde rookie stared at the house and the gang on the porch and thought, "That house looks abandoned, but I'm supposed to deliver every package." That was when Moth called out to her.

"I'll take the package, lady. You've come to the right place," then he handed her a one-hundred-dollar bill which he produced from a roll in his pocket. "You know, for your kids." "Gosh, I really need this money," she thinks. Blondie goes on to deliver several packages to this clearly derelict address, including an encounter with a woman clearly modeled on Michelle Rodriguez from the *Fast and the Furious* movies, who says to her, "Hermosa, you know we both work for Moth!" There are hints of a lesbian relationship forming between the Letter Carrier and Michelle Rodriguez. More and more parcels come to the squat, and Moth is paying her more and more. At this point, my fellow trainees all start muttering, "Hey man, that's a shitload of money. I would be taking that." Finally, Blondie is arrested by a combined task force of the DEA, the FBI, and, of course, the US Postal Inspectors.

This was followed by more on the Postal Inspectors. How they were

America's original federal law enforcement agency. How they broke up child porn rings, mail order drug operations, but seemed to spend most of their time arresting people trying to steal from the mails, particularly letter carriers and mail handlers who stole from the mail. How they could spy on you from the mirrored windows above the mail sorting area. How many were once carriers, and could blend in perfectly undercover. There was a lot of talk about federal prison and long sentences. This was not mopping up spilled spaghetti sauce at the Kroger. This was not a goofy sitcom mailman. This was an organization that took itself very seriously, with its own secret police force.

Right before our first break, the woman who had been running the PowerPoints swapped out with a fireplug of a man in his early thirties wearing a postal blue city carrier's shirt-jac with the sleeves rolled up, like he was the postal version of James Dean. This guy was absolutely on a different wavelength than everyone else in the building. High energy, high speed, and low drag. Some serious ink on both arms and a big Casio G Shock on his wrist. He had ex-military coming off him at high intensity. Hank spoke a strange patois that was a mash-up of Boston and Roanoke.

"Real quick, real quick before your break! I'm Hank. I'm a city carrier, and I'm here to help educate you suckers who have been bamboozled into being rural carriers. First off, this is the easiest money that you will ever make at the post office. Second, and listen up. You in the baseball cap, open your eyes and listen up, because I can already tell you are going to need to hear this. You cannot have your gun on federal property. I'm going to say that slowly, one more time, because in my experience you people have difficulty with spoken instructions: You . . . cannot . . . have . . . your . . . gun . . . on . . . federal . . . property. Not even if it is locked up in your car."

Jackie nudged me, then whispered, "Should I tell him about the gun in my purse?"

"Jackie, whatever you do, don't say anything about the pistol," I said.

Hank looked over at me. "You have something you want to share with the class?"

"Nope. Just discussing the unique nature of federal property," I said.

"Great, a barracks lawyer. Okay, now, as a separate conversation, does anybody need to take a break and move their car?" About half the room raised their hands.

"For the love of Christ, put your hands down! Did you notice all the trucks parked out on the city street, just outside the wire? Those people work here and have a weapon in their vehicle. If you ever need a gun to do a crime, just break in out there. Half of those guys don't even lock their cars. It's legal to have a weapon in your vehicle in Virginia but not on federal property, right? And when you get outside, and you are parked in the USPS lot, DO NOT TAKE YOUR GUN OUT IN THE PARKING LOT. If the FEDERAL security guys see it on video, they will call the postal inspector, who will arrest you, and you will not get to work at the post office because you will be up on federal weapons charges."

Jackie gave me a look and silently said, "Thank you." Then she went outside to catch a smoke, and presumably move her car and leave her gun there.

I had been taking notes all morning, having brought my old leather briefcase. I was the only one doing it, until Jackie asked to borrow a pen and started taking notes on a small spiral pad, the kind my mom used for making grocery lists. The next day she showed up with a full-sized notebook, then handed me two Bic ballpoints. "Repaid! With interest!" She was a lean-forward kind of person, wide awake in a room full of people where a couple of folks were intermittently asleep, or if you were the kid in a trucker's cap, asleep for 95 percent of the time.

The first couple of days I headed out to my truck at lunchtime and ate the rice and lentils Alicia had made for me. But then Jackie asked me if I wanted to eat lunch with her, and after that we ate together. I learned a lot about her place down in Alum Springs. Her old job was putting the headlight assemblies into big rigs down at the Volvo plant in Pulaski. Her miniature ponies. Her chicken and goats. At lunch one day, she told me how violent her ex-husband had been, how he had shot her in the arm with a shotgun. People don't usually live through being shot with a shotgun, but as Jackie said, "He was drunk, and he wasn't a good shot sober." Two kinds of people: those who can shoot and those who can't.

Toward the end of the first week, while we were settling in before the morning's unit of instruction, she told me a story about driving home on Interstate 81 the night before. A guy in a black Mercedes with Florida plates sped ahead of her, trying to beat her to the merge before the construction at the New River Bridge.

"Well, I wasn't going to sit there and let this guy just show me his ass. So I floored it. And I caught up to him," Jackie said.

"Did you give him the bird?" asked Claire, a classmate. Claire was a big blonde lady who loved animals, who had also been a bartender in Virginia Beach and was on familiar terms with aggression.

"I showed that Black son of a bitch my gun! I slapped it right up against the window so he could see it. He hit the brakes after that, let me tell you what."

The room got quiet. This was too much, even for the local crowd. I saw Jackie's eyes bouncing back and forth like pinballs, the externalization of whatever bad loop was replaying in her brain.

There were a lot of things I could have said. That any of us could have said. *Jackie, I'm sorry that happened. Hey Jackie, you cannot flash your gun at people just because they pass you in traffic. Hey Jackie, on the freeway in the big city you keep moving at maximum speed until the lane closure; the dude wasn't doing anything wrong. Jackie, have you ever spoken to someone about what happened with your ex, like a minister or a priest, or a shrink*?

Instead, I just sat there.

I was thinking about where I'd seen those eyes before. My father and I had been pulling the canoes down off their rack in the backyard, a classic piece of Grant overengineering that suspended the canoes above the forest floor on spars of marine-grade treated lumber, held in place with galvanized hardware, the posts set three feet deep in concrete. The holes had been an absolute bitch to chop down into rock-filled earth with a post-hole digger. According to Dad the secret was "brute force," and he wanted a deep hole because what he built he built to last. The boats were stored keel-up, so they could shed the rain. An acorn fell from a scarlet oak and crashed down on the big aluminum Grumman canoe. It didn't ring like a bell but sounded almost like a metallic crack, a gunshot. And I watched my father drop into a crouch, his hand out and at the ready, to fend off an attack, to reach for a weapon, his eyes with that same panicked pinball motion I saw in Jackie's eyes. We are not big huggers and touchers, the Grants. But I remember reaching out and holding Dad's shoulder as this spell passed. My father, with his physical size, strong, supremely competent, almost comically confident. But in that moment, he was terrified. The university had provided a psychologist after the 2007 Virginia Tech shooting and Dad went a couple of times. When he stopped I asked him why and he said, "She just wanted me to write a bunch of stuff down. I wanted to get back to work. So I went back to work."

So, I didn't say anything to Jackie. I knew I couldn't comfort her. I just sat there like a bump on a log, not feeling sympathy or sadness. What I felt was familiar, because even though I was middle-class all the way through, the Grants middle-class for more than two hundred years, I was still Appalachian. I knew this feeling. It was hopelessness.

In our second week, we started specific training for rural carriers. I was a little sad at this, because it meant no more Hank and no more Hank stories. He was an impressive guy, alive and wide awake. But his replacement was pretty awesome as well. Our new instructor, Tom, was about the same age as Hank. Bearded, lean and an avowed Libertarian. How he was able to square being a Libertarian but working for the largest federal service is beyond me. If you're wondering how I knew he was a Libertarian, then you've never spent any time with Libertarians, because all you need to do is wait five minutes.

He was a good instructor, patient and kind. But like Hank, there were things Tom did that clearly served no other purpose than to amuse himself.

"I am a veteran of the United States Army."

"Thank you for your service!" Piped in the Youth Pastor, a man who brought the whole class Bo-berry biscuits from Bojangles one morning.

"Serving in the military was the worst mistake of my life," said Tom.

Dead silence.

He shared this view with us multiple times over the course of the week. Sometimes as he repeated it, a micro-smile would leak through. I knew he was enjoying watching smoke curl from the ears of some of my classmates as deep impulses began fist fighting in their heads. "He's a combat veteran!" would furiously trade blows with "He's running down our military!" But that tiny smile told me that Tom was paying himself back for a debt owed to him by the United States military and the US government, one small jab of cognitive dissonance at a time. He had worked in explosive ordinance disposal, and more than once he shared that he wouldn't have had to dispose of anything if "we hadn't been there in the first place." If you had been sent to Iraq to dispose of IEDs by the US government, maybe you would be a Libertarian too.

"You want any Oreos? I got a bunch," Jackie asked. We were taking a short break for the smokers. At lunch on the internal USPS website I had seen a listing for an RCA position in Blacksburg. When I had first applied, there hadn't been anything listed, just openings in Cave Spring. I immediately put in for it. This would take my commute from forty-five minutes down to about six.

Between pulling apart Oreos, I told her I put in for an opening in Blacksburg. "Now I just got to wait for the email."

"Wait for what email?" asked Jackie.

"Yeah, the system will send me an email if I get the position."

"Honey, you need to go to Blacksburg today—today! Talk to that postmaster. Because the system isn't going to do shit. You can't trust it. You got to look out for yourself."

When we were all headed home at the end of the afternoon, Jackie grabbed my arm in the parking lot. "Go straight there, Steve. Go right to talk to the postmaster." Two kinds of people: people who take care of themselves, and victims.

Jackie did not trust the system to do the right thing. I think her mistrust was part blue-collar—when you do a lifetime of work as a replaceable part, you know deep down the system isn't looking out for you. Her mistrust was also part Appalachian. When you are culturally isolated—the butt of every squeal-like-a-pig, marry-your-first-cousin joke—you might develop the impression that the professional managerial class doesn't hold you in the highest regard. Who was the realist here? Mr. Corporate Kool-Aid, or the Wild-Eyed Mountain Woman?

I drove down to Blacksburg that afternoon and asked to speak with the postmaster. I got reassigned. It took maybe ten minutes and working out of the office at the foot of the mountain, just five minutes from my house probably made the difference between me being able to deal with the job and being broken by it. I didn't know it at the time, but Jackie had just saved my naive ass.

One day after training at the Academy, I had picked up groceries for Mom and Dad and was dropping them off at their place. Early on in Covid, it felt like my brothers were in a constant panic about Mom and Dad. They were worried about them getting exposed. So I would go to the Kroger supermarket with Dad's credit card and buy whatever they put on a shared iPhone list. I was dropping off the groceries when Dad came out to help. I kept my distance while he unloaded the car, speaking spread out, in the driveway.

I told him I got reassigned to a position here in Blacksburg. I told him about Jackie and the gun.

"These people from Florida don't get it. You can't provoke a hillbilly like that."

"I think the dude was just driving down the freeway, Dad."

"I'm not saying she was right. I'm just saying it's not a good idea to provoke a hillbilly with a gun. And they've all got guns." This from a man who would threaten to shoot the home health care worker we sent to the house a couple of years later.

"The main thing that people don't understand is that most folks up here just want to be left alone," he said.

"You can't even tell them to wear a mask. Nobody in my training class will wear one."

Dad was never going to let a chance to critique technique slip by. "You've got to know how to wear them. You've got to create a seal. Nobody bothers to learn how to wear them the right way."

"Oh, in my class they were saying that the masks are actually causing Covid."

Dad put the bag of groceries down, looked me right in the eyes. He had a way of shaking his head when human ignorance took him by surprise. "You cannot do anything with these people. They have been trying to do it since that son of a bitch Johnson and it doesn't work. These people are just too goddamned stupid to help."

My dad was born in Weston, West Virginia. He spent every summer hunting and fishing with his grandfather and uncle and his cousins up in the Cranberry Backcountry. He could rebuild a car engine, dress a rattlesnake, can vegetables; do masonry, electrical, and carpentry work. He knew how to read the weather, every tree in the forest, could call birds and track signs, and work a pump shotgun like an extension of his body. He swam the Kanawha River, shore to shore, there and back, on a bet. He could sharpen an ax fine enough that he could shave with it. He knew all the bugs and when they hatched, he tied his own fly patterns based on a lifetime of careful observation of the natural world. He could dry-flyfish small water with wizard-like accuracy, a thing of beauty to watch; it was funny to see something so graceful from a big quiet man. He could split wood from sunup to sundown. Run a chain saw like a surgical instrument and drive a car like a NASCAR driver. He was tough, a no-quit person who seemed unaffected by heat or cold, even into his eighties. He was all of that, the genuine article, a mountain man. He just happened to have a PhD and be a college professor. But he was an Appalachian all the way through, like a potato, the end product of two centuries in these mountains, directly imported from the Highlands of Scotland. That's why Dad gets to say this.

Everybody else can fuck right off.

When the day of our final exam came, Jackie was agitated. Really agitated. More agitated than when she pulled a gun on a stranger in what was effectively a hate crime.

"I'm going to fuck up this goddamned test." Her hands were shaking.

We had finished the general training week, our driver's training, and now our rural carrier training, which in addition to knowing the classes of mail and how to do forwards involved a lot of dog and driving safety, along with some of the peculiarities of the rural craft, like selling stamps and envelopes on our route, functioning as a mobile post office.

All that was left was the big test, effectively our go-no go. If we passed, we were letter carriers.

In the test we would be given a simulated load of mail—magazines and other flats, "raw mail," the machine-sorted mail we called DPS, some small packages, and a couple of large parcels. This was to show we could figure out what was deliverable and what wasn't, what needed to be forwarded and how to bring back outgoing mail. Basically, we were being tested on the three things you have to do as a letter carrier—process mail from multiple mailstreams for your route, carry and deliver that mail, and return with outgoing mail. We would sort all this mail to get everything into route order, check the pigeonholes for hold-mail cards and vacant address notices, load it into our bags, then take it out on the "street"—a series of mailboxes that had been screwed to the walls of the hallway outside.

This was a simulation of delivering the mail the way that a high school physics problem is a model for reality, accurate but horrifically oversimplified. As my father would tell you, all models are broken. In the test scenario for our final, there was no aptitude score for driving on the right-hand side in a left-hand drive car or delivering in 100-degree heat, no questions on how to recognize when a mailbox is concealing a black widow spider, no evaluations on how to recover a mail truck from an ice-filled ditch, how to deal with armed citizenry, dog attacks, or literally psychotic customers who keep yelling "Tell me your name!" and chasing your car. These lessons are only available live and in living color. If they told you all of that stuff at the beginning the attrition rate would be even higher than it already was.

I cased up my mail and delivered it. The letters and magazines were all addressed to characters from 1990s TV—George Costanza, Homer Simpson. There were a number of trick cases they threw in—hold mail, unforwardable letters, and standard-class mail that was faked up to look like it was first class. In twenty minutes I was done. I got a 100 and I was proud of myself. Because the test was genuinely hard, you had to really think through each piece of mail. Then I looked over at Jackie. She was still bouncing her leg up and down, her eyes back in their pinball panic circuit.

"I am going to fuck this up."

"Jackie, you're going to be fine. It's really straightforward."

"You're good at this shit. I'm bad at tests. I'm going to fuck this up."

"Jackie, listen to me. There are only a couple of curveballs. There's a magazine that looks like *UBBM*. But it's not. It's a publication, so that's handled like first class. You'll need to take that back to the case and forward it. There's a letter that's addressed to a former occupant, but if you check the forward cards at your case you'll catch it before you even leave on your route. It says Jerry Seinfeld, but you'll see about halfway down the case that he's moved. So file that in your forwards before you head out on your route."

Jackie was writing all this down in her notebook.

"Jackie, my dad used to tell me that if you can't be good, be smart. You hear what I'm saying?"

She put the notebook away and collapsed into her chair.

"I'm going to fuck this up."

Jackie passed with a 100.

I have a thought experiment that I run sometimes. It was something that I came up with in 2015 when Trump was first running for office. It's very simple: If an emergency came up, who would you let watch your kids for the weekend? Would I let Barack and Michelle watch the girls for the weekend? Absolutely, because the girls would be in good hands, and I would want the bragging rights. What about Mitt and Ann Romney? Easy yes. They have a ton of grandkids, and even if they are pretty square, I think the girls would have a good time. Sure, we're talking about Mr. System himself, someone who used to "harvest" companies when he ran Bain Capital, getting rid of all those pesky workers and their expensive wages and benefits. But one-on-one, I think they are likely honest and good-hearted people. Ditto George and Laura Bush. Yes, he's directly and indirectly responsible for the deaths of over one hundred thousand Iraqi civilians, but I think I would prefer the Bushes to the Romneys because my kids are artistic, George is a painter, Laura's a teacher, and if I'm being honest I will admit that my own bias regarding the Romneys' Mormon faith weirded me out more than the fact that George Bush stole an election and used the Constitution as a doormat. That's the thing about bias.

Leave the girls with the Trumps for the weekend? No fucking way.

But I would leave my kids with Jackie for the weekend. The girls would love the ponies and the chickens. I knew the kids would be well fed, and Jackie would guard them with her life. Alicia and I were taking a walk after dinner and when I shared this opinion, her response was immediate.

"Are you fucking nuts? She waved a gun at somebody over traffic because they were Black! She's racist! She's dangerous!"

"I don't think it's because they were Black, more that they pissed her off?"

"Steve. She pulled out a gun and waved it at a person. It doesn't matter why she thought she did it. She's crazy."

"I don't think she's a bad person."

"Steve, you just love people from Appalachia."

"I'm from Appalachia. I'm Appalachian!"

"You are not! What you are is blind."

I was. I am.

Two kinds of people. The sort who things happen to, and the sort who go out and make things happen.

Some people give up after things happen to them. Others get back up, over and over again. We think of this as a strength, as grit, determination, willpower. We think of this as an American virtue, but this kind of toughness has always struck me as essential to the Appalachian character. To get up every morning and go at it, hammer and tongs. Try and fail. Fail again. Try harder. Just don't quit. The virtue is in the trying. Try, try, try.

If you get laid off or shot, or people yell at you and call you an idiot or tell you that you'll never amount to a goddamned thing, don't think about it. Just get back up and try again.

Don't think about it. Just get back up. Try harder.

And you wonder why people think you're too goddamned stupid to help?

Don't think about that either. Just get back to work.

Chapter Five

WITHOUT ANY MENTAL RESERVATION

ON OUR LAST DAY OF ORIENTATION, THE SLIDE ON the PowerPoint showed the image of an American flag. The caption at the bottom read, "The Oath of Office."

Don Cooper was there, a recruiter at the P and DC who'd shown me around while he sorted out my fingerprinting and background check.

Standing next to him was Ms. Bentley, the Roanoke postmaster, a Black woman in her midthirties. Mr. Cooper was the one who told me the background check for letter carriers is just a notch below federal law enforcement, because you are in a "position of trust" handling the mail. He was a big, friendly man, formerly of the United States Marine Corps, right down to his Captain Kangaroo walrus mustache. Before he would let me go get fingerprinted (by a guy I used to skateboard with in high school), he wanted to talk to me.

"Steve, I don't say this to everyone who comes through. Just the folks who are going to carry the mail. Stuck behind this desk here, I'm envious," he told me. "Letter Carrier. That's the soul of the Postal Service. You'll get to know your customers. You'll know when people move, get divorced, have birthdays and graduations. Babies born and people passing on. Life's rich pageant and all that." He'd told me a story about the

Hope Diamond being delivered to the Smithsonian by Registered Mail. There was an evangelistic light in Cooper's eyes while he spoke about the Postal Service. A glimmer of something unforced and real. Not your usual onboarding.

Mr. Cooper had also rhapsodized about Postmaster Bentley: "What a mind! She knows it all, Steve. A mind like a computer. In my twenty-five years in the Postal Service, I've never met anybody that knows the system like she does. She won't be here in Roanoke for long, she's going all the way." Standing now at the front of the room, Cooper seemed to be glowing, mustache and all, simply from being in her presence.

"Okay, carriers, the postmaster is here today to swear you all in as letter carriers in the United States Postal Service. We're going to start with the Pledge of Allegiance. So go ahead, stand up, and face the flag. Postmaster Bentley?"

The gold-fringed Stars and Stripes were next to her, the pole in a floor stand. It had actually been there the whole time, but I only really noticed it now.

"I love swearing in new letter carriers! Please place your right hand over your heart . . ."

Mr. Cooper whirled on one of my classmates, a young kid who always had his ball cap pulled low and had slept through two weeks of PowerPoint.

"Take that hat off! You're saluting the flag of the United States!" In two big steps Donald Cooper USMC (ret.) was in the kid's face, his hands chopping the air in a classic parade-ground-sergeant's knife hand, a gesture that suggested simply pointing wasn't enough. The kid pulled the hat off his head and suddenly seemed very young and very scared. This wasn't saying the Pledge of Allegiance at a high school football game.

I stood up drill-field straight, feet together, left thumb carefully aligned with the seam in the leg of my jeans, just like they had taught us in ROTC. It was all I could do to keep from putting my right arm into the Boy Scout three-fingered salute. There was something different there this time. Something I hadn't felt in decades.

"Okay, folks, time to take the oath," said Mr. Cooper.

I was becoming a sworn agent of the US government.

Ben Franklin was appointed as the first postmaster general by the Continental Congress in 1775. He helped build the post road system that joined together the early American nation. Along with Washington's Continental Army, the Post Office was effectively the very first service of our young nation's government. President Benjamin Harrison tried to appoint John Wanamaker, the father of the modern department store, to secretary of the navy in 1889. Wanamaker refused, telling him, "I can't do it . . . if I take anything I will take the hardest place you have got." So Harrison appointed him the nation's thirty-eighth postmaster general. Wanamaker brought in a coast-to-coast postal telegraph system and rural free delivery, which added ten years to the average lifespan of Americans thanks to easy access to garden vegetable seeds, and helped usher in universal literacy in the bargain. Later the Post Office added airmail, where Charles Lindberg learned to fly. And now me. Who wasn't going to do much of anything important. But it now felt like I was at least *part* of something important.

"Everybody turn in your hymnals to page 12-5," Mr. Cooper said. "It should read 'The Oath of Office.'" We all opened up our white handbooks. There it was. Not a pledge, but an *oath*. As legally binding, morally charged, and spiritually consequential as a wedding vow. Except that instead of being between me, my wife, and whatever higher power I recognized, this was between me, the Constitution, and the American people.

Just like at my wedding, I felt nervous. Not because I was planning treason, but because it felt serious. This wasn't a contract. This went way beyond a paycheck.

"Everyone raise your right hand, and repeat after me," said Postmaster Bentley.

I, Stephen Grant, do solemnly swear that I will support and defend the Constitution of the United States against all enemies, foreign and domestic; that I will bear true faith and allegiance to the same; that I take this obligation freely, without any mental reservation or purpose of evasion; and that I will well and faithfully discharge the duties of the office on which I am about to enter.

The room was silent for a moment.

"We got you now!" cracked Mr. Cooper. An old military joke. Everyone laughed, but I could still feel it.

It was that old feeling. The old dumb feeling of patriotism, but changed now. This wasn't dumb. This wasn't the same thrill I would feel when I would salute the flag at Camp Ottari during reveille, or when I was an Army ROTC cadet in college, something I saw as Boy Scouts with guns. Before I walked away from ROTC the feeling I got when I looked at the flag was one of belonging, a sense that America was the last, best hope of the free world. It was a simple thing, and maybe not that deeply held, which is why I could surrender the idea of service so easily. The abstraction of the flag couldn't compete with an actual live woman who didn't think my aspirations as a writer were compatible with a military career. In her mind, writers were creative and sensitive, and the military was the opposite of those things. That's all it took to talk me out of it. In the years since, I have often wished I'd stuck with it. By the time I was in my thirties I had resigned myself to the fact I would never be much use to my country.

Now that feeling was back. Like something that had been casked inside me for decades and was now being uncorked, having matured and complexified.

America is the greatest country in the world, a shining city on a hill, windswept, God-blessed, teeming with people of all kinds living in harmony and peace, humming with commerce and creativity. Being born as an American was like winning the lottery of life.

America is a steroidal monster, consuming a quarter of the world's energy while only holding 5 percent of its population, exporting our misery to the world, waging war for our own self-interested ends, our talk of democracy a soothing doublespeak, an opiate we compulsively consume to quiet the interruptive guilt we feel for the things done in our name between eating Domino's pizza and bingeing Netflix.

Both versions of America are true.

What I was feeling was an adult version of patriotism. An adult version of love, where you love something for its best parts. Where you have faith that enough people are acting in good will that the nation will eventually make amends for its failings. An adult mind can hold two seemingly contradictory thoughts at once. Because they don't actually contradict each other.

Patriotism is not an old-fashioned value, but rather an old value, a foundational one. It is the virtue of critical loyalty, the ability to feel deep affection for one's country and a simultaneous willingness to critique its failures. I don't know if past generations were more patriotic. I think our view of the past gets oversimplified. But what I do know is that this contradictory idea is something that would have felt very contemporary to the Founders. They wanted to establish a government that would be answerable to critique, that would evolve and respond to the new needs of a changing world.

The Founders of 1776 would find the America of today unrecognizable in many ways, but I think they would also be deeply gratified to see the expansion of liberty's franchise. The pursuit of liberty has never been painless. We have been deeply divided in the past, and when our civil process has broken down, violence has been the instrument of change. It was a struggle in 1776 to be represented by our government. We succeeded but wound up tolerating the intolerable in the form of slavery for another ninety years. In 1865 we finally abolished that great sin, but only at a terrible cost. And in 2020 the country was struggling again, with an unknown virus and a great sense of grievance in our body politic. There have always been things dividing us, from the moment of the nation's inception. The country has always had shortcomings, injustices, and yes, even sins. But we must find a way to continue as a liberal society of laws, where we provide the most freedom to the most people but also protect the different and weaker among us.

There has to be a starting point. It is love of country.

America is an idea. Without love of country, how will we ever muster the energy to perfect that idea? Without love of country, how will we grow the moral strength to tolerate what can be tolerated, and to change what must be changed? How is anything going to improve? The nation requires more than cynicism or blind allegiance. As your standard-issue citizen, I didn't think about these things on a daily basis. But standing in the interactive-learning room of the Roanoke Processing and Distribution Center of the United States Postal Service, the stakes felt present tense and very real. I felt bigger than myself, a Whitmanian expansiveness that twenty-five years of consulting had certainly never brought me.

The Oath of Office is a sacred trust, a form of prayer—a prayer for the Constitution, a prayer for America and her people. But there is no unearned grace. For the prayer to mean anything, America has to be acted out. Nature's God endowed us all with inalienable rights. We were all created equal. It takes institutions like the Postal Service to make that statement come true.

In the eyes of the Postal Service you are all created equal: You will receive the mail, irrespective of who you are and where you live. You are all invited to be part of the nation's commercial, legal, scientific, and artistic conversation, entitled by the simple fact that you are American. The Founders wanted us to be neighbors. They wanted us to talk to each other.

Delivering the mail was dumb and anachronistic. Delivering the mail was a vital act of normalcy.

Both things were true. That's the whole point of prayer. It's not that God looks down and grants your wish. Your prayer is an intention to undertake what is required, to do all the work that follows. To make it true.

I was going to be part of that prayer.

Chapter Six

FNG

"WHO'S THE NEW GUY ON ROUTE 10?" I COULD hear Kathy ask Terri. Kathy was a short-haired, short-tempered woman who during my time at the post office only spoke to me to tell me what I was doing wrong. Later I learned she lived down on Route 3.

Terri, the regular on Route 8, the route I lived on, stage-whispered over her case. "He's named Steve Grant. He lives on my route, and you should see his house! He's rich! I don't know what he's doing here. It's weird."

Kathy said nothing.

A city carrier walking by asked, "Isn't he a little old to be starting as a carrier? Was he a professor? You think he's a postal inspector?"

"No," Terri answered. "He's some sort of economist or something. He gets magazines about economics, but he's not a professor. Two young girls, two new cars. He used to work for Prudential. His folks live over on Greg's route. It's his dad that's the professor."

Jesus, what else did she know about me? I was stacking parcels onto a wheeled float, pretending I couldn't hear them. I encountered my first real-world secret about letter carriers: If the carrier knows your name, they know your address. And if they know your address that means they know what you get in the mail. And even in the age of the internet, that means they know *you*.

It was my first day working in the Blacksburg Post Office, and being thought of as weird and suspicious was not helping my "new guy" jitters. My supervisor, David, told me that I was going to be delivering as the substitute, the sub, on Route 10. All routes have a regular and an assigned sub, so that each has a "home route." The regular covers the route five days a week. The sub is typically scheduled to cover the sixth day, often a Monday because it's got such high volume.

Route 10 covered a couple of residential neighborhoods, apartment complexes, and the Corporate Research Center campus, an office park and lab complex home to many of the businesses associated with the university, like TechLab, Regeneron, Torc, VPT, and other intellectual property spinoffs from research at Tech. I was told that my regular had been waiting to go on vacation for months but couldn't because there was no one to sub for him, so once I had gone through my day of on-the-job training, I would be carrying the route six days a week for two weeks. The idea that this was going to be a one-day-a-week job survived a grand total of ten minutes. Still, I told myself, this is because my regular needs to go on vacation. After this, things will go back to normal. This would prove to be exactly wrong. I was starting at "normal" but was too green to know it, because I was an FNG, the fucking new guy.

Cash was my regular. He "held down" Route 10. A good-looking Black guy in his early thirties, Cash just made the job look easy. He was a kid's soccer referee on the weekends and built like a soccer player, tall and lean.

The first time I met him, I introduced myself and he said, "Steve Grant from 1872 Pratt Drive?"

"Yes. That's me."

"There are two Steve Grants in Blacksburg, but the other one lives on a city route."

"Yeah, that's right." I tried to hide my shock. I knew about the other Stephen Grant, as he once paid my library overdue fees and the dry cleaner had tried to give me his shirts.

"Aren't you some kind of economist?"

“Some kind. Not at the moment.”

“So you’re going to be delivering the mail to yourself.”

“Yeah, I guess so?” The strangeness of that hit me.

“Well, it’s good you know things out at the CRC”—the Corporate Research Center, where my one-man office was. “A lot of subs get turned around out there. Let’s get you started. How about you put your briefcase under the case?”

I had shown up for my first day with, yeah, my leather satchel and a cup of coffee, as if I were going to take a couple of meetings and then work at a hot desk. Standing there, I realized what an asshole I must have looked like. The way Cash said it was kind and face-saving. He was just a quality human being. And with that we got to work.

The case is home base for a carrier, the workstation where every morning starts and every day ends. Cash’s had pictures of his wife and kid magneted on the side. Other carriers had pictures of their grandchildren. One of the city carriers had a Ronald Reagan calendar she hung from her case.

I had a couple of friends ask me, “So do you just pick up your truck at the post office and hit your route?” as if there were a whole other team of people sorting and loading the mail. Honestly, if all you had to do as a carrier was deliver the mail, working as a letter carrier would be one of the greatest jobs in the world. But the fact is that every day, each letter carrier effectively builds a library, loads it into a truck, and then disassembles that library in route order. We all worked in a big warehouse room with intake loading docks on one side and outbound loading docks for the mail trucks on the other. Everything smelled like machine oil and cigarette smoke, but there was something else. The smell of ink and paper, the smell of the mail.

It takes a lot of people doing very hard work to support the carriers, but it is the carriers who integrate the mailstreams into order, load the trucks, learn their route, deliver, encounter customers, collect the outgoing mail, forward the mail that needs forwarding, and hold mail for customers who are out of town.

All of this starts at the case. Each route gets its own case, and each case is unique to its route. Imagine a set of metal bookshelves wrapped around a standing desk. The cases were fabricated from brown powder-coated sheet metal. If that sounds vaguely Victorian, people sorting paper into pigeonholes, something out of a Dickens novel, that's because it is. Cases from the late nineteenth and early twentieth centuries were wooden and looked like pieces of utilitarian Victorian furniture. But they are completely recognizable to any modern-day letter carrier. The case for Route 10, my main route, was a row of pigeonholes that if lined up end to end would probably equal about sixty-some linear feet, with a slot for each address on the route, in route order. If you live at 707 Southgate Drive, there is a slot in the case, just for you. It sits between the slots for 705 and 709 Southgate, your neighbors.

Casing up the mail was physical. Because there is a slot for every address on the route, the case for short routes with only a few stops is small. The case for big routes with many addresses and stops is big. There was nothing abstract about it. You could see that Route 11 was a baby, just one vertical module, the endcap to the rural-carriers area, the size of a starter apartment's bookshelf. Route 10 was comparable to most of the other routes. There were monsters like Route 3, so big it needed an extra case bolted onto the left-hand side. You could see it was a beast if you had a carrier's eye. The first time I carried Route 3, I wasn't much of a carrier, so I didn't understand just how big it was.

Every few years, management comes through and evaluates the routes. They take into account the mail volume, the number of delivery addresses, if the route should be classified as rural or not. The routes are supposed to be sized by how much mail the average carrier can deliver in an eight-hour working day. In practice, the evaluations don't happen very often, making the route sizes irregular, and some of their classification as city or rural seemed arbitrary as well. My route, Route 10, was mostly cow pasture when I was a kid, so it made sense it was initially classified as rural. But the explosive growth of the CRC and new developments of detached homes and apartment complexes to house an expanding university turned it into something that looked a lot like a city route, where most deliveries were dismounted. Rural carriers hated it because it was so unlike the other routes. I liked the walking nature of the route. It got you out of the truck and out on the sidewalk.

Once a route was set, an efficiency study done by Operations Research types at headquarters then created the route order, which in turn dictated the layout of the case. Each route had a big three-ring binder outlining every address and every turn of the route. This was kept at the case, and I never saw anyone use them. The only real way to learn a route was to drive it.

Being a mailman is one of those jobs that, from the outside, seem straightforward. Most folks don't really know what a statistician does or how to fix an air conditioner. Unfortunately, like being a teacher, letter carrier is one of those jobs that everyone seem to think they could do. You pick up the mail, you travel the route, you drop it off. How hard could it be? Years of television have left people with the impression that there are a lot of coffee breaks, three-hour lunches, bored housewives, and union-fueled goldbricking. That's all bullshit. There were always people working at the post office when I arrived in the morning, people who had been there since 4 a.m. And there were always people working when I left at the end of the day. But the public doesn't see this. All they see is a letter carrier dropping off their mail and packages, hopefully smiling, picking up the outgoing mail, and then disappearing again. That part, the sticking of the mail in the box, the chitchat, being friendly but not getting stuck with a customer, even that is harder than it looks.

All this work is invisible because the post office isn't a Krispy Kreme shop where you can watch the donuts roll off the automated assembly line through a Plexiglas window. There is the sanctity and the security of the mail, and that means keeping what happens in the carrier area private. At the Blacksburg Main Post Office, or MPO, there is the public area with the clerks' counter, a desk for filling out forms and addressing envelopes, and the lobby holding the outgoing mail slots and the PO boxes. But the magic all happens offstage. Behind the counter wall is a hangarlike open space containing the route cases, the parcel sorting area, the receiving area next to the truck loading dock, all the various racks where the carriers pick up mail, desks for the supervisors, the holding racks for parcels that went out for delivery and were returned, and then a rack of sorting bins for returned mail, each labeled with obscure codes like ANK, NSN, IA, UTF. It all flows in a carefully choreographed dance, part American scientific management, part folk practice.

That's the other way in which the post office differs from Krispy Kreme: Donuts are all uniform in shape and size. They all get the same glaze. The mail is anything but uniform. There are limits to the automation that can be done. To an outsider it looks like a mess, but under that chaos is order. Order created through great effort, every day.

Everything in the USPS runs on a clock. White-collar work is highly scheduled, but it doesn't have a rhythm. Knowledge work is project-based. Delivering the mail isn't knowledge work, it's skilled labor and operations, doing the same thing every day. Delivering the mail requires a rhythm. While there is variance to it, carrier to carrier, everyone still basically follows the same bass line. That bass line is driven by the handlers, who work the second and third shifts from the afternoon and through the night and into the dawn. They bring in what we call the mailstreams.

At the Academy, they told us to show up at the office around 7:30 a.m., the idea being that we would arrive just as the night shift from the previous day was wrapping up. Much as a sous chef preps materials for the chef, the handlers have the invisible, indispensable job of getting the mailstreams ready so they can be organized and carried across the last mile by the carriers. The city carriers were part of a tightly managed operation. They needed to show up exactly at 7:30. Every second of their day was on the clock, one big time-motion study. But the rural carriers showed up all over the place, as we were paid by the route, not the hour. Tommy, our rural shop steward and the most experienced rural carrier (carrying since the 1980s, when I was in high school), would come in the same time as the Greensboro mail truck, around 5 a.m. The moment the parcels were released, he was out the door. Wade ran a similar program. Both of them had long routes that took them deep into the mountains. Cash was such a pro that he could cruise in around 9:30 a.m. and still finish his route early. For rural carriers, as long as you got the job done, you had a lot of freedom in terms of when and how you wanted to work.

Every time I hear someone complain about the USPS messing something up, I have to repress the desire to yell "Shut the fuck up! You have no idea what the USPS accomplishes every day!" Post offices should have glass walls like a haute cuisine restaurant, so that the citizens can see what's getting done for them every morning. FedEx? UPS? They simply cannot do what the USPS does. All they carry are parcels. *Letter carrier* is a misnomer, which conceals the fact that we carry everything for everybody, with 99.993 percent accuracy. In fact, we carry many parcels for FedEx and UPS because they simply can't do it. They don't have our scale and reach. We do it all.

The USPS has several mailstreams that the carrier is responsible for each morning, and till my last day, I would have to get nudged by Wade, Kat, Greg, or another old hand to make sure I didn't leave something at the case, or forget to pick it up from the mail handlers. Ultimately I made a simple checklist for myself, and every time I tried going off book, the old hands would need to save my bacon. It was only by the very end of my year that I was mostly (mostly) mistake-free when casing the mail.

First-class mail and standard-class machine-sorted mail is called DPS, or delivery-point system, and it arrived every morning, presorted into long, translucent plastic gunboat trays, all in route order, as neat and organized as a brand-new deck of playing cards. This was all done at Blacksburg's P&DC down in Greensboro, North Carolina. The electromechanical wizardry that allows them to do this is incredible and BIG. Machines that deal with the analogue world can only get so small. P&DCs are huge buildings located near the freeway because they physically process the mail the way a microprocessor processes information. The outgoing mail goes into a hopper the size of a small house and is then vibration-sorted into stacks, with the letters all facing the same way. Most mail has a bar code that runs along the bottom of the human-readable address, printed on by the address-processing machine, and from there scanners do the rest, and they do it fast. Scanners read the bar codes, or if needed the printed addresses and even handwriting, to sort them by region, town, post office, and finally down to the route level. They zip through the computer-controlled tracks at the P&DC like the bullets in a machine gun, each letter traveling at around 25 miles an hour. Only a computer can read each letter quickly enough to make this work. Long before your iPad could recognize your handwriting, the USPS could read everyone's handwriting through optical character recognition. The USPS actually helped develop the technology using a branch of mathematics called cellular automata, which was developed by John von Neumann, one of the brains behind the atomic bomb dropped on Nagasaki. The man behind mutual assured destruction is also hiding in your mailbox. In 99.99 percent of the cases, a human hand doesn't touch a letter you drop into a blue box until your carrier delivers it to the destination address.

At 4:30 or so in the morning, the first trucks from the P&DCs start arriving. One truck usually brings all of the machine-sorted DPS mail along with the flats and raw mail. The DPS goes on racks in the carrier area, and the clerks sort out the rest to the route level—it's then up to your friendly neighborhood carrier to sort it all into route order at the case. All the different classes of mail, magazines, and larger envelopes got sorted—it's called "putting up the mail." In big cities, carriers get their magazines route sorted by machine, flat sequence sorted. But our magazines and flats came bundled at the route level in an otherwise random stack. Getting those flats into order was up to the carrier. The same with "raw mail." Raw mail was just a loose grab bag of stuff that hadn't made it into the DPS. Maybe the address was only partially legible, the envelope was an irregular size, it was a late arrival or a "sleeper," a letter that had been misplaced. Regardless of how it wound up as raw mail, it was the carrier's job to case it.

As I followed Cash around each of these stations—flats pickup, raw mail, hot case, DPS—I thought to myself, *How the fuck am I ever going to keep all this straight?* And we hadn't even reached the case yet.

Casing. You stand in front of the case, pick up an issue of *Sports Illustrated* addressed to Nathan Dagger at 2001 Plantation Road, apartment B-1. You remember that Plantation Road is near the beginning of your route, just above your left shoulder. You stick Nathan's magazine into his slot. When you pick up Laurie Buendia's seed catalog, you know she lives at the end of Ridge Road, down near the desktop on your righthand side.

If you are thinking, *But how does the carrier know that's where Southgate is?* the answer is that you just memorize it. Yes, you can slowly scan the address names until you find the right street and street number, like a dumb meat robot. But the reality is you simply have to learn the route by heart. That's the only way you can possibly get everything cased up in any reasonable length of time.

Casing is one of the hardest things you do as a letter carrier. You need to be meticulous and focused, and so it was an hour of hell for my ADHD-ass every morning. But it is one of the most critical things you do, in that there is a serious path dependency to it. Get it right and the rest of your day will go smoothly. Get it wrong and you will be on the struggle bus for the next ten hours. Casing the mail is unforgiving and it will dictate your success or failure as a carrier.

None of this was apparent as I watched Cash put up the mail that first time. He was talking to me continuously, telling me about the route. "At Smith's Landing you can always get a drink of water and use the bathroom. Don't forget to drive down to the frat house, even if they don't have any mail. Sometimes District will do spot checks, so just drive it." He was so fluid as he did it, never pausing. He would reach down to his left hand, grab several pieces, and then slot them into place. Left right center. Left right center. In a smooth rhythm.

"Hey, you try it. I'll be right back."

Cash went to talk to a couple of the other carriers. I picked up the mail and stood in front of the case.

Okay. A copy of *Forbes* magazine for a Ben Lee on Pamela Way.

Where the fuck is Pamela Way?

There was no table I could look it up on. No grid coordinate or index. I knew it wasn't on the streets at the beginning of the route, because they were all on Plantation Road. And it didn't sound like any of the roads I knew from the CRC. So that eliminated the first half of the case. After that, I just stood there and scanned from left to right, street by street until I found Pamela Way. I have slight numeric dyslexia, so I had to repeat the street address over and over again, in a singsong. This brute-force search technique took a while, since Pamela Way is near the end of the route.

Christ have mercy, and this was one piece of mail. I could feel hot panic bubbling up. I had to do this by myself tomorrow?

Parcels are big, so they are sorted into a cage for the route, a random jumble of boxes. It's the carrier's job to get them into route order, laying them out on a long, wheeled dolly called a "float," like a parade float. Some carriers will stick a parcel card for each parcel into their case. That way as they work their way along the route, they get a fluorescent card in the stack reminding them they have a package to deliver. As I got better at delivering the mail, I found I could typically just remember where I had packages to deliver. My brain had built a computer that could automatically keep track of them, but for this trick to work, you needed to know the route from memory. The first time I saw a seasoned carrier do it, I was amazed. One day with Route 10, I was sorting parcels onto the float and I realized I had it. I had learned the route. After that, I only needed parcel cards if the route was totally new to me. There was now a map of Route 10 inside my head.

Once all the mail is put up, you then "take down the case," pulling it down into plastic trays. Everything is now in route order. You put the trays into the truck in the order you'll need to get to them, then load the packages into the truck LIFO, or Last In, First Out. If my route was mostly residential, I would work my way back from the cargo-deck bulkhead behind me in the mail truck. On Route 10, most of the route was dismounted, like a city carrier, so I would load the end of the route first. That way I could open the roll tailgate and grab what I needed from the outside as I went.

"Okay, we're almost ready to go," said Cash. He had been carefully taking me through every step. Compared to what we had done at the Academy in our simulation this was literally fifty times the mail. Cash showed me how to lay out everything on the float. The long trays of DPS mail. My gray waffle trays of hand-sorted mail and magazines. My tall Media Mail trays of spurs, small packages like the bubble envelopes you get from Amazon. And finally all the parcels, laid out in stacks from end to end.

For the parcels, Cash had a system using hods—the double-handed translucent plastic bins the size of a small laundry basket. Hod is not an acronym; it's the name bricklayers use for the wooden boxes and baskets used to carry bricks on the job site, an old Middle English word for an old job. Good ones were hoarded by each carrier and kept clean. They were official government property but carriers used them to hold everything, not just packages and flats, but lunches, jackets, tape, and tools. Hods are one of the five fundamental forces that hold together the USPS—rubber bands, Priority Mail tape, hods, Red Bull, and tobacco.

On my first day, my head was absolutely spinning. I remembered what Mr. Cooper said during recruiting about my first weeks on the job: "Don't go tilt. Don't get your blinders on!" I was absolutely going tilt. My notes as I followed Cash around filled pages of my notebook. I talked through the order of operations with him one more time.

"Jesus this is complicated," I said.

"There are a lot of stages to it, but it'll be automatic before you know it. Just take your time and don't skip steps," said Cash.

We got everything organized on the float, and I took out my phone. I wanted to remember how we had organized everything, because tomorrow Cash wasn't going to be here to help me.

Kathy spun around from the Route 9 case, head spinning *Exorcist*-style. "You cannot take pictures of the mail!"

"Hey, it's cool, Kathy. He's just using it to remember how to do it tomorrow."

"You can't take pictures of the mail. That's how you get fired."

That's how you get fired. I heard a lot of talk about getting fired at the USPS. I saw people do stuff I thought would get them fired. But I never saw someone actually get fired. Even after they lost a mail van over a cliff, they still didn't get fired.

Kathy was barking at me because the life expectancy of new carriers is low. I could hear talk on my first day about a carrier who had started the day before me and already quit. Management can give out all the psychological screenings they want. Only some people will have the grit, intelligence, and real-world problem-solving skills to be letter carriers. Not everyone gets to be a Green Beret or play in the NFL, and not everyone packs the gear to be a letter carrier. It is an invisibly difficult job, which is why it should be better compensated. Much better compensated. It is a hell of a lot easier to stock shelves at Target and the pay and benefits are practically the same. The old hands don't bother getting to know new folks, because the overwhelming majority of FNGs aren't there very long. Other carriers only started talking to me once I had cleared the two-month mark. The folk wisdom was that two months was the watershed. If you stuck around that long, then you could make the long haul.

Could a machine do what a letter carrier does at the case? Maybe. But the Postal Service already machine-sorts everything it can—first-class mail, magazines. And when it comes to the edge cases, the curveballs, that's where an individual carrier's knowledge of their route comes in. I once got a piece of raw mail for my route that had the customer's name, the right street address, but no apartment number. Now, technically I could have marked the envelope IA (inadequate address) and thrown it back before I ever left the station. But I knew exactly who they were and what apartment they lived in. That's skilled labor. Mr. Cooper had told me that hand-sorted first-class mail is the most expensive mail in the world. Now, if loading individual route trucks could be automated, that would be transformative. But it would require huge robotic facilities and a massive injection of capital, and are you really going to get excited about the price of stamps increasing to five dollars to fund that?

If the process that I've described sounds long, arduous, complicated, and painstaking, that's because it is. It is the opposite of whistling in the sunshine and delivering the mail to smiling customers. It is the opposite of being greeted at the door by female customers in their bathrobes. It is the opposite of kids on your route wanting to get a look at the inside of the mail truck. It is the opposite of resting in the shade and eating a sandwich on a remote back road. It is the opposite of watching the sun set over the beauty of the world. It is standing under fluorescent lights on a hard concrete floor, doing a repetitive, exacting task, under time pressure, sucking down cigarette fumes and exhaust from the loading docks.

Casing the mail is the worst goddamn thing about being a mailman, and it is the only thing about delivering the mail that I don't miss. Not once. When I delivered my last letter, I thought to myself, *Well, whatever else happens to you in this life, at least you'll never have to case the mail again.*

And yet. By my count, I spent at least a couple of hundred hours casing the mail during my time with the Postal Service, maybe more like three hundred. I remember the procedure and could still probably walk up cold today and case up Routes 10 and 11.

But I don't really *remember* doing it.

I remember software manuals I've written. Coming up with ideas for brand campaigns or designing experiments. I remember some of the answers I gave on essay tests, from thirty years ago.

Casing the mail? Nothing. Blank tape. Down the memory hole. My brain simply rejected it.

We think about memory as episodes of a TV show, or a highlight reel. But what I remember from casing the mail are my customers. Years later, I met a man at my gym in town, and at the sound of his name I thought:

Fortune, the *Economist, Harvard Business Review.* A generous donor to his alma mater. A registered Democrat. The CEO of his company. One of over a thousand addresses, and I remembered him instantly and silently thanked him for all the times I'd read his copy of the *Economist* before I carefully placed it in his mailbox and locked the door.

Chapter Seven

WILDERNESS OF MIRRORS

IT WAS MY FIRST DAY SOLO AS A LETTER CARRIER. The night before I had all the first-day-on-the-job jitters. I wanted to do a good job. I didn't want to embarrass myself. There's a concept that you'll hear supervisors or career carriers tell the newbies: "Follow the mail." After all, all of the DPS is sitting there in a tray, sorted into route order. In theory you could just move from one address to the next simply by following the addresses on the DPS. In practice that's easier said than done, especially if you don't know the street names.

The day before, Cash had driven me through the entire route, and we delivered the mail together. And I had a huge advantage over the general rookie, in that I had worked out in the Corporate Research Center for almost four years at this point. The CRC had been established in 1985 to help spin out intellectual property developed at Virginia Tech into the private sector. I had been working remotely from the CRC since 2016. I got a one-man office there after it became clear that working from home in our goofy 1970s open-plan house was an impossibility. I sat in the oldest building, the Garvin Center, named after Clifton Garvin, a Virginia Tech graduate, World War II veteran of the Pacific Theater, and former CEO and chairman of Exxon. Garvin was a Virginia boy who had done good, ascending to the commanding heights of the postwar economy, and it's fitting that the first building in the CRC was named after him. He was a bridge between the extractive, heavy-industry past of the American economy and the new knowledge-powered, ultrahigh-added-value industry of America's future. Not one thing being carried out in the Garvin Building had anything to do with fossil fuels, and a good bit of it was actually focused on the technologies of decarbonization. I worked out of a single room, 100 square feet with one door and one window. It was perfect.

The CRC only had a few roads in it—Innovation Drive, Research Center Drive—a maze of nearly identical brick buildings with mirrored glass, completely interchangeable. If you were a rural carrier who had grown up in the country, a landscape of single-story wooden homes and clearly labeled tire shops and supermarkets, the CRC was a wilderness of mirrors, hidden addresses that housed cryptic names where plaid-shirt-wearing scientists did god knows what. But it was my briar patch, my home away from home, and the postmaster knew it when she assigned me the route. Prior to my arrival it was the least-wanted route on the rural circuit, a place where rookie carriers were sent to fail.

I had taken careful notes while Cash drove me in our looping, bumblebee path through the place. Even with my familiarity with the campus, the route was still confusing.

When we were done for the day, I went back and drove the route myself. I made a route map on Google Maps and studied it as carefully as a paratrooper getting ready to jump out over Normandy on D-Day. I read through the list of addresses and street names I had transcribed onto a yellow legal pad in route order. I visualized the route in my mind, turn by turn. If you had given me enough time, I probably would have built a scale model and driven a matchbox mail truck through it.

When I went to bed that night, I tossed and turned, waking frequently, which was unusual for me since I usually slept like stone buried deep in the sod. But the night before my solo route, I would wake up to imagining each building, each mailbox, each CBU as clearly as I could remember it. It felt weird, a familiar place that had been rendered alien by "mailvision."

I wanted to do this right. Part of it was the performance anxiety that comes with any new job, something I had always compensated for by overpreparation. I had a deeply held fear that I was going to screw this up, because of a sneaking suspicion that I was coated with a nonstick coating of job success Teflon, a serial fuckup, and that only massive mental rehearsal was going to prevent me from screwing the pooch on day one. I was afraid of what it meant if I couldn't hack it as a mailman.

By the time dawn came, I couldn't wait to get out the door and just get started, to get the waiting over with. I slammed down as much hot coffee as I could, figured that I wouldn't have time for it on my route, and headed in. When I got to the office, I said one of my oldest mantras. *Slow is smooth and smooth is fast.* I wasn't going to let myself feel time-pressured. I would follow my checklist, be deliberate, and execute step by step. Plan your work and work your plan.

I walked to my case and got started, working slowly, one piece of mail at a time. It felt like doing a jigsaw puzzle where each of the pieces was blank. But I could feel an order beginning to emerge. I kept focused on my work. I was still casing the mail when Kat, a rural carrier in her early thirties, looked over my shoulder.

"Jesus, it's ten a.m.! What are you doing? You've got to get the fuck out of here!"

"That's late?" I felt panic surging when I realized that all the other carriers were already gone.

"That's real late. Let me finish this and you get your parcels loaded."

I got everything onto my float and signed out my FFV key, gas card, and Arrow key from the hot case at the supervisor's desk. I was loading the FFV when Kat came up with my mail, the first of many times that she made it possible for me to be successful at my job.

"Hustle! Go on! Get out of here!"

I adjusted the mirrors, started the ignition, and pulled away from the loading dock. I was finally on the road.

Right out of the MPO parking lot, past my parked truck. Right onto University Center. Right onto Glade Road. If your LLV needed gas, or you needed Gatorade, or were running low on Slim Jims, head on up to the Exxon station and salute Mr. Garvin.

Left onto Old Glade road, past the Dodson Urban Pest Management Laboratory. If it's a living creature bigger than something you need to study with a microscope, and you don't want it in your house, they are tying to kill it at the Dodson Urban Pest Management Laboratory.

Right onto Prices Fork, across the 460 overpass, and left onto Plantation. Then right into the Carillon Family Medicine Center. They were always easy, because all you had to do was dismount, give them a hod full of mail—usually medical journals and the occasional old-school x-ray film—and pick up a hod of outgoing mail. In and out.

Across Plantation to deliver to the hair salon and the audiologist. There were a couple of small apartments above the strip mall. All of that went into a cluster box unit, but sometimes I delivered specialty items to the salon. You could smell the fragrance coming off the boxes.

Down the service road to the Hilton Garden Inn, where they were always happy to let me use the restroom or grab a cup of coffee from the lobby. I asked the general manager about it one morning and he told me there was no need to ask, just enjoy. In an earlier life, I'd had a lot of Hilton Garden Inn lobby coffee, and it seemed strange to be drinking it at home in Blacksburg.

Back onto Plantation and into Smith's Landing, a huge complex of five multistory apartment blocks and an administration building. The good news about Smith's Landing was they had all the mailboxes in one cluster box area. You could park right outside, carry in the mail and parcels, and then pull a chain across the entrance to keep the tenants out while you worked. I would open all the mailbox doors with my Arrow key, an almost comically large bronze slab of metal that could open every mailbox in the 24060 zip code. That's why carriers were sometimes being mugged or shot for them, because they unlocked a parcel pirate and identity thief gold mine. If you lost your Arrow key, your career with the USPS was over. I always kept mine clipped off to my belt with a chain, or locked inside the FFV.

At Smith's Landing, you could watch different people come and go as their leases turned over. There were retirees there who got magazines about hot rods, golf, *Field & Stream*. A lot of foreign grad students, who would receive packages from home with customs declarations: SOUP, POWDERED. FACE CREAM. RELIGIOUS ITEMS. These packages sometimes smelled of spices that were exotic to my white guy palate, something essential to a familiar dish for a homesick student.

Back on Plantation Road, there was a quick series of mounted curbside deliveries to students living in university bungalows next to the experimental live-animal farm. These must have been agriculture students, as they were getting their own magazines about horses, cattle, dogs, and beekeeping, true to Virginia Tech's original roots as an ag school.

Then down to the end of Plantation and left onto Smithfield Drive, a dirt road that cut under the freeway and through horse pasture. Some of that open space now held the Virginia Tech Drone Park, which was enclosed like an urban golf driving range, a black cube of netting rising a hundred feet into the sky. The area between Blacksburg and Roanoke was one of the FAA's six national "drone zones" where drones could operate alongside general aviation and commercial aircraft. Google had a drone hub in Christiansburg that would deliver burritos from Chipotle and prescriptions from CVS right to people's backyards. There was a big drone that could deliver blood and critical medications to the far southwestern part of the state, the first remote medical drone in the country.

Smithfield Plantation was here, Colonel Preston's plantation from the colonial era, handed down to his family until one of his descendants lost it by fighting for the Confederacy. Now it was a living history museum that bored me in middle school and was still successfully boring my children thirty years later.

Along this dirt road I would sometimes run into my father and his best friend, Gary Brown, taking a walk together. Gary was a radar research engineer and may be the squarest, most solid guy I knew. Dad always seemed delighted to see me driving the mail truck, and of course he and Gary demanded a guided tour the first time I ran into them.

"Look at all these rivets," Gary said.

"It's primitive, like an old airframe. Really something," said Dad. Nothing made him happier than knowing how something was put together.

After that initial encounter, Dad always wanted to talk, and Gary wanted to keep walking. Dad was curious about the work, something concrete and comprehensible after my years in the corporate puzzle palace. He never seemed to judge the fact that I was now a mailman, which surprised me. Later he told me, "You know, when you're an engineer, that's what you do. You've gotten to do all sorts of stuff."

Gary interrupted us. "Come on, Wally, we've got to get moving. Sorry, Steve. You've got mail to deliver."

"Gotta go, Steve," Dad whispered in through the open door. "Gary gets cranky if we're off the pace."

Past the outdoor obstacle course for the Virginia Tech Corps of Cadets. Right at the Duck Pond, down to the roundabout. Slide down Southgate and deliver to a few homes there, just outside the town limits.

Out into the CRC, down Research Center Drive, past a small patch of old-growth hardwood forest, just a few acres of it. The oaks there must have been more than three hundred years old. With the slowdown in vehicle traffic from the lockdown, this mini wood was full of pileated woodpeckers, blue jays, red-tailed hawks, robins, finches, rufous-sided towhees, wild turkeys, white-tailed deer, great horned owls, foxes, woodchucks, squirrels, and corn snakes. I would drive slow through here. As things opened back up, all of this wildlife melted into invisibility again, but at the beginning of my time on Route 10 it was as if I were the last mailman on earth, and this was life after man.

I would deliver to Advanced Propulsion and Power Lab, a squat brick building where occasionally you could hear them start up something on the test bed outside, howling like a chained demon. There were tanks of propellant and liquefied gas in back, the kind of muscular science I had imagined doing when I was a kid, building model rockets.

There was the Torc Robotics R&D center, where they were building self-driving trucks for Mercedes-Benz and the Department of Defense.

Across the parking lot was the Hume National Security Center, "educating the next generation of national security leaders." They did drones, cybersecurity, and something with a laser mounted on the roof.

The buildings were separated by manicured grass and landscaping. The next big cluster opened up on a soccer field and picnic ground. In the center was the 1901 Group, a US government IT contractor. The next building was Intuitive Surgical, where they built the Da Vinci thoracic surgery robot. I know this only because I spoke to one of their manufacturing engineers in the parking lot one day.

Across the road was the National Weather Service, with their satellite dishes and weather balloons that would rise into the dawn and dusk skies. The satellite uplinks had been under construction when I was in high school, and the land was nothing but bullrushes and concrete pylons to hold the parabolic antennae and their control systems. It was one of my preferred makeout spots—remote, dark—and lying out on those mute concrete structures I felt like I could see into the future. I wondered what my seventeen-year-old self would make of fifty-year-old Steve delivering the mail here, a man in sneakers and a ball cap, listening to podcasts about economics on a portable wireless networked computer smaller than a Walkman. *Jesus,* he would think, *that poor bastard. What an incredibly boring job!* It was part of the reality shear that stalked me around Route 10.

There was BlockOne, the blockchain company that had installed two industrial-grade air chillers, a data center, and a 360-degree camera coverage around the building's perimeter. I occasionally saw one of the two armed guards, wearing body armor and carrying Glock 17 pistols with several spare magazines. The only time I went inside the building was near Christmas. My super told me that BlockOne had a pickup. The armed guard took me inside, and in a conference room were hundreds of identical packages, all about the size of a shoe box, all Priority Mail, addressed to Singapore, France, Saudi Arabia. BlockOne developed technology for secure transactions in the capital markets, and their building sat right on top of the Virginia Tech fiber optic data backbone. It was a silent outpost of global capitalism in the middle of an old cow pasture, unmanned except for its lethal-force-authorized caretakers.

In the middle of it all was TechLab. My mother worked there as the head of product for almost twenty years, making tests to detect harmful pathogens in municipal water systems, deadly stuff like amoebic dysentery, *E. coli*, giardia, cryptosporidium. All of these dangerous microorganisms were inside the production lab, a biological hot room where the staff worked in bunny suits and had to follow sterile procedures. Over the course of her two decades there, everyone Mom worked with got contaminated and wound up in the hospital. Everyone but Mom. She was so present-minded, so detail-oriented that she never made a mistake. Not once in twenty years. When I would deliver mail to TechLab, I thought about the careful, exacting woman who oversaw all those tests, keeping millions of people and their drinking water safe. The kind of mind it takes to do that sort of work. She was always the HBIC, and that lab was her seat of power. I wondered what that woman would think if she could see herself now. The unquestioned queen of her dangerous domain, reduced to what she became. That steel trap mind was gone. Today she would get flustered, disoriented, her procedural memory shot, lost to vascular dementia. There was a kind of mercy to the fact that this past version of my mother had no idea what was waiting for her. By the end, she would sometimes mentally be back in New Orleans, sometimes back working at TechLab, and the room where she stayed at the memory center would become a "hotel room." All places and times coequal and coincident. It was impossible for me to enter TechLab without feeling a sense of loss.

There was the new osteopathic medical school, a music school, a shuttered yoga studio, a sports merchandising business, a company that designed 3D printed helmets for the NFL. A company of former Virginia Tech students who built automated kiosks that could print greeting cards—students I had actually helped teach. There was a cloning company that grew transgenic organs for transplant in pigs, and a beverage startup that brewed up an undrinkable "fermented health beverage." Unsold cases of it were stacked in their conference room, gathering dust.

Hiding behind the credit union was the blank facade of a suite of rooms that apparently contained the university's sensitive compartmented information facility (SCIF), where professors who were consulting on classified projects could hold remote secure meetings.

More apartment buildings, including one apartment with a woman who got a steady supply of live insects, which she wanted delivered directly to her door. She had a totemic staff planted in her front yard, topped with a webcam and adorned with feathers. You were to place the insects on her doorstep, press the wireless doorbell she had screwed to the staff, let her see you on the webcam, and then leave. I would always back away from this camera, maintaining eye contact, because the vibes in that place gave me the whim-whams.

There was the daycare center where my daughter Walker went before kindergarten, and again I could see a past version of myself, driving my Tacoma when it was brand-new from the factory, Walker and I holding hands as we headed into Rainbow Riders. Next-door was an apartment complex with the worst mailboxes in Blacksburg, flimsy aluminum cracker boxes that would burn your hands in the summer and freeze your skin in the winter. In the wind the doors would slam shut on your fingers. I thought about writing their manufacturer, but they had long since gone out of business. Some measure of justice in the market, I guess.

There was a house that's been turned into a cell phone tower station, the antenna tower spouting from the top like a fungal growth. There was the home of a retired cop and full-time ballbreaker whom I was always careful to avoid if I could. There was one last huge apartment center that never let me use their bathroom, claiming Covid.

Almost done. Down past the Virginia Tech airport, where I would fly a Cessna in more prosperous times. My old flight instructor was now the executive director, and if I had a parcel I would drop in and say hello. On game days, the private jets of wealthy alumni would line the runway.

Past the airport was the Center for Packaging and Unit Load Design, where they were building the future of just how to package and move all the stuff the planet was building, buying, shipping, and consuming. Out front was a stainless-steel sculpture of a globe, sitting on top of a load pallet, the humble hardwood platform that let forklifts move packaged goods in bulk. The base of the sculpture reads PALLETS MOVE THE WORLD.

On the edge of the airfield was a small brick bungalow, a private residence with an abandoned Toyota 4Runner in the front yard that never moved in more than a year, a vehicle that I thought about towing off myself as legitimate salvage under the Law of the Sea. I remembered this house from high school, how it would have looked more at home up some distant hollow, complete with a refrigerator and washing machine on the front porch, totally unchanged while this garden of gleaming postindustrial work grew up around it like a time-lapse film.

The last of it: another daycare center, then a frat house that only got mail three times in the year I delivered their mail, the skip dumpster always seemingly filled up with a freshly incinerated sofa. This was followed by a Montessori school, and finally the cancer care center that later my father would only grudgingly visit, until his cancer finally killed him.

The deepest whirlpools of time shear surrounded my offices at the Garvin Building.

At the Garvin Building was my one-man office, where I would work remotely, putting together graphs and PowerPoint presentations. As Cash noted, I was delivering mail to myself. Really, I was delivering mail to my past self. I stood outside and looked in the mirrored window at my desk with its two monitors. My couch and my bookshelves. My mini fridge. The old TV on which the girls could come over and watch a movie while I worked. I could always use the bathroom in this building, because I had a key card. I just couldn't bring myself to surrender the lease. I hung on to it, a promise to myself that I would make my way back to the interrupted narrative of my life. It was a hopeful thing, but it also felt like a stalking horse.

Sometimes I would take my lunch break in my office, sitting at my desk eating a Slim Jim, staring out the window at the mail truck. I would type words into a blank Google doc, just for the feeling of writing words at a keyboard. *Now is the time for all good men to come to the aid of their country.* I would think about Clifton Garvin and his building, my building. Mr. Garvin, fellow Eagle Scout and past executive of what was once the most valuable company on earth, and I'd wonder what he thought about the whole situation.

"You've gotten yourself into one weird pickle here, Grant."

"I have, Cliff."

"What are you going to do about it?"

"Not much to be done at the moment. I'm going to deliver the mail."

"Keep your eyes open, Steve. In my experience, the world is wide. There's oil everywhere. Peak oil? My ass! King Hubbert was a moron for being such a smart man. We're never going to run out of oil. The whole world is floating on it. It formed over hundreds of millions of years, two hundred trillion barrels of the stuff just waiting! People can't even conceive how much opportunity is out there, just underground. Keep looking. When the time comes, you'll find it. Have an oilman's faith. You'll tap a gusher."

There was old Steve, a living middle-aged Eagle Scout sitting at his desk, talking to a dead Eagle Scout and oil executive.

And then there was me, the mailman, in whatever this new timeline was. Lost in layers of time and space, but also as at home as I had ever been.

I knew exactly where I was, even if I wasn't sure who or when I was.

Outside, alone, and at home.

Still, I had done it. Maybe I felt weird. Maybe I felt unstuck in time. Over the year that I delivered the mail on Route 10, that feeling never fully left me. But by the end of my first day, I had done it, all of it. It took me till 6 p.m., pulling in right under the wire, but I had carried the whole route myself, without help. A couple of the other carriers told me this was unprecedented. I was incredibly proud. *You're a natural, Grant,* I congratulated myself. All my note taking, map study, checklists—it had paid off. Every day for the next two weeks, the route got easier and I got a little faster. As far as I was concerned, I had delivering the mail licked.

That's the thing about a wilderness of mirrors. Is that success, or merely the reflection of it? Is the image you see a direct perception of yourself, or some funhouse projection? Bounce the light between mirrored panes of glass long enough, from building to building, reflections of reflections, and a sunset can appear as a false dawn.

Chapter Eight

FROM THE PEOPLE WHO BROUGHT YOU THE F-14 TOMCAT AND THE GRANT FAMILY CANOES

DURING THE TIME THAT I BECAME A LETTER CARRIER and in the years since, when folks who have never known someone in the Postal Service learn I was a mailman they always ask me the same questions. While these questions are being asked by grown men and women, they are somehow rooted in childhood. Delivering the mail is a "Halloween job," like doctor or firefighter, an occupation with a uniform, immediately recognizable, even by children. Part of the everyday fabric of things. Not just walking down their street, but a staple of childhood TV. *Mister Rogers' Neighborhood* had a mailman, Mr. McFeely. Grover was not just a generic mailman on *Sesame Street* but an honest-to-god badged USPS letter carrier. My kids watched the mail arrive on *Blue's Clues*.

Women would always ask about the uniform. Did I wear a uniform? No, I only wore part of one, to make sure that I was visibly a letter carrier of the USPS, so nobody would shoot me. Only city carriers are required to wear official USPS uniforms. It's a good question, however, and one that people are curious about, as uniforms have retreated from American life.

Men never asked about the uniform. Ever. They could give less of a shit. But there was one thing they always asked about: "the little truck." It's funny, but men never called it a van or delivery vehicle; it was always "the mail truck" or "the little truck." My theory for this is that the "truck" was the metal toy you could play with in the sandbox, like a Tonka dump truck. And, as an object of childhood fascination, that's what grown men wanted to know about.

The little truck that all these guys were referring to is the Grumman Long Life Vehicle. When I was a kid, the USPS was still driving the DJ-5 Postal Jeep. The *D* stood for *dispatch* and it was built especially for the USPS. I even had a Matchbox car of it, with a mailman sitting on the right-hand side of the die-cast model. Those were phased out in the late 1980s. While they were very capable on all sorts of roads and in all kinds of weather, the USPS decided it needed a purpose-built vehicle for delivering the mail that could carry one thousand pounds, was tough, agile, and could last a long time.

The jeeps were phased out and replaced with the Grumman Long Life Vehicle, in all its slab-sided, wedge-shaped glory. There are a lot of things in life that don't live up to their name, but when it comes to service life the LLV is maybe only surpassed by Boeing's B-52 bomber (born 1954) and the AK-47, Mikhail Kalashnikov's peasant-proof masterpiece that is still in service in war zones around the world. The LLV entered service in 1987, my junior year in high school, and is still on the road. There aren't many industrial artifacts that have such longevity. Cast-iron skillets, your great-grandfather's duck gun. Stuff made from machined metal that only requires occasional lubrication. No finicky electronics.

The LLV and its cousin the FFV are the single most important pieces of equipment that a letter carrier uses. They are a wonder of built-for-purpose design. They are also a slow-motion, decades-long disaster.

Originally the LLV was built to be in service for twenty-four years. But in 2009, the USPS came to grips with the fact that it didn't have a replacement, so they extended the service life to thirty years. That only gets you to 2017, and there are still over 125,000 LLVs on the road at the time of this writing. The Grumman LLV is so long-lived that it actually outlasted the company that built it, Grumman having been absorbed into Northrup Grumman in 1994. When I think of Grumman, I think of the three canoes my father has accumulated over the years, all fabricated from sheet aluminum and carefully riveted together around Grumman's proprietary "Ball T" keel. "It helps the boat track straight in the water, that's why they don't turn worth a damn," according to Dad. Grumman got into canoes after World War II, trying to find a consumer market for things they could build out of sheet aluminum, since the US Navy was no longer buying thousands of carrier-based fighter aircraft.

I mention these canoes because some of my earliest childhood memories are of floating down the river in them, and the first time I got inside an LLV for my driver's training, I recognized the distinctive Grumman rivets. In fact, I could recognize everything about how the vehicle was constructed—the same way the canoes were built, rib and sheet-metal construction, riveted together, the same way that an entire generation of World War II aircraft were built. What it does not look like is any automobile you've been inside in the last fifteen years. It looks like an upside-down aluminum Grumman canoe, bolted to a GM chassis and powertrain, hammered into shape with no concern for aerodynamics. Because that is exactly what it is.

The LLV is right-hand drive. You can drive down the right-hand side of the road and easily reach out to slide the mail into a curbside mailbox. Where the left-hand seat would go in a normal vehicle the LLV has a large, purpose-built tray that can hold three plastic gunboats of mail. You could store three hods of other mail on the floorboards beneath it. It had two sliding panel front doors, and under 25 miles an hour we were allowed to drive with them open. It made reaching for mailboxes easy. It made dismounting to deliver a parcel easy.

In the LLV you sat high up, with excellent visibility. It had a rollgate rear door to access the big stuff in the back with ease, or you could crouch down and walk into the cargo area from the flight deck, thanks to a locking bulkhead door. With its body-on-frame construction it was tough as hell and easy to maintain, and the narrow stance of its front wheels gave it a golf-cart-like near-zero turning radius. You could thread a needle with its handling, even if it was tippy at any sort of speed. It was good in the city, and despite the grumbling I heard about its age, it was my impression that it was much loved.

I hated the LLV. I loved its many excellent features designed to make delivering the mail efficient and fast. But nobody who grew up understanding that machines were meant to be updated, refined, and ultimately replaced could love it. I say this as a red-blooded American shade-tree mechanic who loves cars and the internal combustion engine. Our delivery vehicles were like democracy, the worst of all possible vehicles, except for the alternatives. There were so many flaws; deep flaws. The LLV was long-lived because it was primitive, a living automotive fossil, a horseshoe crab kept on the road by phased maintenance and Priority Mail tape, the universal fix-it-all adhesive that keeps the USPS running.

The LLV was built on a General Motors chassis, with a barking dog of an engine, the 151-cubic-inch cast-iron straight-4 "Iron Duke" with a single-point fuel injector, cranking out a miserable 90 horsepower, which would negotiate with the wheels via a three-speed GM slushbox transmission. With a real load of mail on board, it was wildly underpowered. A real piece of shit, except that it was somehow the best piece of shit in the USPS delivery fleet.

What was remarkable about the LLV was the design features it did *not* have relative to any contemporary vehicle, even the cheapest domestic grocery go-getter. In the automotive industry there is a measure of passenger comfort called NVH—noise, vibration, and harshness. Most cars have sound insulation in the body and the floor of the car to isolate the driver from road and engine noise. The LLV has none of this. Zero. It was an empty aluminum shell, and the acoustic experience of driving it was like riding inside an empty beer can bouncing free in the bed of a pickup truck along a washboard dirt road. There was no air-conditioning; the heater was anemic—and that was when it worked. The vehicle was a thermal-stress-test unit for human endurance, astronaut-training stuff.

It was toaster-oven hot in the summer and practically refrigerated in the winter. There were no collision-avoidance sensors, just a space-station lattice structure of mirrors around the outside. The only warning you received if you were running something over was the sound of impact.

Turning the mirrors to produce real 360-degree visual awareness around the van was an art. The big A-pillar-mounted side-view mirrors did just what the mirrors on your passenger car do: they let you look into the blind spots down the sides of the vehicle. It was the "pot lid" mirrors that were the real marvel. These were round, convex mirrors that gave a wide but funhouse-distorted view of the world. One was mounted on an arm above the front left bumper and allowed you to see down to the pavement in front of the forward bumper, into the blind spot created by the nose. But it was the rear pot lid, mounted to the upper left-hand corner of the van that required the most optical magic. The relic of an age before cheap digital sensors on cars, the USPS relied on this UFO-shaped mirror to give you situational awareness of what was going on behind the totally opaque roll gate at the back of the truck. You adjusted your left-hand driver's mirror so that you could see into the rear pot lid. You now did a visual bank shot, bouncing light from the rear mirror to the side mirror and then into your eye. It was then up to the visual cortex inside the brain of your humble letter carrier to assemble a spatial model of what was happening around the vehicle.

For me, a lifetime of rural driving, driving in the UK, flying light aircraft, and, most importantly, playing videogames meant I could synthesize all of this together pretty quickly. In our training, older students like the youth pastor, who had spent years driving a school bus, adjusted his mirrors like a pro and drove the obstacle course perfectly his first time out. If you had grown up driving the cars on the road in the 1980s, you were going to be okay driving the LLV, as sort of performative living history, the automotive equivalent of Colonial Williamsburg. But younger drivers struggled mightily with it. During training Hank would grimace as one orange traffic cone after another was mowed down by Millennials and Gen Z. "You just ran over somebody's dog! You just ran over little Jimmy!"

Delivering the mail requires driving, a lot of it, along narrow roads, in parking lots, with pedestrians, bicyclists, and kids playing out in the street. During our driver's training they wanted us to know that driving was the most dangerous thing we would do as carriers. We were shown internet doorbell footage of a carrier who was texting on his phone inside his LLV. He was in a leafy suburban neighborhood. While the vehicle was in motion, he fell out of the open sliding door, because he did not have his seat belt on. The LLV rolled on and crashed into the garage of the house with the internet doorbell. The carrier got up, got into the LLV, backed out, and drove off without his front bumper. About thirty awkward seconds later, he drove back into the frame, collected the bumper, and tossed it in the back of his LLV. When he got back to his home office, he told his postmaster that someone had hit his vehicle while he was taking his lunch break. By that point, the owner of the house had been alerted by his AI that someone hit his garage, and he had already called in the accident and shared the footage with the postmaster.

"What should he have done? What should the letter carrier have done here?" asked Hank.

"He should have immediately called the police."

"He should have immediately called the postmaster."

"No," said Hank. "He should have immediately called his shop steward. The only words out of his mouth should have been, 'I have a drinking problem.' If you have a drinking problem, I can save your job. You'll even get a paid trip to rehab. But this guy lied and was caught on camera, so they canned him. What's the moral of this story?"

"That he should have been wearing his seat belt."

"That all accidents are preventable."

"No, the moral of this story is that if you wreck your LLV and it's your fault, you have a drinking problem. CALL YOUR SHOP STEWARD. Come on, people!"

In the wisdom of the USPS, all motor vehicle accidents were preventable.

All.

At the Academy, this struck me as an almost metaphysical statement.

"Everything? Like, what if somebody runs into you?"

"That's preventable. You should have had better situational awareness," said Hank.

"What about if we were struck by lightning?"

"Preventable. You must have done something because God is angry at you."

"I mean, you can't see anything out the back of that thing. How is that supposed to work?"

"Tell that to the kid who was run over by a letter carrier in Boone's Mill. I bet he wishes someone had paid attention to how preventable these accidents are. *All* accidents are preventable."

"That's a statistical impossibility!" I blurted out. I couldn't help it anymore.

"Oh yeah, Dr. Science? Listen up! If I can teach an eighteen-year-old to drive an M-1 Abrams main battle tank in an urban combat environment, you can drive an LLV safely and without accidents. Because . . ."

". . . all accidents are preventable?"

"Yes!"

Management had to believe this, because this certainty of human error as the sole cause of accidents was the only form of driver protection the LLV had. The LLV was, in the language of the automotive industry, decontented and underfeatured. There was no radio—after all, you're supposed to be imagining all possible accidents, not listening to Journey or talk radio. There were no airbags and no crumple zones. In a wreck the whole vehicle was one big crumple zone. I never visited a post office that did not have LLV crash photos posted on the bulletin board, rear-ended postal vehicles that resembled aluminum piñatas, smashed open to scatter parcels and mail across the road.

There were decades of safety technology that were *not* engineered into the LLV. Once, on the 101 in Los Angeles, I saw a Lamborghini hit a bridge abutment at aircraft speed. The car was absolutely totaled but the passenger compartment survived "unintruded." In fact, the two passengers, an older white dude and a very tall Black American model in a cocktail dress, climbed out of the driver's-side gullwing door with nothing hurt but their pride. That is the miracle of crash engineering.

That engineering miracle was nowhere to be found in the LLV. I would not have wanted to be in any sort of collision in an LLV. If you had your seat belt on, it seems that the survival rate for carriers was good. If you didn't, then you were headed to the big postal route in the sky. You were supposed to have your seat belt on the moment you started the ignition, because that's your training and all accidents are preventable, right? The reality was that at slow speeds, dismounting over and over, it was very easy to let your seat belt discipline slide. The LLV was so old that I never heard a safety buzzer in thousands of hours of operation. Either it didn't have one, it had been disconnected, or it just died of old age. It was all on you, the letter carrier, because all accidents are preventable.

The front greenhouse, the windshield and the side windows, was designed for high visibility, and it did a good job at that. But with age the gaskets around the aluminum framing had a tendency to leak, a design flaw. And that leak would form directly above the fuse box for the vehicle, mounted just behind the firewall on the right-hand driver's side. Rain would get inside and leak down into the fuse panel and the whole machine would go up like a Roman candle. Do you know what aluminum does in a fire? Ask the British sailors on the HMS *Sheffield*, when an Argentine Exocet antiship missile struck the starboard side of the ship and set the ship's aluminum superstructure on fire. The ship burned like a flare, the metal itself catching on fire.

Magnesium, used in illumination flares and fireworks, is also commonly used as an alloy in aerospace and automotive metals. It is light, strong, and ductile but burns with a ferocious, brilliant heat. And that's just what an LLV will do when it catches on fire, except it's stuffed with highly flammable paper products. For the curious, the internet will happily supply you with pictures of burned-up LLVs.

The LLV and the FFV, its slightly larger Ford-built cousin, get terrible gas mileage. The only microchip in this thing was the ECU for the fuel injector, as opposed to the hundreds of embedded microcontrollers in a modern car. Between this primitive fuel management system and its total piece-of-shit powertrain, it got around nine miles to the gallon. Nearly 75 percent of the fleet is LLVs and FFVs, and annually they use over 150 million gallons of unleaded gasoline. Depending on the price of fuel, that means the USPS is paying around a half a billion dollars a year in gas. That's not the whole transportation budget—that's unleaded gas for part of the delivery fleet. Over 90 percent of the fleet travels under forty miles a day, ideal for an electric vehicle that can recharge overnight. The technology was here to do this twenty years ago. What I'm describing does not require some sort of exotic battery technology. Electric postal vehicles, with airbags and air-conditioning, could have be on the road in the early 2000s.

Crashes kill letter carriers, crashes that airbags could prevent. So does heat stress. Sending letter carriers reminders on their scanners to "look out for heatstroke" is like telling someone in the trenches in World War I to "look out for being shelled." There were times here in the relatively cool mountains of Virginia that it got so hot in the LLV, I thought I wasn't going to make it. I cannot imagine how hot they must get in the Southwest in the summer. I know that in Houston, where the heat index was 116 in June 2023, sixty-six-year-old letter carrier Eugene Gates died of a heart attack brought on by heat stress. This wasn't a matter of training. He had been carrying the mail for thirty-six years. It was a matter of him not having air-conditioning in his vehicle. The regulatory fine for his death was $15,625, and the USPS is "reviewing the citation."

All accidents are preventable. Except for the ones built into a forty-year-old delivery vehicle without any real safety equipment. And in the hotter, wetter, more extreme weather of climate-change America, air-conditioning *is* safety equipment. Why doesn't the USPS replace the LLV and FFV? Because it can't afford to. Because it doesn't take any money from the US taxpayer. Because it isn't allowed to capitalize itself like a private firm, or appropriate funding like the military.

If US soldiers and marines start getting blown up by IEDs, the Defense

Department buys mine-resistant troop carriers. And it does this quickly, because taxpayers insist on keeping our service people as safe as possible. The USPS simply does not have the administrative freedom to do this, and it is a crime that the country where engineers invented the airbag and modern collision-avoidance systems, the country that put crumple zones and the shoulder belt into mass adoption, continues to send hardworking people out on the road in these death traps. It is, in fact, an unconscionable moral and political failure. But as letter carriers, we drove these vehicles because they were what we were issued, and all accidents are preventable.

The official attitude toward road safety is very Lutheran: you were born a sinner, and only constant vigilance prevents further sin. If your LLV exploded into flames, that had to somehow be your fault. This complex of multiple safety failures would never be allowed to persist in private industry. Ironically, the federal government, in the form of the Occupational Safety and Health Administration, would have shut down any business that sent their people to work in these conditions. But because of legislative restrictions and the quasi-independent nature of the USPS, these institutional failures are allowed to persist, year on year, along with the insane policy of rural carriers driving left-hand drive vehicles from the right-hand seat, because letter carriers are invisible.

The reality is that the world is hard to change. Material culture has a life of its own, and the things we build often last longer than we could ever imagine. Some artifacts, with their moving parts and motors, only last a short time. The Walkman I carried on my paper route in high school only lives on in memory. This idea that industrial goods are transient adds to our perception that the world is always changing, particularly technology. But there are forms that persist. My great-grandfather's cast-iron skillet will still be in use by my great-grandchildren. The AK-47 will still be killing people one hundred years from now, adding to its body count of millions of souls. The horseshoe crab has been an evolutionary success for some 445 million years, effectively design-stable since the Paleozoic era. The world is full of manufactured stuff we wish we could get rid of: asbestos, coal-fired power plants, plutonium, polytetrafluoroethylene, also known as Teflon and Gore-Tex. We didn't use them because we're stupid. We created them because they were great at their job, until we learned better, yet we are effectively stuck with them forever.

I have always thought of aluminum as an American metal, but that's not historically accurate. The first aluminum was reliably extracted from bauxite ore by a Danish chemist in 1825 and was so rare that Napoleon had dinnerware made from it as an extravagant gift for his guests. But it was America that put it to work, smelting it with cheap hydroelectric power on the Columbia River and then fabricating it into airplanes, automobiles, beer cans, the LLV, and the Grant family canoes. The nine-inch-tall pyramidal cap at the top of the Washington Monument is made of aluminum, where its corrosion resistance and conductive properties help it double as a lightning rod.

It is the rare material that can be perfectly recycled. Recycled aluminum is as pure and as strong as the fresh metal smelted from bauxite. It is a material that can be crushed, heated, and returned to use without loss of strength, ductility, or flexion.

With care and engineering, it can be transformed from obsolescent junk into something new and better. We simply need to care enough to try.

Chapter Nine

PRIVATELY OWNED VEHICLE

RURAL ROUTE 3 WAS A MONSTER. AT OVER SIXTY miles in length, with 724 deliveries, it wound through pocket suburban neighborhoods, past a coal-mining memorial, up dirt roads that threaded along high-grade hollows into dense hardwood forests. The whole middle section of the route, a long slide downhill to the river, was so remote that it received no cell phone service, a place where my trusty scanner went off the grid and I might as well have been delivering the mail in 1920 and not 2020. It snaked through old horse farms, along a stretch of the New River, through the unincorporated town of McCoy, where nearly everyone was named McCoy. While I knew that a lot of the McCoys I went to high school with lived in McCoy, I had no idea how many of them were hidden down there, or that they had their own miniature post office. The route then turned back to town, where another community was hidden, the unincorporated town called Wake Forest, a historically Black community settled by Black American freemen, complete with two historically Black churches. The whole route was a world unto itself.

I was a month into the job at this point, and technically I was considered ready for solo work as a rural letter carrier anywhere in the US. I had been successfully carrying Route 10 without help, and management figured I could handle Wade's route, maybe with a little help. Wade was an Alaskan who somehow wound up marooned in Blacksburg, Virginia. He was maybe in his late fifties, lean, and nice in that Canadian-adjacent way that almost every Alaskan I've ever met is.

After all, I was the rookie carrier who had successfully delivered Route 10 without any help—from day one. We had one carrier quit on their first day, in tears. Some of the career carriers were impressed. "Honey, you're doing great. And on your first day." But other than memorizing the addresses to case up the mail, after a few times it just wasn't that hard. *Of course I finished!* was my thinking. Sure, it might take some getting used to, but go ahead and give me the biggest route in the office. I was a mail-carrying prodigy. A month in, I was convinced that I knew how to deliver the mail.

Management and Wade wisely thought otherwise. So I was given two more days of OJT, doing a ride-along on his route so he could take a long-delayed vacation of three weeks. For two days I helped Wade case and load, and then deliver, his long, serpentine route. It's a lot of time to talk with someone. I learned that before he delivered the mail, he had once owned a Domino's Pizza franchise in Anchorage, Alaska.

"Did you like that work?" I asked.

"I did, I liked it a lot."

"Did somebody buy you out?" I was trying to understand how he wound up down here.

"Well, the guy I ran the place with, he wasn't a nice guy." And that was it. If I had gotten screwed out of my franchise, it would have consumed me in revenge scenarios and self-recrimination for months, years. Wade wouldn't even bad-mouth him. I never did learn how an Alaskan winds up delivering mail in southwestern Virginia.

Despite it being a college town we only had one other distant transplant as a mail carrier. He was a city carrier, a tall, pale guy about my age who had grown up in the Soviet Union. I once overheard him say, "I like post office. Is faceless bureaucracy. Very comfortable for me. Is like communism."

Wade was one of the guys who seemed to have eyes in the back of his head. It was never part of his official duties, but he was the one who always caught the mail I had forgotten to case.

"Hey, Steve. Don't forget to check the hot case."

"Thanks, Wade."

"Hey, Steve. Check on your raw flats."

Out of the hot case, the raw flats, the parcels, the raw mail, multiple trays of DPS, there was always something I was missing, and Wade was the one who caught it. It became a game for me, to see if I could remember everything without Wade catching something, and it was only toward the end of my year that I occasionally got it right. Occasionally.

The truth was that I was never a very good mailman.

During my training with Wade, I watched him effortlessly case a route that was 50 percent larger than mine. I watched him automatically sort the parcels into route order. I watched him eat a sandwich in the right-hand seat and deliver the mail at the same time. It's one thing to know academically that process fluency helps people become unconsciously competent at complex tasks. But to see it in action is something else when you know enough to understand the mechanics of what is happening and to appreciate the skill behind what you are seeing. I will admit I felt a kind of awe watching Wade work. He was simply really fucking good at delivering the mail, and looking back I think he and Cash were the best carriers we had in the rural craft in Blacksburg.

Unlike my route on Route 10, a rural route in name only, where I had regular access to a postal van, Route 3 was the real deal. Wade drove his own POVs—privately owned vehicles. Rural carrier associates are required to have a POV to deliver the mail, as well as a backup vehicle. I never bought a dedicated delivery vehicle and skated on it, but the real pros all had one—my friends Kat and Erica drove boxy Honda Pilots, beloved for their flat floors and front seating where you could just stuff a cushion between the seats to drive and sling the mail. Tommy and Wade were in the old Ford Explorer camp—the SUVs were easy to work on, cheap, and tough. I once saw Tommy, our shop steward and most senior rural carrier, drive to work in his personal pickup, pull a new rear axle for his Explorer out of the bed, drop the old one in the parking lot with his Explorer up on jack stands, and swap in the whole assembly, right there in the parking lot. The cool kid in this bunch was Diana's purpose-built right-hand-drive Jeep Wrangler. Jeep had done small production runs of this vehicle every year for a couple of decades, but finally stopped producing them in 2021. Diana's ride had permanent flashers, US Mail magnets, and was even white, like a government-owned mail truck.

Wade had not one but two Ford Explorers as his personal mail fleet: the newer and nicer one that we rode in, and the older black one as his backup. He kept both inside the wire in the MPO vehicle lot. On my training day I helped Wade load the jeep, carefully stacking the mail on the float and pushing it out to the loading dock. Wade called out the roads on the route as he fit the parcels together in the cargo area like a four-dimensional game of *Tetris*. I tried to absorb what I could, but it was like trying to absorb what Jesus was doing when he turned a couple of baskets of bread and fish into enough food to feed five thousand people. Nothing overtly miraculous happened, but a hugely complex operation with a lot of spatial cognition and procedural processing was over in a moment as if it was just another day with the twelve apostles.

We drove the route, and really I should have been paying attention like a hawk. Instead I paid attention like a fifty-year-old with ADHD who was enjoying a guided tour of the country. Route 3 was all close-shouldered two-lane country roads, where it wasn't gravel road. This was what I had imagined when I signed up to be a rural carrier. We pulled up to a row of five identical black mailboxes, at the top of a snaking single-lane track with a locked gate at the top of it.

"These mailboxes were really a mess, so I replaced them."

"You mean the USPS sent someone to replace them?"

"No, I told the owners that I would replace their mailboxes with these Gibraltars, so they could get their parcels."

"Did the Postal Service pay you for that?"

"No. But this way I didn't have to drive down the access road, and they could get their parcels."

The Gibraltar is more typically known as a "farmer's mailbox," a huge, cathedral-vaulted black mailbox big enough to hold a Thanksgiving turkey and a couple of side dishes. Later, as a carrier, I held a special place in my heart for anyone who was thoughtful enough to put one up. They are beloved by all letter carriers everywhere. I was trying to imagine coming out here on the weekend, installing these mailboxes for someone else. But then I wasn't the regular. This route was Wade's home. He saw it every day. I was just the sub and, as I was to come to learn, doomed to wander the face of the earth. That's the difference between a regular and a sub.

If something has suddenly gone wrong with the delivery of your mail, it is probably the sub's fault. Or the product of Postmaster General Louis DeJoy's latest "efficiency" project.

Wade introduced me to Mrs. Adele James, who was at the halfway point on his route. She was a lean active woman in her eighties. She was wearing slacks, the only thing I ever saw my Mamaw in. Never a dress.

"Mrs. James, this is Steve and he's going to be delivering the mail here for the next few weeks while I'm in Florida."

"You're going down there with your son?"

"Yeah, going down for soccer camp."

"Well, Steve, if you need a drink of water, or to use the phone, you just come get me," said Mrs. James. I thought that the offer to use her phone was quaint. It was actually very practical. Later I realized that most of the route was so remote it didn't get cell service.

"I always check in on her," Wade said. "If I don't see her, I'm supposed to call her son."

That is the other difference between a regular and a sub. The sub just delivers the mail. The regular is delivering something else. Continuity. Safety. Normalcy. Companionship. Civilization. You know, the stuff that a government is supposed to do for its people.

Adele waited for me every single day that I carried the route. She would come out and wave, ask how I was doing and if I needed water. Check up on her? She was the one making sure I was OK. Once I figured out how hot it was, I always took her up on it—served in a glass with ice that I would drink in one gulp. Apparently, she later told Wade that I was "Always late, but he did okay. A polite young man."

Wade pointed up at a small bungalow house with a bass boat on a trailer in the front yard. "A retired carrier lives there. She was city side." I looked at the Tracker bass boat, pretty much the one I had fantasized about owning for years.

"She must be doing pretty good, to have a nice bass boat like that."

"Oh, if you put in the time, it really adds up."

If you can do the job and work your way up the ranks, and max out your Thrift Savings Plan (TSP), you can have a very comfortable middle-class retirement from the USPS. A carrier who has worked a full career could expect to get $40,000–50,000 annually in the form of their pension. If the carrier does the smart thing and starts compounding early with their Thrift Savings Plan, essentially the same as a 401(k), they will have hundreds of thousands of dollars saved up. Millionaire mailmen are not a myth, just hardworking people who put their money to work for themselves in the capital markets. For someone without a degree, or without skilled labor, the Postal Service offers not only a path into the middle class, but security in retirement. If you were in the military and did eight or twelve years, that counts toward your retirement as well, which is why the USPS was full of folks like Hank who were in their early thirties, having put in a couple of hitches in the service, and were now running up their numbers with the post office. There are a lot of ifs in that equation, but there is a path there that people had figured out.

I spent the next part of the ride trying to imagine the counterfactual of me moving to Hawaii at age eighteen and working as a letter carrier for thirty years. I would be forty-eight when I retired, so already two years into my retirement by now, maybe married to a local with four kids. I would teach English part-time at the high school in Waimea. Of course, I couldn't have told you Kauai was one of the five Hawaiian Islands when I was eighteen. And it is a neurological fact I could not do the same job for thirty years, even in a place as beautiful as Kauai. Clearly the idea of spearfishing in a mask and fins, reading books from the public library, and spending time with my imaginary grandchildren was what I liked thinking about.

How would delivering the mail for thirty years change a person? I don't know, but the odds suggest rotator-cuff injuries, a compressed lower back, and for me in Kauai, skin cancer. What I can tell you is this long reverie about bass boats, skin diving, and my fictitious Hawaiian family was time that should have been spent learning how to deliver this route. Time I would later come to consider as radically misspent because honestly, Route 3 came very close to breaking me.

Wade had one last thing to say to me before heading off to Florida.

"If you need my black Explorer, just text me. I'll leave the keys in my drawer at the case."

It was Saturday. I would take over Wade's route on Monday.

As a rural carrier, I was supposed to supply my own vehicle. This was a problem. At first blush, it seemed like El Cabrito—my trusty Toyota Tacoma—would be perfect. Great on dirt roads, nimble, and all mine. However, as a vehicle with a lot of ground clearance, the Tacoma had a high transmission hump and a cramped cockpit. It would never be able to hold all the mail on a route. At home I spent a very painful hour of self-contortion trying to figure out how to reach the left-hand drive controls from the right-hand seat. Even with my long legs there was just no way for me to reach over the gearshift to get to the pedals.

But I could fit into my late grandmother-in-law's 1999 Toyota RAV 4.

The car was like a toy, giving off beer-can vibes in that unique way that only borderline antique Japanese cars can. Compared to my big, solid V-6 Tacoma, it felt like I was driving a go-kart. But I could reach the pedals from the passenger side with my left foot. I got my new car magnets—US MAIL—and my white and yellow utility flashers on top as required by Virginia law. I had my letter from the postmaster declaring that I was a sworn letter carrier and should be considered "essential personnel" by law enforcement. I drove down to the post office, cased the mail, and loaded up the parcels. The load completely filled the interior of the car, but it all fit.

It's important to note that at this point, I'm still driving from the left-hand seat, as the laws of the commonwealth of Virginia and the engineers at Toyota intended. I am feeling bullish about my first day on a big-boy rural route. I pull up to the parking lot of the picture-postcard white clapboard church at the start of the route, move my DPS into the driver's seat, and set out.

I make it down the first curve toward Tom's Creek with no problem. Then, misremembering the route, I rocket up a dirt road that quickly becomes a rutted-out washboard. I lose traction and the RAV begins to roll backward down the dirt road. I am desperately trying to keep my painstakingly sorted tub of magazines and the trays of DPS from falling to the floorboards.

I fail. The floorboards are now covered with slick, glossy magazines and a half a tray of first-class mail and the RAV is increasing its downhill backward roll. The RAV is now headed into the woods, where I can see an oak tree on a collision course with the rear bumper. I had not told Alicia I was going to borrow her grandmother's car. This is going bad fast.

My desperation move is a combination of someone clinging to the helm of a clipper ship in a storm and the yoga position of "bridge"—shoulders pressed back against the ledge of the passenger-side window, legs pressed forward like a high diver, back arched into maximum flexion. In this state of bow-string muscular tension, my left foot, by the grace of

God Almighty, finds the brake pedal, my hands spinning the wheel left and right to bring the car back into the center of the road bed. Then, in a shower of limestone dust so thick that I can taste it at the back of my throat, the car stops.

I stay there, stuck in dynamic repose for what feels like a very long time. The dust settles. I'm able to slowly take my right hand off the steering wheel and reach under my lower back to the gearshift, and by feel I move it into Park. Then I collapse into the right-hand seat.

What the fuck? I probably hadn't been in any danger of dying, but I was sure as hell in danger. Maybe wreck the car, a car we needed and could not afford to replace. Maybe wind up with a broken leg or lacerated arm. In my employment history to this point, on-the-job injury was a chance at carpal tunnel and repeated bouts of depression. This was something very new and very real.

I cut the ignition and looked down at the floorboards. All my magazines are in a randomized heap in the footwell. A full tray of DPS is scattered like fiddlesticks. There was no friendly software here, asking me if I was sure I wanted to delete a file. No undo command. The only operating system here was thermodynamics, and I could see its second law hard at work. All systems tend toward maximum disorder. Entropy was the enemy at the post office, and I had just colossally fucked up. Two hours of hard work was now scrambled eggs on the floorboards of a compact car that just wasn't going to work on this route.

All of the confidence I had from my success on Route 10 was gone. What had bitten me in the ass was the egotism to think, for the ten thousandth time in my life, that I was smarter than the people that I worked with, that the rules—take your pick: standard operating procedure, the need to pay attention, Robert's Rules of Order, the laws of physics—did not apply to me. Sure, regular people might think this job was hard. This was a headfirst impact with reality. Route 10 was manageable, my briar patch. Here on 3 I began to get a sense of just how outmatched I was—procedural overload of the job, physical discomfort, the time pressure, driving on the wrong side of the car. It was the aggregate power of all these things hitting at once that made new carriers quit. But not me, I was special. I had told myself this was going to be easy for me. Because, you know, I'm so goddamned smart.

No. I was a fifty-year-old fuckup whose arrogance had just shuffled a deck of cards the size of a compact SUV. Welcome to the real world, Grant.

Chapter Ten

DOWN BY THE RIVER

"YOU'VE GOT TO FORGET ALL THAT STUFF THAT they taught you at the Academy. You've got to set up the mail to be nice and flowy."

"*Flowy?*" I asked.

"I know that's not a word but it's my word." That was Kat. She was waiting for me at the post office and was helping me get everything out of the little Toyota and into Wade's spare Ford Explorer. Wade had texted me from Florida, and we found the keys to the spare Explorer in the sheet-metal cabinet under his case. Now Kat and I were splitting up the mail, since the route was so long and I was now starting so late, after 10 a.m., when most mornings the goal was to be on the road at 8:30, if not earlier. Kat would carry the back half of the route and I would carry the front. The assumption was that as a rookie I would not be fast enough, and this proved to be highly predictive.

Five foot six, blond, with a milkmaid complexion, in her early thirties, Kat had a very serious West Virginia accent, strong enough to remind me of my mamaw. Full of sass and Bang energy drink (when Red Bull just isn't strong enough), and more than willing to get into it with management, Kat was my guardian angel and savior. A mother of three, married to one of the city carriers, she was an RCA-79, a fully vested career rural carrier who did not yet have a full route of her own. Her husband worked a city side route. They were a post office love match, so Kat was working in a floating career role until one of the regulars retired and she could bid on the route. Kat held down a half route, Route 11, and was responsible for filling in across routes as help was needed. And man did I need her help.

Kat taught me a lot of things. To dress for the weather, to drink water, to bring PowerBars. From her husband I learned to take Slim Jims as a snack because "they don't smush up" and were immune to the summer temperatures. In fact, Slim Jims really came to life in the hot weather. Heated on the dash to a temperature just below sizzling, their rinds would sweat with food-science industrial lipids, a marvel that if plated in a Michelin-star restaurant could be served as molecular gastronomy.

Kat was always on the go, always hustling, and if you watched carefully she was saving seconds to make minutes, minutes to make hours. It was a philosophy of action. Kat taught me how to make things *flowy*. Because making things flow, at the case, in your vehicle, at every stop: that is the key to delivering the mail. In the morning when you arrive at the post office, you flow through all the different sources of mail and lay them out at your case. At the case, you carefully make a single pass through all those sources to get them in route order, stacked and rubber-banded so that you can actually handle the mail out on the road. Cash had taught me to carry Route 10, essentially a park-and-loop city carrier route. It was Kat who taught the "real world" rural-carriers academy, the practicum. She taught me how to work through all this stuff in a Ford Explorer or Toyota Tacoma, keeping everything orderly and accurate; how to actually get the job done out in the sticks.

There is no one thing about delivering the mail that is hard. There is no virtuoso component. Nobody has to be able to throw a sixty-yard touchdown, paint in the chiaroscuro style, work with Seiberg-Witten invariants, or carry out a light aircraft crosswind landing on instruments in zero visibility. It's a matter of one big sequence problem, doing things in the right order. When you do it the right way, the Kat way, flowy, things run smooth, and smooth is fast. Flowy builds process fluency, the postman's friend. Flowy maintains the fragile construct of order over washboard dirt roads and high winds and time pressure.

You know, flowy.

"So make it flow?"

"Yeah, you want to be able to just go in a circle before each stop, so get your DPS, check and see if you've got a parcel, grab up your spurs, then get that parcel and set up the next one if you can reach it. You get all your flats out of your tub, and get it all in your right hand. Pull up to the box and then throw that mail."

"What kind of tub?"

"You're going to need to get you a tub. I can loan you one of mine but go to Target tonight and get you one. Because people will steal them, but if you keep your own in your truck then you'll have it when you need it."

She was referring to a Tupperware-type tub you would keep between your legs while you drove, loading it up with magazines, the little packages we called spurs (an acronym that was never defined for me), and our DPS. The tub keeps everything for the next five or ten houses or so in order, right between your legs. You would drive along from the right seat while you delivered from your tub with your right hand, your left hand stretched across the cab to handle the steering wheel. I would keep the next couple of parcels under my elbow on the center console. But it was the tub, jammed between your legs, that kept things organized, fast, and flowy.

The morning in the shop, or the house as it's sometimes called, is critical. If you can get your casing right, the rest of your day is going to be a hell of a lot easier. I had taken my best shot at casing the mail that morning, but for the next three weeks Kat helped me get it cased up. The time spent in the Kat Pepper Postal Finishing School was fundamental to me surviving my year as a mailman.

In economics there's a phenomenon called "path dependency." In a time series, something happens in the past that has a powerful downstream effect, typically constraining the kind of outcomes someone might enjoy in the future. For example, the adoption of QWERTY keyboards is something of a historical accident. But it has had the contingent effect of creating a population that has learned how to type on QWERTY keyboards. So the switching cost to move everyone to something new and faster is now not just mechanical (replacing a keyboard) but neurological (the collective muscle memory for an entire population of touch typists), along with the material fact of all those physical keyboards now sitting on desks around the world.

The path dependency inherent in casing your mail the right way in the morning is very, very strong. And there are some real challenges to it, especially when you are on a route that you don't know. It is always worth taking the time to get it right. That first morning casing Wade's route, I had a piece of personal correspondence in my hand from the raw mail. It looked like a birthday card addressed to someone on JE Jones Street. I didn't remember a JE Jones Street from my two days of ride-alongs. I remembered the moonshining Mash Run, coal-mining Big Vein and Tipple, the patronymic McCoy Road, floral and lyric Mockorange and Ladyslipper, and the biblical Mount Zion. But for the life of me I couldn't remember anything about a JE Jones. I stood there and quickly scanned the case. Nothing.

I looked again. Very slowly this time. There was no JE Jones that I could see.

I walked over to the parcel-sorting area. In the middle of the floor, where you took the packages out of the cages from Greensboro and scanned them, there was an old-school alphabetical table of all the roads in Blacksburg, each with its assigned route number. It was so big that it covered the entire surface of a card table and had been laminated down to the tabletop. The type was tiny, but there it was: JE JONES ST R003—Rural Route 3. So this wasn't a missorted or missent letter. JE Jones Street was on my route, and this letter was supposed to be delivered to it. The mail handlers didn't make many mistakes when it came to the raw mail, and they hadn't made a mistake this time.

Diana worked at the case next to mine. She was the carrier with the white right-hand-drive Jeep, the real Cadillac of the privately owned vehicles.

Diana was in her late fifties. She always wore a tennis visor. She must have slept in it. In the summer she worked in her visor and a tank top and shorts. In the winter she wore an old blue city carrier's fleece jacket over her sweatshirt and . . . a tennis visor. Once, when we were sorting through our parcels and came across one too many missorted packages, she pulled out the clinker and said, "I could walk this SOB over to the right route, but my give-a-damn's busted."

"Oh man, the old Joe Diffie song!"

"Joe Diffie? What are you talking about, that's Jo Dee Messina's song." She started telling me about how, in the video, Messina had just gone through a bad breakup with her manager, so she was in revenge shape and her arms looked awesome. Between the tennis visor, this very appreciative evaluation of Ms. Messina's arms, and the Jeep, Diana was pure local product. One morning we were casing mail next to each other and after looking at her phone she growled, "My husband is at the damn gun store?"

"Oh yeah? What's he getting?"

"He said he was thinking about a new rifle."

"Target shooting, home defense, hunting?"

"Deer rifle. Winchester .243. He's always wanted one."

"I had a buddy in college that used a .243 for white-tail."

"All I know is that if he's getting something, he better get me one."

A lady deer hunter. It was more common than you might think. A lot of dads took their daughters deer hunting. Dad never took me. I wanted to, when I was a kid, but my father would only reply, "A deer. That's a big animal." He offered instead to take me turkey hunting, which also never happened. Deer hunting was so popular when I was in high school that half the student population would play hooky in November and walk the halls for weeks after with homemade venison jerky, which I was always wildly envious of. I wanted a giant Ziploc bag of venison jerky.

Back to casing up Route 3. Diana and I were friendly, friendly enough that I knew from previous conversations that she had once carried Route 3 earlier in her career. And now that I knew for a certainty that JE Jones Street was somewhere on 3, I figured it was worth a shot to ask her where.

"Hang on, let me think. Shit, wait a second, I've got to actually stand in the case. It was years ago."

Diana came over, stood in the case, and then closed her eyes. She held up her hands like she was at a tent revival, and then pulled them down like she was taking laundry off the line. They were now a pair of dowsing rods, and she turned to her left, index fingers on an intercept course until they fell directly over a label on the case.

JE JONES ST.

The "street" was just two mailboxes, jammed between Long Shop Road and Mount Zion. There was hardly room for the label on the case. No wonder I couldn't find it. A sliver of a road.

"Sweet Jesus, Diana. How did you remember that?"

"Hell, I felt like I was slipping that it took me so long to remember."

I had just witnessed a feat of spatial memory that I have only seen equaled on the streets of London. When I first moved to the UK, I didn't actually believe that the cabbies could do it, that The Knowledge was some bullshit they told tourists, the British zeal for licensing and regulation as marketing. London is a maze, how could any driver know every little alley and capillary? I would tell the cabbies I worked in Farringdon, near the intersection of St. John's Lane and Clerkingwell Road. They would dutifully drop me off, until one day, an older cabbie said, "Listen, mate, how about you just tell me where you actually want to go?"

"Okay, 6 Briset Street."

"Oh, so around the back then, between St. John's Lane and Britton—just around the bend from the Jerusalem." The Jerusalem was a pub with a sign out front of the head of St. John the Baptist on a silver platter. I was astonished. Briset Street was barely a short block. There was our crummy office building and a dorm for the University of London, 150 feet in length, if that. It was true, they really did know every street, every pub, every landmark in London.

This kind of spatial memory was exactly what letter carriers had. They would refer to homes by their address. "You know the place at 401 Deercroft?" No, I don't. Because I haven't memorized every single home on your route. But even in just my year on the job, without trying, I began to absorb it. When my daughter Walker wanted a ride to a friend's house on Horseshoe Lane, I knew exactly where she was talking about, on Route 2 off Mount Tabor Road. Now imagine covering routes all around Blacksburg for a decade. You would know everything.

The most remarkable thing about this place memory is that the carriers saw nothing remarkable about it at all. They all had this level of understanding. Everyone who was a regular carrier had memorized their routes. They had a house-by-house understanding of each mailbox and customer. The carriers who didn't make it didn't make it for a number of reasons, but I would argue that one of the biggest was that if you didn't have the ability to mentally map abstract information like street addresses and names onto four dimensions—the route itself and the time it takes to carry it—then you were just never going to make it as a letter carrier. Just as remarkable was their humility about it. Everyone had this power of recall, but also a get-it-done, let's-not-make-a-big-deal-out-of-this realism. In corporate America, if people had memorized the contract values and forecasts around an account, they would shove it in your face. At the whiteboard there would be acrobatic displays of calculation, or org charts drawn from memory of the client's power structures. Because everyone was desperate to demonstrate cognitive mastery and dominance. At the post office the other carriers just wanted to know if you would show up and were capable of doing the work.

What carrying the mail taught me is that modern life has made us strangely weak in many ways. Weak memories for space, for numbers, for language. Our bodies are capable of walking tens of miles every day, of memorizing every fold of huge territories, of tolerating great heat and great cold, yet in our modern life all these capabilities are latent. When I think about the way that carrying the mail changed me,

I wonder how much of it was tapping into this different experience of being human.

Kat and I had split up the work and I was ready to make it "nice and flowy." It was about 10 a.m. at this point, and there wasn't a carrier left in the office, so I knew I was way off the pace. But Kat assured me that with the work divided in half we could get it done. At 10 a.m. it was already getting hot, unseasonably so for June in the mountains, but that would be okay. I had a better vehicle, Kat had helped me organize things, this was going to go smoothly. I hit the road and I was hopeful.

Olinger Road with its homes that had been converted into student apartments out in the boonies. Big Run with its chicken coops at the end of the road. Down Brookfield, past the blueberry farm where my mother went blueberry picking with the girls when they were little. The stone house with the crazy old woman who wanted every package delivered to her porch, where they joined the stack of other unopened packages. In three weeks of delivering to that house I never saw the stack of packages change, but someone was getting the mail out of the mailbox, and the one time I put some small parcels in the mailbox, the old woman complained to my super about it.

Down Old Creek Road, which was a long dead end, down past a couple of backyard auto shops, horse pastures, trailer homes on some good bottomland acreage with kids bouncing up and down on trampolines. I was pulling out my DPS, putting it together with my flats and spurs, and generally making okay time as I was learning to drive from the right-hand seat. Then I came to a yellow split-level.

Vacant cards and their role in casing the mail are about to become very important in this story. Let's say someone on your route is going out of town for the week and they want you to hold their mail. We would stick a hold card in their slot on the case, pull their mail out, and hold it there under the case until they got home. The same thing was the case with vacant homes. Once a home was listed vacant, you would get a yellow card, which would go in the case at that address to let you know that that home was not meant to be receiving mail. Sometimes this was a change of address, where you would need to forward some of the mail and deliver the rest. But a vacant card meant that you needed to take care of the mail right there at the case. If you were an experienced carrier you would get ready to pull down your case for delivery, but right before that you would pull out the DPS mail, the cased mail, and then walk down to the Forwards area, where you could forward everything—theoretically the computer should have caught this stuff, but when it didn't it was up to the carrier to forward it. If we didn't have any forwarding info at the case, we would code it UTF (unable to forward). If we knew the house was vacant, the mail would be coded VAC (vacant). Ideally, forwarded mail doesn't head out on the route. Everything you load into your vehicle is meant to be delivered.

This is what happens if you are an experienced carrier. I was not an experienced carrier.

This is how mistakes stack and compound. I was not familiar with the route. Despite Kat's help, I had not cased the mail correctly. I had not seen the VAC card. I was feeling time pressure. It was hot. I was thinking about lunch. That is why I thought nothing of grabbing up a handful of mail on Old Creek Road, rolling up the next mailbox, and shoving it in. Which is what I had been doing as fast as I could since I'd left the post office.

Three things happened simultaneously that were a very real-time reminder that honest-to-God, open-ended anything could happen in rural America. Old Creek Road was at the bottom of the valley, in a floodplain, with horse pasture left and right. I remember pulling up to a run-down two-story house with yellow vinyl siding at the top of a dirt driveway and set far back from the road. The grass out front needed mowing.

My robot brain was in charge. On autopilot it was assembling a stack of mail in my left hand, rolling up to the mailbox at low speed, feathering in the brake with my left foot while my right hand opened the door mailbox. My eyes were already down, looking into the tub to double-check the address. Left hand grabs DPS and tub mail, left foot brake, right hand opens and takes the mail from the left, right hand shoves the mail in the box, fast. There was a bit of crunchy tactile feedback from inside the mailbox as I did this.

My left hand had already reached back over to the steering wheel, in the autopilot groove, when my apprehending brain, the "me," was looking out at horses, houses, the road, the clouds, keeping track of the clock, thinking about Slim Jims. My executive function picked up on the strange bit of feedback from my hand and quickly snapped a look inside the mailbox.

Credit to my automatic brain: it recognized what was going on and had already mashed the accelerator to the floor with my left foot while my left hand was fighting to keep the car on the road. My prefrontal lobe caught up to the situation: the entire interior of the mailbox was one big hornets' nest, and I was looking right into the heart of it. The crunch was from my crumpling the hexagonal paper matrix of the eggs with a fistful of mail. The inside of the box was a seething, glossy black nightmare of insects crawling all over each other. In my mind's eye, I could see the vacant card in its case back at the MPO, laughing at me. Nobody was supposed be delivering anything to this mailbox, and clearly Wade hadn't done so in a very long time. The sky behind the car went dark with dust and hornets, a black mass of them. The Explorer was rocketing up empty road as my thinking brain finally categorized what I had seen.

I am terrified of wasps. When I was in college, I spent a summer as a camp counselor at my old Scout camp, teaching the Weather and Environmental Science merit badges and riflery in the afternoons. We were taking the camp out of mothballs at the beginning of the summer, and while I was painting under the eaves of the buddy board at the waterfront I whacked a hornets' nest with my paintbrush. In the noonday sun I couldn't see it hiding in the dark. A handful of hornets fell on my forehead and went to work. The only thing that halted their nonstop stinging was me running full-tilt into Lake Ottari and diving headfirst under the water. Over the course of the next couple of days, both my eyes swelled shut, and my father eventually had to drive me out to the ER in Radford.

I had never liked wasps. Who does? But after being blinded for a couple of days by them as a young man, I was genuinely phobic. And the pop-quiz nature of this latest encounter, along with the magnitude of the response from the mailbox nest, completely bypassed any sort of rational ability to control myself. I was in a full-body, screaming freakout, standing in the middle of a dirt road.

Somehow I had gotten away without a single sting. I was a good hundred yards from the nest now, had thrown the car into Park and jumped out before I was even conscious of it, running my hands up and down my arms and legs and shouting "MOTHERFUCKER! MOTHERFUCKER!" The black cloud of hornets had formed a tornado-like murmuration, the physical embodiment of animal rage. I could feel how bad they wanted to kill me, even from a football field away. I felt nauseous.

Not a single additional human soul had witnessed this. On the other side of the barbed-wire fence along the road, a chestnut horse looked over at me, completely unbothered. His expression said, "I bet you check the vacant card next time, dumbass."

I had already been getting hot as the day warmed up. Now my whole body was drenched in sweat. The AC in the Explorer was tepid at best, not nearly up to the task of cooling me down after the kind of physical reaction I'd had, and now I had the windows fully buttoned up. Old Creek was a dead end, which meant that after I delivered to the row of eight mailboxes on a plank at the end of the road, I had to turn around and drive back through the biological death cloud that still swirled over it. I did it at speed, running a full 60 miles an hour through the mass, listening to the wasps clack like castanets on the windshield. And I didn't stop till I was back on the main road.

By the time I had made it down Norris Run to the banks of the New River, I was so overheated and lightheaded, I wondered if I was having a cardiac event. There was a small park there, really nothing more than a couple of picnic tables and a place you could put in with a canoe or kayak. It was a Monday. The banks and the river were pretty empty. The New River runs over a limestone bed, which gives the water a green-blue color. The hills that rise up steep from its banks are heavily wooded, with few homes. So unless a train is coming through, along the tracks on either bank, it is a quiet place where you just hear the wind moving up the valley and the water running down over the rocks. It's a peaceful spot, maybe my favorite in the whole world.

I dunked my whole head under the water, kneeling on a big flagstone on the bank. I stayed underwater until I needed to come up for air. Then I sat there on the grass and looked across a couple of hundred yards of water. I was soaked, but I felt cool for the first time since I'd started my shift.

I sucked at this.

My phone rang. It was Kat.

"Hey, are you okay?"

"Yeah, I'm okay. I mean, I guess so."

"The supervisor has been blowing up my phone. They were about to send me down Norris Run to find you. They saw your scanner go in but you never came out."

"I'm out. They should be able to see me now." My scanner had a single bar of reception. "I'm just slow as hell, Kat."

"Well, keep going and then we can meet up at the church on Centennial and split up what you've got left."

I was near my breaking point. She talked tough—hell, she was tough—but she was a warmhearted person, and I think as long as she saw a carrier trying, she was supportive.

"I can't do this, Kat."

"What's going on?"

"I got attacked by hornets. I'm slow as fuck. I can't do this. It's just so goddamned hot out here. I'm going to quit."

"Didn't you say you needed this job?"

"Yeah, but I am fucking terrible at it."

"Didn't you say your family needed the health insurance?" I had kept the fact that I was the one who really needed it to myself.

"They do need it, yeah."

"Then do it for them. Don't quit."

"Fuck this."

"I get it. It's like this for everybody. Just show up one more day. Just deliver the rest of this stuff and you'll be done for today."

"Okay."

"Don't quit today."

"Okay, I'll keep going. I'll see you at the church."

By the waters of the river, with the kind words of a sister carrier, I brushed the sand off my knees and got back in the Explorer, and for one day more I didn't quit.

Chapter Eleven

LEST I TEAR YOU IN PIECES, AND THERE BE NONE TO DELIVER

"ABSOLUTE HELL."

Those were the words in my logbook.

The log I had been keeping was just that, a pilot's log. I recorded the route I was delivering, the miles driven, or if I had registered or certified items. When I arrived at the MPO, when I left the loading dock, when I had returned to base. If there was something I needed to follow up on for a customer, I would note it down. The only subjective note in my logbook from this time period were the words "ABSOLUTE HELL." It was the kind of thing you recovered in the tent of a missing Antarctic expedition, their bodies and their gear located after a century under the ice by a National Geographic Society team using ground-penetrating radar.

I thought about quitting every single day of the three weeks I carried Route 3. As a "senior career professional," I wasn't used to sucking this much at my job. It had been a long time since I had sucked at all in my work. For decades I had been—at the risk of sounding like an egomaniac—very good at what I did.

More importantly, I wasn't used to things being this hard. On the competence scale, from unconsciously incompetent—so bad that I didn't even have the tools to understand how bad I was—to virtuosity, when it came to delivering the mail I had at least graduated to the consciously incompetent stage, lost in the burning wasteland of self-awareness that I was really not very good at delivering the mail. It was a profoundly uncomfortable place to be.

Early in my agency career, I was part of a leadership on-site where they had us all learn to juggle, so we could all reexperience the discomfort of being a novice again. Of being bad. By the end I could maybe juggle for three cycles before losing control of the balls. During that same period of time, my friend Pete, the creative director, who had only one hand, had not only learned to juggle but had also added a number of tricks. This was counter to the lesson the coaches wanted us to learn. What I took away from the exercise was that contrary to the American idea that hard work can overcome any obstacle, natural talent trumps everything.

The place I actually learned the coaches' lesson was out here on the road, with an important corollary—yes, you could learn new skills as an adult, if you simply stuck with it and embraced the discomfort of feeling incompetent. What the coaches didn't speak to was just how uncomfortable and unfamiliar that feeling was. People might ultimately quit because they lack grit, but the immediate impulse to quit comes from the desire to stop profoundly painful feelings of embarrassment and inadequacy.

I had worked jobs in my twenties, thirties, and forties that I had wanted to quit so bad that it created a physical sensation like tinnitus, a palpable bodily unease similar to but distinct from depression. I say this with a connoisseurship of both job hatred and depression that has been cultivated over a lifetime of experience.

This was different. This was about actually trying and coming up short, and it was really fucking with me. The reality of just how slow and inaccurate I was dominated my waking thoughts. At night I dreamed about losing the mail, of being behind. Confronted with the real challenge of delivering Route 3, I became convinced that there was something intrinsically flawed in my makeup. I started feeling sorry for myself and my old "secret loser" self-talk was now running the show. I wasn't better than the average starting carrier—I was worse. I lacked focus. I hadn't paid attention. I was slow and error-prone. I was going to get fired, and let down my family. I was going to fuck this up and it would be nobody's fault but my own. I was lost in the wilderness of my own bullshit.

It's worth pointing out that Route 3 was rated at nine hours—Wade frequently did the whole thing in just five, while fielding phone calls, eating the lunch he had packed for himself, and chatting with customers along his route. I was struggling to carry half of it in eleven hours, with help. This is the difference between mastery and incompetence, of a few days of doing something versus years of it.

For three weeks I would meet Kat at a pullout along the road near Community Christian Church, not Centennial Christian Church, with its nearly identical red-brick construction and white steeple. There we would split up what I had left.

"I'm probably going to quit tomorrow," I'd say.

"I'm going to take everything from Big Vein on."

"Yeah, I'm going to quit."

"You're not going to quit today. I'll see you back at the house."

And that is how I made it through. I learned to bring a cooler full of Gatorade. I wore my most cooling fly-fishing shirts, unbuttoned to the sternum, driving in shorts and running shoes. But mostly it was Kat. I made it through alive because of Kat and the grace of God.

The one day that Kat had off during this period, the postmaster got so freaked-out that he came out for me with a rescue team. The four of us split up what was left, and with it cut into quarters we were able to get the outgoing mail back for the truck to Greensboro, because one of the performance metrics our office was measured on was outgoing mail for each route making the truck to Greensboro each day. I had a moment of real panic that I might get fired over this, but the reality was that nobody was going to fire me or make me drive the late mail to Greensboro, like they used to threaten at the Academy. I hadn't yet internalized this truth—all I needed to do was show up, try hard, and not commit any crimes. But at the beginning, every day was still a panic. A panic where I confronted becoming the kind of person who got fired from the Postal Service.

Route 3 seemed ever ready to supply a bottomless supply of curveballs and edge cases. About halfway through the route was the unincorporated town of McCoy. I had a big box of what looked like protein powder, too big to fit in the roadside boxes. So I drove down a dirt driveway into a broad field, surrounded by small homes. A quick scan revealed that not only was everyone living on that acreage named McCoy, but nobody had numbers on their house. I was just about to give up when I saw an old man working in a huge vegetable garden.

"Excuse me, sir, I'm trying to find the right McCoy. Package looks like some sort of bodybuilder's protein powder?"

"You go up there around the cornfield, down around the bend, and you'll see a fork. Take the left fork. There'll be a blue trailer. That's where Jimmy lives."

"Thank you, sir."

"Hang on!" said old man McCoy. He plunged into the garden, and when he came back he handed me a paper grocery bag full of beefsteak tomatoes.

I followed the old man's directions. At the blue trailer a guy who had clearly spent a lot of time in the gym was waiting on the deck, doing overhead dumbbell presses. I gave him his package and told him about the old man giving me directions and a bag full of tomatoes.

"Well, hell. Now he's just giving them out to anybody," said the bodybuilding McCoy. Yes, your mailman will learn the human terrain of your neighborhood so well that he will even know your interfamily squabbles and bad blood.

When I described getting these tomatoes to Kathy, who lived on Route 3 and was married to a McCoy, all she made was a kind of spitting sound. "I bet they weren't any good, nothing he grows is any good." It was one of those blind mountain statements that said there was a lot more to the story than flavorless tomatoes.

The tomatoes were actually pretty good.

Wake Forest was at the end of the route, the only surviving historically Black community in Blacksburg. The other community was forcibly absorbed by the university decades ago. Wake Forest was a small town all on its own. It had two churches, a community center, and a place that must have been a general store at some point.

I collected the best names from my routes, and one of my favorites lived back in Wake Forest—Sunshine Frisbee. Early in the summer, I delivered an inflatable pool so big it must have been right at the seventy-pound weight limit. Later I delivered pool noodles and other float toys. Her kids played in that pool all summer long.

One of my last days on this route was very hot but very beautiful. Big white Maxfield Parrish clouds covered the valley, the trees a vivid green. You could feel them breathing out water vapor and oxygen. Kat and I had divvied up the last of the mail, and by this point I was fast enough that I could carry all the way down to Big Vein, a dead-end road that led to an old coal mine. (The Appalachians were never big on fanciful place-names.) Big Vein led to a now-mined-out vein of hot-burning hard anthracite coal, the highest grade of coal there is, metallurgical grade, perfect for smelting iron and forging steel. My folks lived off Coal Bank Hollow, where you could still see a seam of black coal along the road-cut.

I had delivered the last of my share of mail for the day and was mentally ready to head back to the MPO when I saw a lonely parcel resting on the floorboard. A sleeper I had forgotten. The address was on Anthracite, another dirt road up the mountain where you could still see chunks of coal lying on the ground. I looked at my watch. I had finished with enough time that I could quickly run back down McCoy, take a quick zip down Big Falls, and deliver. Then I would have delivered them all—every single letter, flat, spur, and parcel I had been assigned. Maybe I really was getting better at this? I can still clearly picture the box. Brown cardboard with brown, fiber-reinforced packing tape. The box was a perfect cube, the size of something that would hold a machine part or a couple of pounds of coffee. Whatever it was, they were getting it today.

I blazed back down toward the river. I could feel the humidity and the heat build back up with every foot of elevation I lost, the air gas mix in a piston being compressed toward Top Dead Center, right before the spark plug detonates the whole mix.

Up through a green tunnel of trees on Anthracite. The address was just to my left. I swung through the tree line into a clearing, the hot blue sky overhead. Across a broad green lawn was a well-kept brick ranch house, neat as a pin.

I jumped out of the car with the cubical parcel and my scanner.

I took two steps across the lawn.

The wind hit me and I felt the perimeters of myself fall apart.

The whole New River was below me, everything open after a day trapped in the Ford. I could see the valley extend to the horizon, stretch, and elongate through space.

I took a knee. Deliberately this time. Steadying myself. Like I was a quarterback catching his breath after a frenzied drive to the end zone. I didn't hear music exactly, but I was perceiving sound like it was moving right through me. Wind. The molecular motion of heat. The train across the river carrying coal.

This was my breaking point, it had finally arrived.

I was experiencing what Romain Rolland, a colleague of Freud and Jung, called the "oceanic feeling," or alternately the "spontaneous religious feeling" described by William James in his book *The Varieties of Religious Experience*. It started as a whole-body euphoria, and I felt a oneness with everything. I could see the world organizing itself. Seconds later came the terror of the sublime.

I burst into tears, right there on the customer's lawn. I held the package under my arm and close in, a cardboard football in a touchdown only I could see, and wept. And in the first time in decades, I broke my embargo against all higher powers and prayed.

Lord, if you will just grant me the strength to keep going and do this for my family, I'll do it. It's hard as hell but I'll do it. Just give me the strength.

Sometimes winning is the act of not losing. But there was more than that here. I was being shown something: all that was required of me was not quitting.

I stood and took in the river, a broad ribbon of silver in golden light, following the path prescribed for it by geology, running away at just a couple of miles an hour, standing still in movement. The McCoy Falls were visible from here, the surface of the water disturbed by limestone humps that were still part of the living rock below, unmoved for millions of years. I could feel the water flow all the way to the Kanawha, the Ohio, the Mississippi, all the way down to New Orleans, where I was born, all the way down into the Gulf of Mexico, returning to the ocean.

Someone could have stood here two hundred years ago, or two hundred years hence, and we would all see this same thing. Water, bounded by the steep green slopes of home. In this particular moment of time, the act of seeing fell to me. I was here to witness this, and all these forces—economic, geologic, atmospheric, social, neurological—they had all reached a perfect equilibrium in this accident of now. A river in summer sunlight at late afternoon in Virginia, in America, in the early twenty-first century. As seen by a mailman holding his last package on the last stop of a hot day.

I stood, scanned the bar code, laid the package on the front porch, rang the doorbell, and turned back toward the Explorer.

I felt it, right then. A battle joy rose inside me, a holy flame.

I knew to a cast-iron certainty that I was out of my fucking mind.

But so what? Maybe that was the thing holding me back, some internalized norm of how my brain was supposed to work that simply wasn't doing it for me any longer, a task-oriented spotlight of intellectualization that kept trying to turn this job, this moment, into a management consultancy exercise, Mr. Systems Thinking, when really all I needed to do was deliver the fucking mail. It had taken me three months to shed my old self, the self that had clung to this notion that my selfhood was something you could write up on LinkedIn and that I deserved to exist because I was good at something. It's right there in the word we use—*good*. Being *good* at something somehow held equivalent to possessing goodness, possessing virtue. In America we are praised for it, from early on—kindergarten, even earlier. We call it the pursuit of excellence, "self-actualization," becoming your best self. My best self. Contingency had stripped me down to the chassis, bare metal. Dad, husband, vice president, strategist, pilot, English major, Eagle Scout, winner, loser, fuckup, superstar, disappointment. In that moment it was all gone.

Being great hadn't led me to my essential selfhood. Sucking did.

This wasn't some insight unique to me. This was Dante at the beginning of the *Inferno*: "Midway on our life's journey, I found myself, / In dark woods, the right road lost." You don't get there by being awesome. I got there by being terrible. The story I had told myself, of being really good at my job? That story was over. The new story, the one that was waiting for me if I would just let go of the old one, was the story of a man about whom there was nothing special at all. I was slow. I made mistakes. I needed help. That person was named Steve, and the main thing he had going for him was that there were people who loved him and the persistent audacity to exist.

Just go from one mailbox to the next and deliver the mail. Then get up again and do it tomorrow.

Crying on my knees on a stranger's lawn, not giving a single fuck. That's when I knew I was going to make it.

Chapter Twelve

NAMASTE

IT WAS ALWAYS A STRANGE EXPERIENCE TO MEET PEOple that I knew on my routes, and even stranger when they were a pretty strange person themselves. Years earlier I had been introduced to Amanda Cleveland, PhD, as a yoga instructor. I think it's important to be clear that Amanda's doctorate wasn't in something like computer science, from Stanford. It was in consciousness studies, and it was from a spiritual institute that I had never heard of. In addition to teaching yoga she was also a "nondual therapist" who specialized in "family constellations work." Alicia had taken yoga classes and teaching instruction from Amanda, which is how I knew her.

Amanda was something like a therapist, but in reality she was a witch. Not like the Wicked Witch of the West or your evil fifth-grade teacher who wore the same sundress everyday and hid candy in her trash can so she could eat it in solitude while the class was at recess. No, I'm talking a witch in the way that Gandalf is a wizard. An ethereal presence who seems mostly but not entirely human. Amanda had long brunette hair with streaks of white, and gray eyes that I was always careful not to stare into for too long, because I felt like she was x-raying the inside of my skull. She moved like a dancer, each step deliberate and fluid. Sometimes it seemed like she was moving through water, in a slower flow of time, while the rest of us were just sweating in the air like the apes we were. She was constantly surrounded by young women, most of them in their mid to late twenties, but always women, which only added to the coven atmosphere. Amanda seemed to be offering something that drew this flock in. Healing, understanding, maybe the promise of taking on a share of the obvious power that she commanded. Some of these women were clearly more wounded than others. All of them adopted Amanda's long scarves and flowing clothing, maybe from the same catalogs that Amanda got. In another demographic, these young women would have prayed the rosary for peace, or seen a shrink, but instead they were here in the deep end of the yoga pool.

I had seen Amanda as a therapist of sorts when Alicia thought she might help me manage my anger. I had reached a point where my rage was so volatile it was making me unemployable. My actual therapist (not Amanda) had diagnosed me with intermittent explosive disorder. At other points in my career I'd gotten pissed enough to get a reputation for being hair-triggered. I was unable to tolerate other people's mistakes. Under pressure, I was happy to let people know just how inadequate they were. I could be a real asshole. But this was different. I found the first place I worked in Blacksburg consistently infuriating, half frat house, half startup cosplay. At one meeting with HR, having been stood up one time too many to discuss equity, I had gotten angry enough that our head of HR felt threatened. After that I had to attend mandatory anger management classes. It was a desperate situation, and it meant I was willing to entertain desperate measures. This was when I started conventional therapy. And if Amanda could offer additional help on the road to emotional regulation, I was willing to try.

I found time with Amanda to be disconcerting. Her therapeutic method involved a lot of direct eye contact, and there were times I felt my selfhood dissolving like a pat of butter in a hot skillet when she was engaged with me. I did not believe in any of what she was saying at the time, about glowing fields of light and the subvocal muttering she would engage in as she "moved energy" in my body, and I still don't. I was raised by scientists, and until I delivered the mail I had resisted metaphysics as a matter of principle. My ultimate rejection of her therapies probably had more to do with my ego and an Appalachian sense of boundaries about where my space starts and the rest of the world stops. But I have to admit that what she did worked. She helped me. Magical thinking, placebo effect, or some unknowable mechanism of action, my time with her made me less angry, less explosive. She helped me stay employed. I was, and am, grateful to her for her work.

Amanda lived on Route 3, along Mount Zion road, along the banks of Tom's Creek, with her husband in a very normal-looking brick ranch. Next door was a one-room log cabin that overlooked the floodplain of Tom's Creek on its snaking, oxbowed last mile down to the New River. The cabin's porch faced the creek. It was a beautiful place, grassy and cool in the summer, where you could spot the occasional great blue heron on its way down to the New River, along with cardinals and Carolina wrens. When I was her client and I got bored waiting out on the porch, I would try to imitate the birds' calls and see if I could get them to answer.

I had been delivering mail to Amanda's place for over a week when I caught her outside near the mailbox.

"Hey, Amanda!"

There was a very long pause.

"Hey, Steve—what are you doing here?"

"I've got your mail."

"Why do you have my mail?"

"I'm a letter carrier. I'm carrying this route for Wade while he's in Florida."

"But you aren't a letter carrier. You're some kind of economist."

"I got laid off, so I joined the Postal Service. So I'm delivering the mail. I'm a mailman."

"You are not a mailman. What's going on?" Her tone now was one of strengthening disbelief.

"No, I'm a mailman! I got trained at the Postal Academy in Roanoke. I work out of the Blacksburg Main Post Office."

"You are not a mailman."

"Amanda. This is Wade's truck. Look, here's a letter from the postmaster general declaring me an essential worker traveling under the color of federal authority." I showed her my credential letter.

"Okay. Okay. This is some sort of weird joke?"

"It's weird, I'll give you that. But there's no joke."

"You are not a mailman."

"It was really nice to see you."

"It was great to see you, Steve. Have a wonderful day." She took a small stutter step toward me, and I could see her begin to reach out to touch my arm. Some part of her wanted to touch me; she wanted the Doubting Thomas proof that I was real. But something stopped her. As she left, she checked over her shoulder twice, maybe for the joke reality-TV reveal that was never going to come, maybe for something more sinister, whatever follows the kind of grotesque category violation that breaks someone's everyday model of reality. The comfortable conviction that we live in a country where people don't one day lose their jobs at fifty and have to start over from the bottom rung of a totally new career.

But if they didn't know me, people had no trouble believing I was the mailman.

Amanda sometimes rented out the cabin where she held her therapy sessions as an Airbnb. One day I was confronted by two people staying there. They were sixty something, skinny and intense, carrying themselves with distinct stridency that suggested at some point in the past they had been in a cult, bombed a research lab, or gone to graduate school in the humanities.

"We had a friend send us a very important letter over a week ago, and we still haven't received it." This was from the man, tall at about my height, lean, in a loose-fitting Patagonia T-shirt that probably cost fifty dollars, no watch (always a statement in a man over thirty-five), and Teva sandals. He and the woman, who was wearing some sort of flowing gossamer dress thing over her yoga clothes, were standing very close to me at this point, New York distances, inside three feet. I took a step back and they kept coming. So I held up my hands, not palms out in a defensive gesture, but palms up, using a technique that Amanda had taught me called "willing hands." It was supposed to signal to them that I was here to help, and to signal to my hillbilly-lizard amygdala that I didn't need to get ready to beat a customer to death with my fists.

"Okay. Let's see what I can do to help you. Is it a letter or a package?"

"It's a letter. From a friend."

"Do you have a tracking number?"

"How would I get a tracking number?"

"If it was certified or registered mail, or if it was Priority Mail."

"I think it was just a regular letter, with a stamp."

"First-class mail?"

"Yes. That's it. First-class mail."

"Do you know where it was sent from?"

"Delaware County, in Pennsylvania."

"Oh, so outside of Philadelphia?"

"Yes. What does that mean?" That wasn't a question so much as anger, directed at me, with a question mark at the end.

I saw myself through their eyes, a lanky white dude in a US Mail baseball cap and an old fly-fishing shirt. I already had the tan, windburned look of a letter carrier. Here they were, months into a pandemic with maybe no end, and now it seemed like even the mail wasn't working. I represented a government that had failed to control this outbreak, and maybe even a world that hadn't turned out the way they had wanted. I had been watching the color rise up this man's neck from beneath the collar of his crew neck, a charcoal-colored T-shirt, undoubtedly woven from organic cotton. It was time to start defusing this bomb.

"Listen, I don't know what your politics are." I was nearly certain what their politics were. "But this new postmaster general that Trump put in, between him pulling out the mail-sorting machines and staffing disruptions from Covid, we've been told that Philly is really jacked up. Stuff has been getting hung up for weeks in there."

They had been very clear at the Academy: don't talk politics on the job. The Hatch Act actually prevented us from any campaign-type speech in the office, and the fact that it was an election year had management on alert. But there were days when we got no DPS, or half of the normal volume, followed by days when it was doubled. Because in the middle of historic strain on the mailstream, I was reading news reports of Louis DeJoy taking machines offline, instead of adding them to keep up with volume. Was it political to talk about someone unplugging sorting machines like a drunken switchboard operator? My only knowledge of the situation was what I read on the internet, but politics or not, I *was* going to talk about it on the job if it made the difference between getting yelled at and perhaps deescalating a difficult situation.

"There are really important pictures in there!" said the man. "We wanted to share them with Amanda." He pointed toward Amanda's house.

"Oh! You all know Amanda?" I said. "She's a friend of mine. My wife studies yoga with her." Immediately everything changed.

"Oh wow, you know Amanda!" The woman smiled. "I think what Trump is doing to the post office is terrible."

"We're doing our best. How long are you here for?"

"We're here tomorrow and then we leave Saturday morning."

"Here is what I am going to do for you. If you all write down your home address, I'll keep an eye out for this letter. If it comes after you leave, Amanda can look at the pictures, and then I'll stick it in a Priority Mail for you and send you the tracking number."

"Wow, that's amazing, thank you."

"We take first-class mail very seriously. Personal correspondence always gets white-glove treatment."

"Louis DeJoy is an asshole!" The man couldn't help himself.

I laughed. If I had wanted to give the couple a new target, it worked.

"Thank you," said the woman. "We were so worried." She reached over and grabbed my hands. I saw this over and over during the pandemic. With so many of the normal contacts with the outside world cut off, the few remaining, like the mail, took on outsize importance.

"You're welcome."

The husband put his hands together over his heart. "Namaste."

And God help me, I folded my hands in prayer and said it back.

Louis DeJoy's status as an asshole is a matter of personal opinion. But it seemed pretty clear to me that he was anti-union, and that union was the only reason I had health care. Correlation is not causation, but it doesn't seem like a stretch to link his appointment with his massive donations to the Trump campaign. When he got the job, he awarded his old company, XPO Logistics, a $120 million contract. Some apologists for him will say he's a reformer. That taking the old mail-sorting machines offline for replacement was already in process. But most of what I've read says DeJoy sped up the timetable. In the middle of unprecedented volumes of mail, in an election year where the Postal Service would play an outsized role in protecting the franchise to vote. It wasn't policy, but when the customer tells you that the postmaster general is a political hatchetman and an asshole, well, isn't the customer always right?

When I looked at this couple, when I thought about how I interacted with them, I felt it—they believed I was a mailman. There was no prior frame of reference to keep them from seeing the thing in front of them. They saw a man in a mail truck, wearing a US Mail ball cap, carrying the mail. A mailman.

Did I believe I was a mailman? I was lousy at my job, still very stuck on how slow I was. I saw myself as a faker being chased by the clock. Time really mattered. The time it took to get ready and out on the road, to deliver the mail, to collect the outbound mail for its journey down to Greensboro. Time not as a professional courtesy but as the medium of orchestration.

For a rookie mailman the first noble truth is suffering. But the best carriers walk the eightfold path of right action with ease. They know the rules, they have the flow, and they make it all look so good.

I got better over the months to come. There were days when the mail was light and the weather good and delivering the mail was the best of all possible jobs, the work a joy, the solitude a gift. I knew I was never going to be flowy in the way that I will never be an NFL quarterback or play electric guitar like Eddie Van Halen. When it came to delivering the mail, the best I ever got was a solid B-/C+, and even with that I think my greatest accomplishment was not quitting.

And yet.

Somewhere in those early months, change did come. I got tougher. I became capable of delivering everything that I loaded into my truck in the morning. There was no sudden gain of function. It was a gradual thing in a world that had taught me most things come in leaps. Letter by letter I was learning. I was still looking for marketing work, and would keep looking. The economics of delivering the mail were unsentimental—paying for my mortgage and groceries cost more than I was bringing in. But out there on Route 3 the job became more than just a financial delaying tactic.

That morning, out on Mount Zion Road, I could feel it. Joy! I wasn't just doing the job, but instead I was inhabiting something real, feeling what it was like to be there for people. I smiled, and the smile stayed with me for the rest of the route.

I had become a mailman.

Chapter Thirteen

CHRISTMAS IN JULY FOREVER

"THIS IS LIKE CHRISTMAS."

"Weird working this kind of volume with the students gone."

"It's all weird. It's all as bent as a dog's hind leg."

"Every day here is like goddamned Christmas now."

It wasn't like Christmas; it *was* Christmas. From the moment that I had joined the Postal Service, it had been Covid Christmas every day, all week long, forever.

Summer was supposed to be the easy time. First, the students all left. That more than cut the population in half. In a college town like Blacksburg, where much of the year-round population is professors, the professors often left town as well, doing research, visiting Europe. If you were a professor from Egypt or Korea, you went back to your home country for several weeks. Not our family. When I was a kid, we were the family from Western Virginia that vacationed in West Virginia. Our vacation was . . . mountains that looked a lot like the mountains where we already lived. But as far as the mail was concerned, when half the population leaves town, it typically means half the mail volume.

This was not my experience at the Postal Service. Every old hand at the Blacksburg MPO told me that from the moment I arrived in the spring, we were at Christmas-level volumes. You didn't need to be an economist to figure it out. Everyone was stuck at home. For a lot of folks, day drinking and shopping online went hand in hand. That was an issue if your job was delivering all that online shopping.

The Postal Service is really good at handling mail, the sort that comes in an envelope. We are good at handling magazines too, and we've got machines that can help us sort both. But when it comes to packages, you'll notice that UPS trucks are big, and have shelves inside. Our vehicles are for the most part, small, and at my post office most of them don't have any shelves inside. That's because they are designed to be good at zipping through narrow streets and sidling up to mailboxes, not delivering toasters and paper towels.

In May I had carried Cash's route while he was on vacation. In June I had carried Wade's while he and his son were in Florida. Now that Wade was back, I still carried Route 10 when Cash was taking his day off, typically Monday, which he chose since that was the heaviest day of the week. But with all this Christmas-in-July volume, management also started putting me on parcel duty other days. That means that instead of carrying the mail—delivering DPS, envelopes, flats, and parcels to every address on a route—I instead just carried packages, as many as I could safely stack in my truck.

"Oh honey, that truck is too pretty to deliver the mail." This was from Crazy Martina, a city carrier whose route started at the Kroger next door. I was loading parcels into the back of the Tacoma, trying to figure out the route with Google Maps and a legal pad.

"It's the only wheels I've got."

"This place doesn't deserve a truck that pretty. You'll tear it up."

"It's tough, it'll be okay."

"That's a crying shame." She walked off shaking her head. After that, she often would greet me with "It's a crying shame what you're doing to that truck."

My favorite time at the Postal Service had begun.

El Cabrito—the Little Goat—my trusty black tougher-than-tough 2012 Toyota Tacoma crew cab, was my friend on these parcel days. If the weather was good, I could stack the bed with carefully organized packages and throw the cargo cover over them. If it was a light mist I'd use a siliconized tarp that in easier times I used for backpacking.

If you drive a Tacoma, you will invariably have full-size truck drivers wander over to talk about your "little truck." They will always say that, personally, they can't see driving a truck without a big, buttery V-8 in it. If you want to understand the challenge that electric trucks face in America, here it is. If it doesn't have a V-8, is it really a truck? As one of my buddies from Ford used to say, there is no replacement for displacement. But these questions about the Tacoma always come in a curious and admiring tone, and they will always conclude with an anecdote about a friend's truck like the one you've got with two-fifty, three hundred, even four hundred thousand miles on it.

Santa has to have his sleigh.

I'm sure that when my customers were children, they were excited to see Santa at the mall, or to imagine him sliding down their chimney. When I slid up their driveway, the response was often active irritation that somehow I was personally responsible for why it took so long for their toilet paper to arrive.

I remember one day I had three huge parcels that needed to go to one address at Smith's Landing, the mega–apartment complex that started Route 10. Looking at the boxes, I could tell it was a flat-packed computer desk, a monitor, and an office chair. Maybe a graduate student who had just moved here and with Covid had nowhere to buy this stuff? A lot of grad students start showing up in the summer, particularly if they are from overseas.

Most of my deliveries to Smith's Landing went into the big cluster-box unit in the mailroom. They had an entire room full of parcel lockers that made delivering there a snap. But Cash had kicked these to me because they were too big for the lockers, and the front office had stopped receiving packages under their Covid policy.

I had a sinking feeling when I looked at the address. The apartment was on the third floor, which meant that it was actually four floors up, because there were ground-floor apartments as well.

No elevators.

There was no magic trick to this. All you could do was grab the box in a bear hug and then hump your way up the stairs. I don't know how a five-foot-tall carrier with short arms could have done this, which was part of the logic behind giving the big parcels to the big guy with the pickup truck. I got the chair up, all four flights. Back down to the truck and did the same with the desk. The chair might have been bulky, but it was relatively light. The desk was flat-packed IKEA-style, a monolith of particleboard and it weighed every ounce of its seventy-pound postal shipping limit. I was sucking wind by the time I got that one to the door. One more trip down to the truck, where I collected the monitor, then back up. According to my Apple Watch, my heart rate was over 160 at this point. I had just completed an impromptu event in the Letter Carrier CrossFit Olympics.

I wiped the sweat off my forehead, scanned all three packages, took a short breather, and snapped pictures of the packages in front of the door as a CYA. I knocked and an Asian guy in his early twenties came to the door, with the chain still on.

"Hey there, United States Postal Service. This is a big delivery, so I need you to sign for it."

He looked at the boxes and nodded his head.

"You come inside."

"No need for me to come inside," I said. "I just need you to sign my scanner."

"You come inside. You set up."

"I just deliver. I need you to sign my scanner, please?"

"You come inside! You set up! Tools!" He was making screwdriver motions with his hands.

"Sir, we don't set anything up. I just deliver the parcels."

His expression changed, as if he had figured out the problem. In a helpful tone he said, "I leave and you set up."

"Sir. I. Do. Not. Set. Up." I pointed to the USPS patch on my sleeve.

He shouted at me in what I think was Chinese, but I certainly didn't need a translator to understand that he was pissed. Maybe the courier set things up wherever he was from?

Across the landing from the grad student's apartment, another door opened behind me. A middle-aged woman was standing there, blond, drinking a gin and tonic in a highball glass, wearing a bathrobe that was barely closed. I could hear the TV playing in the background.

"Hey there, mailman. Did you bring me anything?"

"Uh . . . no, ma'am."

"Made you blush," she said, as she raised her glass in a toast and closed the door.

And it was true, she had me blushing like I was a teenager. I wasn't yet the hard case I would be, come next spring.

I wrote "COVID-19" in block letters into the signature box and marked the packages delivered. Which is what Santa would have done and I should have done in the first place.

It felt like Christmas to the old hands because of the volume, but to me it felt like Christmas because of what people were ordering. Sure, some of it was just because people couldn't go to the store. But people were also bored and depressed. They were shopping to amuse themselves. They were buying their kids toys to entertain them and distract them—Legos, princess dress-up clothes, books, inflatable pools, footballs, basketballs, board games, art kits. The kids were stuck at home and parents were throwing money at the problem. The parents and everyone else were throwing money at themselves too. They were bored. There was a lot of wish fulfillment. With no commute and no prying eyes, they had time to kill and money to burn.

If you think your carrier doesn't notice when you order a sex toy, you're wrong. We carried a lot of sex toys. Most of the distributors of this stuff did their best to make it discreet. But when the box said "Adam and Eve Superstore" as the return address, I was pretty sure I wasn't carrying a book of Genesis trivia game for morally edifying nights around the dining room table.

One morning, one of the city carriers breezed into the rural carriers' casing area, holding a parcel aloft like the Olympic torch. She was a big lady, but this morning she was practically skipping.

"Today, I'm going to be delivering somebody a really good time!"

The parcel was one of those opaque, semi-indestructible plastic sleeves that would carry books, underwear, T-shirts, or prescription drugs. This was none of the above. It was a dildo, thick enough that she could barely close her hand around it, easily over a foot long, with a head and balls on it we could see through the "plain vanilla envelope" like it was the bulge in a seventies glam rocker's blue jeans.

"Whoo! Special delivery! Whoever is getting this is one hell of a woman." She was now holding it, inevitably, in front of her crotch.

"Yeah," deadpanned Kathy, "or one hell of a man."

There was a lot of talk at the start of the pandemic that people were going to learn to knit, or paint, learn to keep bees or make sourdough. So much sourdough talk. But the mail doesn't lie. People were not teaching themselves violin or how to speak Portuguese. People were ordering weed from their friends in Colorado. They were ordering videogame systems. They were ordering Dungeons & Dragons books. They didn't want edification, they wanted escape. In the privacy of their homes, with sabbatical levels of free time, what most people wanted was to be anywhere else, to feel some other way, to pretend to be someone else, to imagine another time. They wanted to go back to an American time where there's no past or future or consequences, but just pleasure wrapped up in boxes waiting to be opened. Christmas, the most American holiday after the Super Bowl. Not the birth of the baby Jesus and all that nativity pageant bullshit. There was very little baby Jesus spirit floating around that summer. No, they wanted American Christmas, where you get the thing you always wanted in your secret heart, and now you were an adult and you could be your own Santa. Swords, drugs, videogames, day drinking, junk food, an unbroken string of multiple orgasms—when nobody was looking that's what people *really* wanted. They wanted to be anywhere but trapped with their thoughts, locked in their homes, in Blacksburg, Virginia, in those seemingly endless weeks and months in 2020. They wanted emancipation from their present selves, and there wasn't much they weren't willing to try in the pursuit of escaping their own humanity.

Sourdough was what wound up on Instagram. But their mail told the secret truth.

Later in the week, I delivered a shoe-box-sized parcel to the front door of a nice home down toward the river. The front door opened before I even reached it. An older man in a white T-shirt and khaki pants was standing there.

"Hi there! Is that package from Midwest Model Railroad Supply?"

"Well, the return address reads MMRR, Independence, Missouri."

"That's it! Yes, that's it!" The old man was beaming. I wish everything I delivered made people this happy. "Say, do you want to see my model railroad?"

I'm going to be honest, if it was the seventeen-year-old version of myself delivering the paper, I would have thought something was up. But I was a fifty-year-old mailman.

"Sure."

"Bring it around to the garage." A minute later the garage door rolled open and revealed a model train set up that filled the whole double-bayed space. There was a long mountain ridge that ran down the middle and a flat valley section with a blue plastic river winding through it. A town with model cars, a bank, a pharmacy. A drive-in movie theater. A massive switchyard, including a turntable like the one they had at the Norfolk Southern Roanoke Yards.

"Wow! That is a setup!"

"I used to work for Norfolk Southern. My models, this is what I do now. Let's open the box!"

Inside was a locomotive engine. "This is a Norfolk Western SD45. Twenty-cylinder diesel electric, thirty-six hundred horses. This is what I worked on when I joined up."

"Were you an engineer?"

"Oh, I was just an apprentice at first. This was a great unit. The fast freight. That was always what I liked." He looked up at me. "Once Jennie passed, I started buying models of all the trains that I worked on, so I can set up different times, like the sixties or the seventies."

"This is a heck of a setup."

He had the engine out of its box and was setting it on the tracks.

"See, you can go back to different times. Just change out the cars and the power. It's all about having the right power."

"The engine?"

"The power. Working for the railroad we called it the power. That's the key, having the right power. You can't just jumble together everything. Not if you're going to go back to a specific time."

"I'm going to go now, sir. You have a nice day."

I left, because Santa never sticks around to watch the kids play with the toys he brings. The old man wasn't even listening to me. He wasn't even in the same room as me. The same year as me. All he could hear were the sounds of thirty-six hundred diesel electric horses on the tracks, his whole life ahead of him, somewhere in the middle of the twentieth century.

When it was Christmas in July, I took my cues from the career carriers. *This is crazy! How can we keep this up?* And it was crazy. But it was also just the warm-up.

Looking back, it was the happy time.

Chapter Fourteen

EARTH'S MOST CUSTOMER-CENTRIC COMPANY!

"JESUS CHRIST! WHAT HAPPENED?" THE MOMENT I arrived at work on August 1, I could tell something was different.

There were a lot of parcels. We had been hanging on with our Christmas in July volumes, but this was different. Boxes were piled up behind every city carrier, boxes piled high in every route cage back in the sorting area.

"It's Amazon, man! They're fucking with UPS and now they're sending all the UPS volume to us!" That was the latest from the rumor mill from one of the younger city carriers.

The Amazon Wars had landed at our doorstep.

Amazon is ruthless. A behemoth that ate Sears and Kmart for snacks. A publicly traded Frankenstein creature, shocked into life by vast flows of data, animated by its robot-staffed misery factories, where the humans trapped inside are stuck in a John Henry race they are never going to win, their every movement tracked to the second in an eternal time-motion study, the workplace as Frederick Winslow Taylor's mutant brainchild. Amazon, where orders are loaded onto trucks within thirty seconds of you clicking that BUY NOW button. Amazon, where Amazon Prime made shipping "free," not free like freedom of speech or free as a bird, but instead an invisible cost you can no longer see. Amazon, capital's new organ for a new age, the purest expression of the connection between supply and demand, connecting . . . everything. After all, Amazon is the Everything Store. Amazon, with its glass bubble offices powered by the clean power of the far off Grand Coulee Dam on the Columbia River in evergreen Seattle, filled with high-octane MBAs, cracked from the best business schools in the world, the pure distillate of American scientific management, all of them running spreadsheets that make numbers scream, chasing down every weakness, every inefficient dollar so that they can work harder, harder, ever harder, chasing the golden glow of expansion forever, no business cycles, no contractions, just eternal continuous growth. Because the mantra is always that *this time things will be different*, there will be no correction, no countercycle. This time the growth party will be all high and no hangover. Because it's just numbers, right? Numbers in a spreadsheet getting bigger. These number are not abstract, however. They start as numbers but end as boxes carried by your mailman. Physical, corrugated cardboard boxes. Like the most dangerous of ideas, they land in the real world and change it.

And if you're wondering? Yes, I'm an Amazon shareholder.

There are no Amazon trucks out in southwestern Virginia. There wasn't enough population density for that to make economic sense. So there was an equilibrium in the regional e-commerce logistics market. The big packages went to UPS, which was set up to efficiently handle parcels. But UPS handed over the little stuff to us at the USPS, and undoubtedly did not pay enough for this service. Why not? We were set up to deliver to every mailbox every day. This gentleman's agreement served Amazon until it didn't. Some VP at Amazon wanted to make his annual bonus, and hoping to squeeze some margin out of their shipping costs, they were looking for leverage to renegotiate their rates with UPS. But UPS held firm. So Amazon simply said, "Okay, we'll give it all to the USPS, because they have to take it."

Because the USPS is not a business. Our charter is not some TED Talk corporate mission statement babble but real, honest-to-God federal law, voted into existence by the United States Congress on behalf of the American people. This law, the Postal Reorganization Act of 1970, says that the Postal Service operates under a "universal service obligation" to provide the same level of service to all Americans at a reasonable price. Not to generate a profit. Not to produce revenue growth. UPS and FedEx are publicly traded firms. They need to generate a profit with each parcel carried, and are accountable to their shareholders to do just that. If a customer wants to send a letter to California from North Carolina, these private firms can charge more, right up to the customer's threshold of WTP—willingness to pay. They can even decide that they won't deliver to some addresses. Not worth their time. The USPS doesn't get to do this.

When you chase down your letter carrier and say, "Wait a minute, Mr. Postman!" and jam a get-well card you handwrote to Grandma into my hand, correctly addressed and with a Forever stamp in the upper-right-hand corner, guess what? I have to take your letter. I work for you, the American people. Congress has not only authorized me to carry that letter but has obliged me to take it, to carry it in trust and under the legal protection of the federal government and deliver it wherever it is supposed to go. If Granny lived in a Zuni cave dwelling at the bottom of a canyon in the Four Corners area, and the address was registered with us, then Granny gets her letter delivered, same as anyone else. There is an actual route in Arizona that delivers to the bottom of the Grand Canyon, by burro. Do you think the USPS makes money on these customers? Profit is irrelevant. The law says your mail gets delivered.

So while Amazon and UPS are free to play games with marginal value, the Postal Service has no choice but to pick up the slack. But while Amazon Prime may offer two-day and same-day delivery in the major metro areas, in rural America Amazon arrives at the speed of the US Mail. That two-day shipping "guarantee" from Amazon is more of an aspiration because it's just not possible to get all those packages into the backcountry any faster.

The contract dispute between Amazon and UPS had been going on for months. But Amazon was not bluffing, and when UPS didn't offer acceptable terms, things changed for us in the Blacksburg Post Office overnight. July, high volumes. August? Insanity. And management was caught totally unprepared.

This massive influx of new parcels had created a low-level riot in our post office. As carriers were trying to get their loads together in the morning, the wheeled floats we used to move packages out to the loading dock were crashing into the stacks of packages by other carriers' cases. They were not precision instruments—the floats were about ten feet long—and accidents were happing in all directions. Cussing was always pretty general in the casing area, but it was constant and hot now. Tempers were running high. People were getting territorial. There were so many additional packages that there just wasn't room to get your day's parcels in order at the case. The only option was to just throw everything onto a float, unsorted, and then sort at the loading dock. Some of the rural carriers were loading cribs, rolling canvas bins, and doing their loading out in the parking lot. Everyone was out of their normal routine, and carriers are creatures of habit. The mood was angry. The shock of it felt unfair.

There was so much parcel volume that I started being called in seven days a week to just transport parcels. The regulars would take the mail and whatever parcels they could carry. I would load up on the big stuff with my truck, get it into order, and get out on the road. Sometimes I would do three of these runs a day. This was great work. I set my own route. I got to do plenty of land navigation, explore back roads, and never had to mess with all the casing up of DPS and the other mailbox mail. Just me and the Tacoma, slinging parcels.

Parcel runs were my favorite work in the USPS, except when they happened on Sunday. With the huge leap in volume, management had activated Amazon Sundays—where the rookie carriers would come in on Sunday mornings and run nothing but parcels. We were apparently becoming a wholly owned subsidiary of Amazon.com Inc. All I know is that this work was fun, my favorite time at the USPS. This did not include sorting incoming parcels, because that work sucked. Bad.

I had just come back from a run in late morning when Sebastian, the city carrier supervisor, grabbed me. "Hey, new guy, go help Serena throw parcels. We just had another truck come in."

"I've never thrown parcels."

"Serena will teach you how."

"Am I even supposed to do this?" I asked. I had never seen a carrier throw parcels before.

"It's covered in the rural contract. Go help Serena."

Serena was a Black woman in her forties. She was built like a linebacker, with short cornrowed hair. It was August and it was hot in the sorting area, so she was wearing a tank top and yoga shorts and no mask, radiating a quiet "don't fuck with me" energy that seemed to repel supervisors.

Clerks don't just work the front desk at the PO; they also help set up incoming mail each morning. They get the raw mail sorted for the right routes, load the trays of DPS into the appropriate racks for pickup by the carriers, and get the parcels sorted into the route cages for the carriers as well. Each of these metal cages is about the size of a playpen for a baby. On a "normal" morning, this was a job that usually took an hour with two or three people working it. Now it was running continuously while yet more cages came in. We were on a wartime footing.

That's what Serena was doing, a job that was normally done by 8:30 a.m. Here it was 11:30 in the morning and she had hardly made a dent. She stood next to an open GPC cage, a tall container for parcels the size of an industrial refrigerator and mounted on casters, one of which looked like dozens that had just rolled off the truck.

Next to her on a long yellow articulated arm was the superscanner, like a seven-foot-tall mechanical praying mantis. The reader head threw a grid of green light onto the ground underneath it. If you got anywhere near it with a bar code it would flash a grid of lasers and call out the destination for the parcel—"C11" or "R8" for city Route 11 or rural Route 8. This would log into the system that we had processed-in the parcel and that it was now in the cage waiting for pickup. In a long arc around the scanner were the route cages, twenty-three for the city routes and eleven for the rural ones, covering the 24,000 addresses that we delivered to every day from the Blacksburg Post Office. Our job was to empty out the GPC cages, scan them, listen for the route number, and then put those parcels into the correct route cage.

"Who are you?" asked Serena.

"I'm Steve."

"That little Mr. Miyagi motherfucker ask you to come over and help me?" I wanted to laugh but couldn't because I wasn't sure if the joke was racist. But Sebastian really did look like actor Pat Morita's Mr. Miyagi from *The Karate Kid*. So I went with my old standby—clueless but helpful country boy.

"I don't know anything about how this works, but how can I help?"

"Start scanning, start throwing, and get the fuck out of my way."

Serena could grab a box, scan it, and loft it into its cage without really looking. It was, as the lady said, important to stay the hell out of her way because she was like the manifestation of a multiarmed Hindu goddess of the mail when it came to sorting packages. We got into a rhythm, looping around each other. If the packages weren't too big, I could grab one in each hand. Then I would take each, right then left, scan them, and sing a song to myself so I wouldn't mix them up—"Right hand, Rural four. Left hand, City twelve"—then, in an NBA-worthy pick-and-roll movement, step back to the GPC and grab two more.

Brianna, a rural carrier, was casing up Route 11, the auxiliary route that Kat usually covered, half the size of a full route. It usually didn't get delivered until the afternoon if we weren't fully staffed up. Brianna had come down from Newport, a tiny town just over the Giles County line, and like my truck, she was too pretty to deliver the mail. She had long curly black hair and gave off a super-relaxed, latter-day-hippie vibe.

"I see you," said Serena.

"What?" We were still scanning and jamming.

"I see you looking at Brianna. You like 'em crunchy, huh? Yeah, she's cute. I'd date her. Good thing my girlfriend isn't here!"

"I wasn't looking at anything!"

"Sure you weren't, Stretch." And from there out, that's what she called me—Stretch. That was when Serena smiled for the first time. When you are moving boxes in a concrete-floored warehouse, you have to take your entertainment where you find it.

We were in a flow now. We cleared one cage and cracked open another. I started counting the number of boxes in each one. I used the stopwatch on my G-Shock to measure how long it was taking us to process a cage.

"What are you doing?"

"Throwing parcels."

"No, I see you counting and timing shit. What are you doing?"

"I'm trying to calculate our throughput."

Serena stopped and just stared at me, hands on hips.

I paused my timer.

"Anybody ever tell you that you think too goddamned much?"

"All the fucking time."

"Okay, genius." But she smiled. "Shit, these route cages are full." She was right, we didn't have anywhere to sort parcels into at this point. Serena turned to Sebastian. "Hey, these cages are full up!"

"You two are done," said Sebastian, looking up from his desk.

"You don't have to tell me twice. We're done, Stretch."

She never said it out loud, but after we worked together, Serena would always give me a little smile when I was back in the house. Sure, I was the strange, too-old letter carrier who talked about throughput. But work is work. Show up, don't sandbag anybody, be humble, play through to the buzzer, and the next thing you know, you're part of the team.

As we headed inside, another truck arrived with more GPCs.

The mail did not stop. It never stopped. Each day, despite heroic effort, the sorting area was filling up faster than we could move things out. Every carrier was a rat in a behaviorist experiment. Every move was a game of *Tetris*. Every movement seemed to knock over someone's stack of parcels, the whole system tending toward maximum disorder, a Hobbesian war of all against all. I would arrive and immediately be sent back to help throw packages for a couple of hours.

One day, they had brought in more help. A new handler was in the scanning area.

"Hey, I'm Steve," I said. "I'm supposed to help you sort parcels."

"So sort parcels then." Glynnis was maybe five feet tall, and had legally-blind-level glasses on, in big aviator frames. They were totally fogged over from her mask.

"You new here?"

"They called me in from Galax. I'm supposed to retire."

"You drove here from Galax?" Galax is at the eastern edge of the Grayson Highlands plateau, the highest part of the Appalachians in Virginia, just north of the North Carolina state line and a solid hour and a half away.

"They told me I had to come. How do you keep your glasses from fogging up?"

"Oh, you got to pinch the wire down really tight across the bridge of your nose."

"Well, I've tried that and it doesn't do shit."

"Ever tried medical tape? When mine fog up I use medical tape."

"Where the fuck am I supposed to get that?"

"Out of the first-aid kit, in the break room."

"The goddamned break room. Like anybody gets a break in this cocksucking place."

Glynnis looked like she would have been at home sewing a quilt in a rocking chair, with her soaps going on the TV. But she swore like a marine with busted knuckles.

"This motherfucking broke-dick machine. I can't understand what the fuck it's saying half the time. Must have been made in Mexico by a bunch of cocksucking Chinese."

It was hot. Who wouldn't be cranky in this heat? I was twenty years younger than this woman and I was cranky. Not racist, but still cranky. The noise of the big fan made it sound like we were on the tarmac of a small airport.

"Every goddamned time I turn around there are more boxes of bullshit macaroni and cheese and fucking Hamburger Helper and every other goddamned thing because these motherfuckers are too big a bunch of pussies to drive to the fucking Kroger and I'm driving three hours every day to sort this shit because they're a bunch of pussies and this post office sucks one big donkey cock, did anybody ever tell you that?"

"That this office sucks donkey cock?"

"Bet they didn't tell you in training that it's one big shit sandwich and what the fuck are you doing here anyway?"

"Same as you, sorting parcels."

"I know why I'm here, to get my motherfucking pension and get out of this broke-dick chickenshit outfit, run by a bunch of peckerwood know-it-alls that wouldn't know how to find their asses with both hands and help from their kindergarten teacher."

"I'm in the same jam as you are."

"No you ain't, because I'm here to get my motherfucking pension, and you're too goddamned stupid to stay at home and collect unemployment."

She had a point.

I kept throwing boxes. Patience wasn't enough. I needed intercession. I prayed to the Virgin Mary to grant me strength. I prayed to the Virgin Mary that some supervisor would spell me off and send me out on the road. I didn't care that it was 90 fucking degrees out there. I would have happily delivered the mail in a motorized pizza oven to make this stop. Anything to get me away from the human fountain of externalized misery that I was chained to in the parcel-sorting area.

"Merciful Jesus, please take pity on me! My goddamned back is killing me. I feel like somebody took a tire iron to me, and I'm an old lady. You can't fucking treat people this way!" It was clear to me that Jesus was not listening to the prayers from the parcel sorting area.

"Glynnis, have you tried taking some ibuprofen or something?"

"What are you, the fucking Peace Corps? You a doctor? If you're so goddamned smart, why are you in here working with my dumb ass?"

"Hey, Grant!" It was David, the rural super.

"Yeah, man?"

"How about you grab a couple of cages of parcels and hit the road?"

"Sure thing!" Maybe Jesus wasn't listening, but at least David was. He gave me a big wink. No words were required.

I will say this about Amazon exercising its rights to negotiate contracts in the interest of its shareholders. I am a shareholder and it sure didn't feel like it was in my interests. They may have been exercising their fiduciary duty to increase the value of my Amazon stock. If you were talking to economist Milton Friedman, he would tell you that Amazon had done its job. What they did was legal but it was not fair. It was not humane. Wall Street loves Amazon. Capitalist Steve loves the growth and Consumer Steve loves the choice and convenience. Business Steve loves Amazon's business model and operational excellence. But Mailman Steve fucking hates Amazon. For Mailman Steve, the externalities, the intangibles around the Amazon logistics chain were not external at all. They were not intangible, but very human in their consequences. All mailman Steve could do was listen to Glynnis bitch, and cry, and swear and suffer, the picture of the future, an old woman buried under Amazon boxes forever.

Everything sold by Amazon should come with a home visit from Glynnis.

Chapter Fifteen

POLO SHIRTS

AT NIGHT, I DREAMED ABOUT PARCELS.

Literally dreamed about them. I could feel myself handling them, different sizes. Corrugated cardboard with black, fiber-reinforced Amazon packing tape.

I dreamed about scanning them. Loading them into cages. Loading them into the bed of my truck. I dreamed of long, snaking routes through new-build neighborhoods and into deep hollows. Walking up groomed driveways, and in mud so deep I had to pull on my Wellington boots. The sheer volume and repetition of it, the hopelessness of it, had taken every bit of fun out of the work. It was bad enough that every day was the same. Now I was having to dream about it too.

In the mornings I would walk into the big carrier's bay at the back of the Blacksburg MPO, and each day was worse, a physical bar chart of boxes climbing to the ceiling. Cardboard boxes stacked on cardboard boxes, six, seven, eight feet high. It was the scene from the end of *Raiders of the Lost Ark*, but instead of crates filled with Nazi superscience and looted antiquities they were filled with facial moisturizer, home electronics, and fast fashion. In the middle of all of this, toiling like something out of a Brueghel painting among these towers of boxes, were people. Carriers working like hell to do their job, load their trucks, and get out of there into the field. But working harder wasn't enough. Every day was harder than the last.

As the weeks wore on in August, my dreams about the physical aspects of the job flattened out into a systems diagram, the post office as abstraction—input, throughput, and output. This was the essence of the problem. There wasn't anything we could do about the input, and we needed not only a 200 percent–plus increase in output, but now we had to clear a growing backlog. This was what had management so on edge. It wasn't that the working conditions had become totally inhumane, it was the fact that their numbers were slipping. Our mail and periodicals were going out on time, but our package deliveries were getting later and later. We were starting to lose track of the age of the parcels in the bay. Some must have been late enough to be triggering alerts up the chain of command.

One day when I came back to reload for my next parcel run, I could hear the supervisors getting absolutely reamed on speakerphone by a woman's voice, from some distant, more powerful office. She was raking everyone else on that call over the coals, referencing a seemingly bottomless series of numbers and saying, over and over again, "This just isn't good enough. You guys need to handle this."

Quality control metrics are one thing; the hard constraints of time and space are another. There was a limit to the capacity of the mail-handling bay, and it seemed to me we were very close to hitting it.

When water or another hydraulic fluid flows through a pipe, the flow is generally laminar, or smooth—at least up to a point. An engineer will tell you laminar flow is good; it means that the fluid can move at its maximum speed from the intake to the output. But if you increase the flow too much—too much pressure, too much volume, too much speed—the flow increasingly becomes turbulent, chaotic. In fluid dynamics this is called the transition, and we were creeping into the upper registers of it, where everything was going to fall into chaos.

That was life in August 2020. Things were pressurizing toward some unseen transition point. I couldn't do anything about the vibes in the country, but I knew I could do something about this disequilibrium in the Blacksburg PO. If I had been hired as a consultant to help with this problem, how would I approach it? This idea set up shop in my head. I was daydreaming about it out on my route, and when I came back into the office, I would count boxes, then estimate volumes by pacing off the stacks and measuring their heights with my thumb at a distance—the old Boy Scout trick for measuring the height of a tree.

I woke up on a weekday morning and I saw the answer with numinous clarity. I knew how to fix the backlog. Sitting up in bed, I winced as I looked at my phone. Were they going to call me in today? I wasn't scheduled, but that hadn't meant shit for the last month. My heart rate was already accelerating, like I was a firefighter or a paramedic on call. But I could see that, miraculously, nobody had called me in yet. Blessed quiet. This was a message direct to me from the higher planes of existence. This was my chance.

I opened up a spreadsheet on my old laptop and started plugging in some numbers. What they needed to estimate was the number of packages left in backlog, which I could do based on what I had learned from pacing off the stacks of backlog packages by each of the route cases. Looking at a two-week baseline of inbound GPCs, I could forecast the total inflow of parcels, and to some extent their distribution across the routes, a curve that was fairly noisy but still pretty tightly correlated to how many residential addresses there were on that route, and the rough socioeconomic status of the folks who lived there. While everyone was still spending the mad money from their pandemic benefit checks, driving all the numbers up, as a baseline the volume still had a lot to do with disposable income. It only took about an hour to generate a pretty good forecast of what was coming in and what was going out.

It felt good to work a problem like this. The old pleasure of sitting in front of a screen, moving around numbers and words.

There are 24,000 addresses in the Blacksburg PO catchment. And we'd gone from nine to twelve of the big rolling GPC cages coming off the truck a day to twenty to *forty* of these cages, so around a 230 percent increase in a system that was white-knuckling it to begin with. You didn't need a master's degree in supply chain management to see the problem—we had too much coming in and not enough going out. The system needed to be shifted into a positive outflow: more packages going out than coming in. The big question was quantitative: How many more boxes did we need to move every day to clear the backlog and get ahead?

If our office went to three full, rolling shifts dedicated just to parcels, eighteen hours a day, while the regulars carried their "normal" route volume, my crude model showed things being cleared up in a couple of weeks. These new parcel routes would cover multiple "normal routes." This would unclog one of the artificial restrictions on volume. Very proud of myself, I printed off a couple of projections, and when the phone rang asking me to come in the afternoon to run parcels, I saw this as my opportunity to pitch a new approach.

I was an Idea Man once again.

David, the new rural supervisor, and Sebastian, the city super, were standing near the rural desk when I came in.

"Can I show you guys something?"

"Yeah, man, what's up?" David was a high-energy guy, whippet-lean, a leg bouncer. He was a serious dip user, likely self-medicating for ADHD and stress. For those unfamiliar with chewing tobacco, I haven't seen anybody chew plug tobacco since I was a kid. Too old-school. The modern dip user is a pouch man—Skol Bandits, Kodiak, Cope—or, for David, since the name-brand stuff was expensive, an off-brand called Wolf. In the chewing tobacco market, you wanted a name that evoked the past, a far frontier, and a manly indifference to long-term risks like oral cancer.

The air around David was always a pleasant wintergreen flavor. He would cram two or three of these Wolf pouches into his lip at the same time, anything to take the edge off the algorithmically fueled goatfuck that had taken over our office. "This is just pure hell, man. Just pure hell," he would sometimes tell me when I passed. The dip gave him the perpetual appearance of a man-squirrel who had found himself trapped under the hood of a car that had just roared to life and was now accelerating toward the freeway.

I handed over the printouts to him and Sebastian, complete with a line graph. “See, these are the parcels coming in. This is the range; median volume is around here. We would need to be beating this number every day to clear the backlog.”

They both looked up at me. Sebastian seemed almost angry.

“Where did you get these numbers?” This wasn’t a question. It was an accusation.

“These are just estimates. I counted the parcels in the incoming cages and how long it takes to process them into the route cages.”

“You aren’t supposed to have access to the numbers. You’re an associate carrier.” Sebastian was now visibly agitated, red-faced.

“Whoa, these are just estimates. I don’t have access to anything. I just kept count when I was throwing packages with Serena and Glynnis.”

“You aren’t supposed to have access to the numbers.”

“I didn’t look anything up. See, if we created dynamic parcel routes, and added an afternoon shift and then another shift after 6 p.m., we could clear everything out in a couple of weeks. Kat showed me this app on her phone that lets you build your own routes. Part of the problem is sticking to the route structure, its artificially restricting our clearance rate. If we build new runs using adjacent routes, we could carry bigger loads. The turnaround time is killing us. We could even use a Freightmaster and a runner.”

“Your job is to carry the mail. Our job is to manage the office.” Sebastian was now pointing his finger at me, raising his voice. And why not? In all likelihood what he saw was a busybody, a smart-ass, a rural carrier associate still in his probationary period who seemed to think he knew how to do things better than a professional like himself. Someone who, with his graphs and charts was seeming to suggest, in red and blue curves, that he thought Sebastian was fucking things up.

David likely saw a guy who had walked in with a bunch of crazy ideas that the Blacksburg PO was not authorized to put into practice. A carrier who, with the sometimes clueless nature of the neurodivergent, was now actively jamming a stick into a hornets' nest and digging it around to see what would happen. "I think what Sebastian is trying to say is that these are a lot of good ideas, Steve, but right now we need you to carry the mail. Thanks for everything you do." I got a friendly hand on the shoulder and a look that I now recognized as "How about you get some parcels loaded and get the fuck out of here?"

Sebastian did not give my printouts back.

Nobody gave a fuck about my ideas. This shouldn't have been a surprise to me, but it was. A great idea can come from anywhere, right? Isn't that what I had been teaching in innovation classes for the last several years?

Thing was, the general rule of the post office was *don't involve management.* Or, if you are management and something has gone wrong, whatever you do, don't tell District. Nobody was going to engage in a process experiment, not when they would need to explain to District and the union exactly why things had gone so far off-book. What were they going to say? "One of our rural carrier associates had graphs!"

Why resort to untested measures when we could all keep believing in one of the most basic of human dreams, that maybe if we all just kept working hard enough, and long enough, somehow everything would just go back to the way it was?

It had been over a month when the men in white USPS logo polo shirts finally arrived.

They came with tablet computers and a portable printer. There were six of them. Middle-aged white guys.

I couldn't help myself. The oldest of the group, balding and white-bearded, seemed to be in charge. The other men with their tablets kept asking him questions. I had a couple of my own.

"Hey, good morning!" I said as I approached.

"Hey there, how can I help you?"

"You guys are here to help with the backlog?"

"Yeah, they sent us down from Pittsburgh. Nothing to it. We're going to start getting everything into W-routes, running continuous shifts until we're back on top of things."

"What's a W-route?"

"You know about the codes?"

"Vaguely, from the Academy. Something to do with route size?"

"Well, that's true for standard routes, but W-routes are dynamically generated. Parcels only. We use them for Amazon Sundays. Lets us create any length of route segmentation that we want."

"So part of the problem was sticking with the fixed route structure?"

"Yeah, it was throttling your throughput. Now we can run much bigger routes just for parcels. What do you do here?"

"I'm a rural carrier."

"Well, if you want to learn more about route generation, let me know."

I was smiling as I walked back to the rural desk. Sebastian intercepted me, and my smile evaporated.

"What were you talking to those guys about?"

"I was learning about W-routes."

"What were you saying to them?"

"Nothing, just saying hello. I'm just here to run parcels."

They reorganized everything. It was beautiful to see. We started hauling huge loads, day and night. Little by little, there was more elbow room, spaces opened up, and things were becoming manageable. Then, at the end of September, like the day after a hurricane, it was over. UPS and Amazon had arrived at a new contract, effective immediately. The deluge of parcels stopped.

I had spent weeks cursing management, the MBAs at Amazon and

UPS, and the faceless systems engineers who had allowed this unforced error, this wholly foreseeable abomination, to happen to our office. To happen to me. Management should have been ready and waiting with a contingency plan if the UPS-Amazon negotiations had broken down; they should have been ready to lead with imagination, or at least with compassion. But the thing that makes me so disappointed in myself isn't the memory of all those sleepless nights, the way those Amazon boxes consumed my life. What disappointed me is not that I was angry, but that I was so grateful to these men in the polo shirts. I admired them. *Finally*, I thought, *there are some experts here who will fix this*. The same expert class that had failed to be ready for this shift in volume. The same expert class that reduces the number of Doritos in a bag of Doritos but said let's charge the same price, because consumers will tolerate it, because another expert like me helped find the sweet spot between reduced cost-per-unit and consumer rage. The same expert class that oversells the seats in a commercial airliner, knowing their loyalty program will keep fliers from defecting to another airline. And the expert in one system is the consumer in another, all of us pushing each other's buttons in a Russian doll of nested loops. The problem is less that the world is malign than that it's complicated. This world we've built for ourselves is complex to the point of being paralyzing. Then we wonder why people feel hopeless and angry. They know all these systems are pushing them around, even if they aren't sure how. I have been complicit in this expert-powered world, and I did it for the same reason everyone does—because I've been in management and now I've been on the front lines, and let me tell you, things are a hell of a lot more comfortable in management. If the world is too complex to understand and too complicated to change, you might as well be comfortable in your nihilism and get as far from the actual work as possible.

There were many hard days at the Postal Service where I dreamed about sitting at a desk, floating high on a cloud of abstraction, far away from the real work, because that's where the money is, and abstractions are just that, abstract, even though I knew someone else would be doing hard stuff and paying for those improved margins out of their own pockets. But that's more than just cynicism. It's the road to a hard heart.

One click might seem simple. And it is. But if you want to live in a world of one-click commerce, somebody still has to carry the last mile. It is the last mile that is the most expensive one. In logistics it is called "the last-mile" problem, the most labor-intensive part of any supply chain. In modern, computer-coordinated supply chains the last mile still makes up 53 percent of the cost of bringing goods to market. America is a huge country. At the time of the American Revolution, it cost as much to ship a wooden chair from England to Boston as it did to transport that chair twenty miles inland to the end customer. To unleash the economic power of the middle class and solve the last-mile problem, Benjamin Franklin created the United States Post Office. It made the world more complex. Arguably it made the world better.

When you order something from Amazon, the "one click" is the trigger at the beginning of a long global chain. And at the end of that click is the last mile. That "one click" queries cloud-based microservices for inventory and finds the closest fulfillment center. Robots pull the items off a shelf. The parcel zooms down miles of conveyor belts. Humans load it into trucks as palletized loads. Computers then coordinate the trucks, or the blue Amazon 737s turning and burning on the runway. Off to a regional fulfillment center, out to the USPS P&DC, down to the local post office, because all of Amazon's market and computing power comes to grief at the last mile. Those clicks are ultimately handled by old women who curse your nighest name and pray for your death, women who drove three hours to sort your stuff into wire cages and from those cages into the back of my 2012 Tacoma truck. It was good that we lived in this world when the pandemic came, or else millions more would have died around the globe. I am proud to have been part of this big system that helped us survive.

But I also cursed your name. Was curbside pickup too much to ask for your chest-of-drawers-sized deliveries of Variety Pack Quaker Instant Oatmeal? Was forgoing your Gatorade Brand Kiwi Strawberry Propel Zero Calorie Water with Electrolytes and Vitamins C & E too big a sacrifice? The floppy flats of bottles weighed just under twenty pounds each, and you drank three of them a week. But my suffering was invisible to you, same as Glynnis, and Kat, and Cash, and Wade, and Diana, and David, and the rest of us. And I suspect that even if our suffering wasn't invisible, you would still order the Gatorade Zero Calorie water. Because it's your favorite, after all, and all you have to do is ask for it, with a single click.

Chapter Sixteen

ANARCHY ON THE HIGH SEAS

IN DIRECT VIOLATION OF THE RULES AND REGULAtions covering my duties as a US Postal Service letter carrier, my daughters sometimes helped me deliver the mail. Only for a short time, and only on one small route. And they were carefully supervised, by me. The sanctity and security of the mail was never compromised. I don't think what I did was strictly illegal, or otherwise I wouldn't be writing about it. But if I get a visit from the postal inspectors, then you will know why.

The reason the girls wound up helping me deliver the mail comes down to my vehicle. As a rural carrier, I was technically supposed to buy a privately owned vehicle that I could use to deliver the mail within six months of taking the job. But when I got hired at the Blacksburg MPO, my original postmaster told me that I wouldn't need one. Route 10 had its own FFV, as did a lot of the rural routes. And she had a liberal policy around the use of other postal vehicles, like the Metris vans. Why just let them sit there? Get them out on the road. Plus, I had just gotten laid off. My plan had been to radically curtail our household burn rate, which ruled out buying a mail delivery ride anytime soon. Which was okay under the previous postmaster's regime. But then Jeremy, the new postmaster, showed up, and he seemed to lack the compassion and imagination of his predecessor. My free-riding days were over. When I picked up Route 11 as a sub for Kat, I suddenly needed a vehicle that I could deliver the mail from, and I knew for a fact it was impossible from the Tacoma.

Route 11 was short, what they call an auxiliary route, or AUX route. In her role as a floating assistant, Kat would run 11 after she got done assisting other carriers. In a purpose-built government-owned vehicle, a good carrier could run it in just under two hours.

Now I was on the hook for delivering Route 11, and Postmaster Jeremy wasn't going to let me use a GOV even if there was one available. I had thought about buying an old Explorer, like Wade ran on Route 3—the Beast. Old flat-bottomed Explorers had been going for maybe three or four grand, but now with the car shortage triggered by pandemic-related supply-chain snafus, anything with an engine and four wheels was going for a record price—and that's if it was even available. The demand for cars was so high that in the Kroger parking lot I frequently had people offer to buy my Tacoma, with its well-loved 100K miles, for more than I paid for it new off the lot. Duncan Automotive sold oddball import cars, including some right-hand-drive SUVs from Australia, like a high-greenhouse Mitsubishi that I had my eye on. I had a recurring fantasy about murdering it out in matte white paint and then painting on the old 1970s US Mail livery. This evolved into a scheme where Dad would buy the car and then rent it to me. Dad could sump expenses into the limited liability company as a tax shelter, and I could write off the vehicle as a business expense.

When I ran this idea past Alicia, what I got in return was the hardest of nos.

"Steve, we're not buying a mail truck. We don't even have money for groceries and the mortgage."

She was right. Even with the pandemic assistance and dropping things like steaks and organic food, we were in the negative. I can't say that we were starving, we weren't. I looked up food assistance and saw that we qualified, but Alicia wasn't having it. She felt like other people needed it more than we did. This was true. We had saved up a significant emergency fund for a layoff event—it had happened enough in my career. When I would get Mom and Dad their groceries, Dad told me to buy stuff for our family as well. We were learning how to be cash-poor and we were doing it with a hell of a lot more support than most folks in our predicament.

It still sucked. Bad. I had always been able to make enough for us. Now I was working seven days a week and we were still coming up short. I had rarely felt jealous of what other people had. We had been a family with everything we needed, and then some. But now, when I heard people complain about Zoom meetings, about day drinking, about being bored, I felt something dark—not just jealousy, but hate. It never fully consumed me, but at times it burned very hot. For the first time as a father I was feeling genuine economic precarity. It scared the hell out of me.

When I got afraid, I did one of two things. Rage was always an option. At the seeming unfairness of it all. But then I would remember what my old man told me—the world didn't owe me a thing. The other emotional course of action was just that, action. Stop feeling sorry for yourself. Make a plan. Make your own luck.

My new plan innovated by breaking the rules to keep the job I had. I would use the truck I already owned and leverage the human capital I was already paying for: my two girls. Mathilda, fourteen, and Walker, twelve. The girls were free because the schools were closed, and besides, they were getting straight A's online. When I pitched the idea, Alicia was an immediate "Yes!" And the girls were excited for something new to do.

The incentive structure was simple: Alicia would get the house to herself for a couple hours and the girls would get Gatorade and granola bars that I would buy with cash from Mom and Dad. Gatorade, with its liquid glucose and automotive-fluid colors, was banned from our house. But as I explained to the girls, this was letter carrier fuel. Deliver the mail, get Gatorade. There were so few artificial flavors in our hyperorganic whole foods hand-made-from-scratch home that Gatorade had the golden shimmer of unobtanium.

It worked like this: I would head into the MPO, case up the mail and the parcels, stick the scanner inside my Faraday bag to block the signal, drive home, pick up the girls and some breakfast burritos, and then we'd hit the route. I would drive and Mathilda would sit in the front passenger seat. Her job was to deal with the DPS and the flats. Walker sat in the back with the parcels, spurs, and the scanner. I taught Walker how to use "parcel look-ahead" on the scanner to show what packages were next, and to get them ready.

Our first trip out did not go smoothly. It was more like sightseeing.

"Jesus, Dad, look at that guy's Trump banner!" shouted Walker.

One of the first houses on our route had a stadium-sized Trump banner stretched across its front porch. It showed our beloved president standing in an explosion, flanked by aircraft carriers, overflown by a screaming bald eagle. In massive block letters under the photomontage NO MORE BULLSHIT! The bullshit being stopped was unclear.

When we got home that night, the banner was all the girls wanted to talk about. The only other Trump signs near our house were the red yard signs that simply read TRUMP, in the front yard of a retired Norfolk Southern executive.

"Mom! It said 'NO MORE BULLSHIT'!" said Mathilda, clearly enjoying the transgression.

"Girls, come on, we don't use that language in the house. Imagine if Doc heard you." Doc was Dr. Kratzer, Alicia's father.

"It's not swearing if you're quoting," said Walker. Always the barracks lawyer.

"If you think that's bad, you should hear Dad in the truck!" said Mathilda.

"I'm giving the girls a real workplace experience" was my defense.

Mathilda's ADHD was strong, very strong. The artist in her wanted to take pictures of collapsing shacks and cars up on blocks when she was supposed to be slinging the DPS and flats. I had to get her head in the game.

"Listen, babe, this isn't a country outing. You need to be anticipating the next box. Finger the mail and look ahead. Get everything into your hand so it's ready when we roll up. That mail isn't going to deliver itself!" I became some fusion of Kat and my dad. Heart Attack Steve, Always Be Closing Steve. This was new for the girls.

I kept driving faster. Eventually I filled a small media tray in my lap with the upcoming DPS and just handed it to Mathilda. "Faster, babe, you've got to go faster."

"Faster, Mathilda! Faster!" Walker never missed a chance at a leg up.

She kept calling out upcoming parcels. "Two more at the next box, then one more on Raspberry Lane." She could have been an air traffic controller or a stockbroker on the trading floor. She loved the pressure.

But it was too much for Mathilda. "This is anarchy on the high seas!" she shouted.

When the girls were little and they would get crazy, running around in elaborate costumes made out of cardboard and repurposed Disney shit, that's the thing I would say. "This is anarchy on the high seas! We don't have anarchy in the house, girls! We have the rule of law." Half joke, all command. Now it was that moment that comes for every parent, when you hear yourself mirrored back by your children, in a totally reflexive, natural way. For better or worse, they are going to be stuck with me in their skulls for the rest of their days. It was a softer version of my own father's "Everybody shut up! Quiet!"

I wondered how this time together would age with them. This wasn't work as fun, as self-actualization, this was work as counterattack, all cortisol and urgency.

Route 11 showed the girls a very different Blacksburg than the one they lived in. This wasn't the affluent college town, full of roboticists and professors. This wasn't Main Street, or leafy residential neighborhoods. This was the real sticks, and I realized that up till now, the girls had never really seen anything like it. On Route 11 people lived in trailers or old farmhouses, or lived next to the small rock quarry they ran as a family business. There were jet-skis and bass boats in the yards. Old cars up on blocks. But things were wilder too, more do-it-yourself. One trailer park had mounted everyone's mailboxes on a wagon wheel, like a mailbox merry-go-round painted red, white, and blue. One guy ran a meat-processing plant out of his backyard.

"What does that mean, meat processing?" asked Mathilda.

"Well, if you take a deer while you're hunting, you've got to butcher the meat. When I was a kid you could just take it around back to the butcher at Radford Brothers, where the YMCA is now. The butcher would cut the venison into steaks or roasts, or grind it for you. It looked just like any other meat at the supermarket when he was done. Wrapped up in cellophane and everything."

"That is redneck as hell, Dad." Walker was trying out "adult talk" with me.

"Kroger doesn't do that?" asked Mathilda.

"No, Kroger is a big corporation. I reckon they don't want the liability exposure." Then we'd have a discussion about liability.

There was the tiny house with the Dale Earnhardt banner hanging from it, the road so narrow you could almost reach out and caress old Dale's cheek as you drove past. The girls were fascinated that you could see the owner of the place, sitting at his kitchen table and eating breakfast. He was right across the street from the houses where the mailboxes were either over a leaking water main or a spring. Whatever it was, the area in front of the boxes was a perpetual mudhole, except when it froze into a skating rink in the winter.

"Wow, they have a pool and a trampoline," said Mathilda.

"Why can't we get those, Dad?" asked Walker.

"We don't have enough flat land up on top of the mountain."

"We couldn't afford it anyway," said Walker.

Ouch.

There was erectile dysfunction guy. Every time we delivered this man's mail, there were multiple pieces in there about ED.

"What's erectile dysfunction?" asked Mathilda.

"Nothing you're going to need to worry about for a long time."

"They covered it in health class, Mathilda," said Walker.

There was the grumpy bastard who yelled at Mathilda from his porch when his mailbox flapped open. Morbidly obese. In overalls. Right out of Hollywood's idea of Appalachia.

"Don't leave my goddamned mailbox open!"

Look, the guy had a point. Leaving mailboxes hanging open is a pet peeve of mine. To this day if I see one open in my neighborhood, I'll dismount and close it. But this guy's mailbox was almost impossible to close because it was all beat up. I closed it for Mathilda and apologized to him.

"Why was that guy so angry at me?" asked Mathilda. She looked stricken.

"Sweetheart, that guy is probably that angry at everything."

She shook it off. But I didn't. The next time I delivered his mail, when I was by myself, I hammered his mailbox closed with the butt end of my scanner. You couldn't have gotten it open with a crowbar, and I later saw that Kat had flagged his box as NMR—no mail receptacle. That meant his mail was going to be held at the MPO until he got a new box. When I asked her about it, all she had to say was "Oh, that guy's an asshole."

Kipps Farm was a new subdivision right in the middle of an old cow pasture. These were homes selling from $400,000 to $500,000, built around a short loop road. The neighborhood was full of doctors and new professors. I recognized the name of one of the oncologists from the Blue Ridge Cancer Center. She got a lot of the same homeware catalogs that Alicia got.

The girls and I figured out a way to deliver this neighborhood very efficiently. Mathilda would take the DPS and flats and load up my postman's satchel. She would walk the route on foot while Walker and I slung packages. Walker would ride on the bumper of the truck. I would stop, Walker would grab the package, I'd scan it, she'd run it up to the customer's front door. She'd hop back on the bumper and give me a thump when she was ready to go again. Remarkably, nobody received a life-altering injury during any of this. We could absolutely demolish the route with this system, and I got paid for completing the route, not for how long it took.

When the weather was nice, folks would come out into their yards to see Grant & Daughters deliver the mail. You've got to remember that this was the pandemic. Things were provisional and people were forgiving. They were happy when something relatively normal and fun was happening. Once, a couple in their seventies were out working in their front yard. It was beautifully manicured, full of flower beds and carefully groomed ground cover. I always got a smile from these folks, but this time the man waved for me to stop. He had gold-rimmed glasses and a Teddy Roosevelt mustache. He was the picture of a grandfather. He walked over to my window from his gardening and grabbed my arm. "Boy, you've got some good helpers there!"

"Thank you. It's been great getting to work with them."

"They will remember this the rest of their lives. They'll remember this time working with you. It's special."

I caught myself getting emotional, but managed to keep it to myself. It was special. And it was fun. In the middle of a crazy time, it was sunshine.

"We all love to see you and your girls. The whole neighborhood."

Not the whole neighborhood. Not Lego Woman.

Lego Woman sent and received packages of Legos and action figures every single day, inbound and outbound. She was some kind of eBay warrior. When the girls asked about her, I said, "There are markets in everything, girls. Anything that people are willing to pay money for, even reselling Legos," and we had a conversation about arbitrage, just the kind of Hallmark moment every adolescent daughter wants with her father.

Earlier, I had actually brought Lego Woman a stack of hods, so she could load up her outgoing boxes the night before and I could leave her another one with her incoming stuff. I had left her the hods with a note, so I guess she didn't really know what I looked like. No thank-you note back, naturally. One day after delivering Route 10, I also picked up 11.

I was by myself, and driving an FFV since Jeremy was out and one was available. I met Lego Woman in person for the first time. She was waiting for me in the front yard.

"Oh good, the real mailman! Are you the one who left me these containers?"

"Yes, that's me. Are they helpful?"

"They're great! Thank you. The other woman never left any for me." She was talking about Kat. "Listen," she said. "I'm part of a walking group of moms here in the neighborhood. We get together and walk and drink wine." I wasn't sure where she was going with this, but so far she wasn't challenging any of my assumptions about her. "We were talking. And there is this guy in a black pickup truck who uses his *kids* to deliver the mail. Do you know about this?"

Now, there were a couple of ways I could have played this. But it's hard to go wrong playing stupid.

"Oh yeah? Really?"

"Yeah, one of them rides around on the bumper and the other one walks. Well, the last time they came through, the walking one got all of the mail wrong by one house. Everybody had to bump their mail down by one house. It was crazy!"

"Everyone?"

"Okay, it was just a couple of houses. But he shouldn't be out here with his kids."

"Yeah, you're right. I'm going to have to write him up."

"What?"

"This is a violation. I'm going to have to write up a 27B-dash-6 on this."

"He doesn't need to get in trouble. I just thought you should know."

"I really appreciate you telling me this. I mean, unfortunately, this is an involuntary reporting situation for me. I've got to file the 27B-dash-6 with the postmaster. Don't worry, this won't be a problem going forward."

"Okay. I really don't want to get anyone in trouble."

Which was bullshit. Of course she wanted to get someone in trouble. If she didn't want to get anyone in trouble, she wouldn't have said anything, like literally everyone else in the neighborhood. But I really did appreciate her telling me this, and not calling in to the post office, because it meant the trouble stopped with me. Even if it meant the end of family delivery service on Scenic Ridge Road.

I never told the girls why I stopped using their help. I guess if they read this, now they know.

After the Lego Woman encounter, I figured out a way to do Route 11 by myself. I had to dismount a lot, and it took longer, but I could do it solo. But one Saturday, Walker asked if she could come with me. She wanted Gatorade and something to do. Walker, always looking for the action. I was going to be delivering parcels on Route 4, out by the Blacksburg Country Club. I figured, why not? We delivered a whole truckload of packages and that was that.

The following Monday, Diana pulled me aside. She was the regular on Route 4.

"Steve, were you out on Route 4 with one of your kids?"

"Maybe?" If there was one thing I had learned working in corporate America, it was to answer direct questions indirectly.

"Johnny called me from the golf course. He's the old shop steward for the rural carriers. He told me he saw a black pickup and a little blond girl running parcels out to the houses at the country club. Didn't you run parcels on Route 4 yesterday?"

"Diana, if I answer in the affirmative, then you're going to have to say you know something. So let me say I've got no idea what you're talking about."

"Well . . . people have gotten caught farming out their route, sometimes to a friend, sometimes as husband and wife, sometimes to their kids, and let me tell you, the union will drop the hammer on you if they catch you at it." She gave me a hard stare and left it at that.

You can get away with something until you can't. Grant & Daughters as a subcontractor for the USPS was officially out of business.

The girls must have told Mom and Dad about delivering the mail with me, because once, when I was picking them up from their grandparents' house, Dad pulled me aside.

"Hey, you know how you use the girls to deliver the mail?"

"Yeah?"

"Well, what if you used your mother? She could drive down and meet you at the post office. She could hand the mail out the window, like Mathilda."

"I don't know, Dad. I'm not supposed to be doing it. I stopped."

"Well, don't stop yet. Your mother needs something to do. She's going crazy here at the house."

Translation: Dad was going crazy being stuck in the house with Mom. What I didn't know at the time was that Mom really was going crazy, or at least slipping into progressive cognitive decline. What I did know to a cast-iron certainty was that hell would freeze over before I spent a ten-hour shift delivering the mail with my mother. My mother, at the height of her powers, could talk endlessly, a one-woman public radio station of gossip, recollection, small talk, and free-form critique. Even at that point in the progression of her disease, she could still do it, even as proper nouns seemed to increasingly elude her once razor-sharp mind. It was an ironic refutation of one of her favorite sayings, that the tongue is the only tool that grows sharper with use.

Still, Dad's request got me thinking. On a family farm, or if your family ran a store, or a garage, the children would get involved in the work as they got older. But when I would visit Dad in his lab in my teens, I never got to pitch in on experiments. I only helped Dad with his work once, and that was as an adult. He asked for my help editing a paper he was having trouble getting published. Same with my girls—were they going to help me review survey data? Put together a PowerPoint? Knowledge work isn't a family business, it is hyperspecialized, atomizing. But delivering the mail was. The pandemic and the US Postal Service gave me the rare opportunity to actually work with the girls. I got to see some flash of their future selves, but I also became deeply aware that I was being given something I could keep with me the rest of my days.

The old man at Kipps Farm was right—we had created something indestructible, joyous, and magical. A moment in time that the girls can keep long after I'm gone. Maybe it's even a story that will enter into family lore, like my great-grandfather Laurence Mehaffee the Mississippi riverboat pilot, or my great-grandfather Titus Grant cutting window glass, the last of the Grant glass men. I think these myths are often about work, because work is how we live, and live on. And maybe, like piloting a steamboat or floating window glass on a pool of molten tin, a father and his daughters delivering the mail house-to-house will fade into history, an anachronism, replaced by robots and the sunshine of another lost American time.

Chapter Seventeen

UNITED STATES POSTAL SERVICE, MA'AM

FROM THE VERY BEGINNING OF THE SHUTDOWN AND into the fall, we moved a lot of baby chicks. Prior to carrying the mail, I had no idea that chickens could be shipped by mail. Stuck at home there were a lot of suburban types who wanted fresh eggs and something to do with their kids, so they started a backyard coop. The Rural King in Radford was closed, a typical source of baby chickens, geese, and ducks. In 2020, if you wanted chickens the only game in town was the United States Postal Service.

Farmers would ship the chicks the same day they hatched. The birds would be boxed up and shipped via Priority Mail, and when we would come in to case the mail in the morning, they were stored in the parcel-holding area on the other side of my workstation. I could hear them peeping away, an organic sound in a loud industrial space. The flat rate for a Priority Mail "chicken box," a special reinforced-cardboard container with ventilation holes and filled with shredded paper bedding to protect the chicks and keep them warm, was just over sixty dollars.

As a rookie rural carrier I never got to deliver any live chicks. They were always handled by Mabel, a former rural carrier turned back-office assistant who handled all the rural-route-based phone calls, plus a few special deliveries. Mabel was in her sixties, and my memory of her is of her wearing a colorful sundress and white sneakers, real granny-wear. She was a sweet lady and knew just about everything there was to know about carrying the mail. I actually carried the mail for her home address on Route 11, and would typically pull it out for her and walk it to her desk. She tried to stop me every time. "Oh now I don't want to make more work for you, Steve." But it was never really work for me. Mabel was one of those people at the post office, like Kat or Cash, that I would have done just about anything for.

When the baby chicks would arrive, Mabel would call over the female carriers. The group of them would hover over the nest box and coo. The male carriers were all performatively indifferent, making sure all the other male letter carriers saw that they didn't give a shit about any stupid chicks and were glad they didn't have to carry them. But when I wandered over to join the women, I detected more than a few flashes of jealousy. Yes, even delivering the mail, it was important to be tough and to be seen to be tough. We men would dip tobacco, smoke, or talk football or cars. Gun talk seemed to be one place where gender parity had been reached—because everybody in the post office seemed to be a gun owner and was eager to talk about it.

When all of the social theater was over, Mabel always drove the chicks directly to the customer's house in one of our climate-controlled USPS Dodge vans.

All those chicks mean chicken feed. It's the kind of thing that a rural quasi-suburbanite like me doesn't think of. As an economist it should have been obvious. Chicken feed is an industrial input to another capital asset: chickens. But the Grants hadn't been farmers for over two hundred years. We made window glass in Scotland, then in West Virginia until the 1950s, and after that we were chemists, engineers, and consumer strategists. So, as the parcel jockey, I was genuinely surprised when I saw three fifty-pound bags of chicken feed sitting in the sortation area. Surprised as in "What the fuck?" To which Diana said, "All those chickens people are ordering have got to eat something."

The USPS will ship anything up to 70 pounds with a combined length and width of 130 inches. As I learned firsthand, there is a lot of stuff that you can fit inside those dimensions. The pandemic had turned back the clock. Everyone was a homesteader now, isolated in the countryside. While the internet was piping bad news, videoconferences, and election hysteria into people's houses without impediment, when it came to getting physical goods into the home it was 1906. A man in a truck was going to clatter up to your farmstead with the outside world in the bed.

The one hundred and fifty pounds of chicken feed were going to the end of a winding spur road off Happy Hollow Road. Google Maps guessed, but for certainty I needed the *Virginia Atlas & Gazetteer* for the final approach. The *Gazetteer* is a book with maps of the whole state of Virginia. All the roads are there, down to the last horse path. More importantly, those roads are laid out on topographic maps, which at least gave me some idea of what I was looking for: a road snaking right up a draw till it crawled along the ridgeline that overlooked Indian Run. So some very high, remote place. Unlike Google, which only discriminated between three sizes of road—superhighway, road, and small road—the *Gazetteer* was much finer-grained. I could see the last stretch was a jeep trail.

These were the sorts of deliveries that were fantasy material for a Tacoma 4x4 driver. I loaded the chicken feed into the bed last, laying the bags end to end so they wouldn't shift around too much. I would make a big loop down Catawba, back up Mount Tabor, then down into the neighborhoods along the foot of Brush Mountain, so I was going to deliver the chicken feed first, FIFO-style, just like they taught us at the Academy.

Happy Hollow is a windy enough road that when I drove Alicia down it the first time, years ago when we were dating, there were enough doglegs and hairpins in it that it made her carsick. The first time an oncoming car headed for us and I dropped two wheels off the pavement to let them pass, Alicia said, "People here are crazy! He's going the wrong way up a one-way street!" And I had to explain that Happy Hollow was not a one-way street, just a really narrow country road. It was a freeway compared to where this chicken feed was headed. The pavement ended about a hundred yards in, and from there it was nothing but gullies and sandbars. There was no part of that road flat enough to even develop a good washboard. It was more like a dry creek bed.

I was watching the address numbers go by as the truck climbed. There were a couple of big new houses, hidden behind thickets of thornbushes and honeysuckle growing in the sun provided by the road break. That didn't last. The road narrowed to where the oaks and tulip poplars touched over top, shading everything. From the air this road would be invisible, hidden under the forest canopy. The houses now were built right next to the roadway—typical of small, high-grade plots where the only place level enough to put a house was basically hugging the spur ridge that I was following in the truck. I passed a trailer that had been hidden inside extensions built on over the years. Then just straight-up single-wides, with kids throwing a ball in the tiny front yard that was more punked-out sandstone than grass. There was a driveway that ran off into the woods with several no-trespassing signs, but according to the address I had written into my notebook, I still hadn't gone far enough up the road.

There was no more cell phone signal, the real sign that you were in the sticks. The track had jumped over to the northern side of the spur—a part of the mountain in perpetual shade. No more big oaks; the woods were now a dense thicket of scraggly pines and cedars. This was about as far off the grid as I'd gotten carrying the mail. The branches were close enough in to the trail now that they were scraping the sides of my truck.

Had I screwed up my map-reading? How could anybody live up here? There was a tight bend around a thick, gnarled-up white pine. Just around the turn was an old Datsun compact pickup, the granddaddy ancestor of my own trusty rig. The Datsun had met a bad end, the tires dry-rotted flat, the windshield covered with pine sap, the body panels gone eggshell matte. It seemed an ill omen to me. If I didn't find a turnout up here, it was going to be a very long, slow reverse out of this place, the kind where if I wasn't careful, I'd wind up tearing a side-view mirror off the truck. Just on the other side of the dead Datsun, someone had screwed brass numbers into the trunk of another pine—hardware store address numbers that had been stuck into the trunk of that tree so long ago that the bark had started to bulge out past them, like dough rising in a pan. This was the address I was looking for. I still couldn't see any sign of human habitation, but this had to be the place.

Another fifty yards and things opened up into a small field holding a cozy house, saddle land on top of the mountain. There was a big equipment shed with a John Deere tractor and a Bobcat excavator, and a dirt lot with two old Chevy pickups and a very well-loved 1990s burnt-orange 4Runner. Two small corgis started barking at me before I even had the ignition turned off. I dropped the tailgate, got the first bag up onto my shoulder, and walked it the rest of the way to the front porch.

An old woman, an Appalachian survivor in sneakers and blue jeans, all smiles, opened the front door.

"United States Postal Service, ma'am."

"Oh my goodness. Nobody comes up here. Nobody. Hell, you're the first person I've seen that isn't kin since all of this started. Of course, it's the post office. You all are the only ones with any guts. The rest of them won't even try it in their fancy trucks."

"Where are your coops? I'm happy to carry this down for you. "

"If you would carry it down, well, it would be a kindness. I have to use a wheelbarrow these days." This woman barely reached five feet tall. She lived alone. She was straight-no-chaser mountain tough, the genuine article, and would have lugged those bags down herself if I hadn't offered. She had the usual assortment of self-sufficiency tools I had come to recognize by now—cords of firewood, a woodshed, a hydraulic log splitter, her own gas and diesel tanks. Maybe helpful grandsons came to run all this heavy equipment for her on Sunday afternoons, but I suspect she could run every bit of it herself.

"I wouldn't turn down that wheelbarrow, ma'am. That way I can do all three bags at once. Just let me get my work gloves."

Down past her home was a shallow grassy hill. The left side of the meadow held a pen with goats, pink ribbons tied in the hair of one of them. At the downhill end of the field was the biggest home chicken coop setup I'd ever seen. This wasn't a hobby, but rather had the look of something being done in deadly earnest.

"You raising these eggs to sell?"

"Got nobody to sell them to, so I mostly eat them myself and give them to my kids."

I rolled the bags down to the storage shed that held all her chicken-keeping stuff, the craft of raising birds a mystery to me.

"There you go, ma'am. You want this back up at the top of the hill?"

"I feel bad for asking. Let me get you a glass of water."

I pushed the wheelbarrow back up the hill and tipped it up against the equipment shed where I found it. When I turned around, she was standing there with a glass of water and a paper bag.

"There's some eggs for you and your family. God bless you, young man," she said, and laid her hand on my arm in that grandmotherly way.

This tough, independent old lady was a pretty different creature than my granny, who wore white gloves and a hat when she left the house. She was much more like my mamaw from West Virginia. Mamaw knew birds, drank bourbon neat, drove a Thunderbird, lived by herself, and only asked for help when she really needed it, like when Dad and I drove up to Charleston to replace her hot water heater. I had thought women like that might have been a thing of the past, but they weren't. That toughness lived on, and it was the most hopeful thing I'd encountered in a season that hadn't been long on hope. When this mountain woman handed me those eggs for my family and told me "God bless you" something deep twanged inside me. Instead of getting choked up in front of a stranger, I just touched the brim of my hat and got back into the truck while my composure still held. For the rest of the day everything else was as light as a feather. I'd have carried chicken feed for her every day of my life. It was my great privilege to do it as her mailman.

I carried everything I could right to the customer's front porch. I always tried to deliver every parcel, to never leave a PS 3849, the dreaded orange slip that customers hated. We had been told at the Academy that we were supposed to deliver every letter, every flat, and every parcel, every day. During the pandemic, our postmaster made it a point to say, "Don't come back with anything. Deliver it all. We're out there so people don't have to come in here."

One day I was delivering the mail in Woodbine, out on North Main. Woodbine is an older neighborhood in Blacksburg. The lots are small, the housing stock mostly from the early 1980s. Once it had been surrounded by cow pasture on all sides. Now it was encircled by student apartments and a rank of new airplane-hangar-style churches with names like Tried Stone and Northstar. Lapsed (very lapsed) Catholic that I am, these new churches seemed more like a place you would rent a log splitter than worship the creator of the universe and his only begotten son. Woodbine was solidly middle-class—affordable homes for young families of assistant professors, teachers, nurses, university staff and administrators.

I had a signature-required package in my hands, so I figured I would walk the mail to the door while I was at it. I was struggling to place the name. It was familiar. Rhonda.

The woman who opened the door, however, knew me immediately.

"Steve Grant! What are you doing here?"

"I'm your mailman. At least today I am."

"Mailman? I thought you were in advertising?"

"The pandemic. Gosh, Rhonda, how are you?" I hadn't seen Rhonda since high school. She had been in the marching band. It took me a while, but I was finally able to place her face. I had slow-danced with her at band camp, the first girl I ever really slow-danced with. I remember how closely she held me. We had always been friendly but just ran in different circles. But we get older, and any connection to the past becomes charged with nostalgia. These witnesses to our younger selves tell us that it wasn't all some hallucination, that our younger bodies once walked the earth.

"Steve, I think you are the first person I've seen face-to-face since this all started. I get my groceries delivered. I don't leave the house really." She seemed to turn inward, then spoke, as if she'd made up her mind to share. "I had a heart attack. I've been isolating myself."

"You had a heart attack?"

"I was in a meeting right before they sent everyone to work at home. My arms went numb, I passed out, hit my head on the table before I fell to the floor. They had to take me to Roanoke in an ambulance."

"Jesus, I can't believe you had a heart attack! But you're okay now?"

"I guess so. I didn't really have a heart attack, it turns out. I had broken heart syndrome."

"That's not a heart attack, I take it?"

"No . . . they call it Takotsubo cardiomyopathy. Where stress can fool your mind into having a heart attack. My heart is actually healthy."

"What caused it, do you know?"

"My ma and I. We were so close, almost like sisters. When she died, it felt like all the color drained out of everything. I've got nobody. I don't know why I keep going sometimes. But I keep going."

I didn't know what to say.

She smiled.

"I'm so happy to see you, Steve Grant. Thank you for bringing my mail."

"I'll see you, Rhonda. Take it easy," I said. Although the honest reply would have been "It's good to see you too. I'm glad that you're alive, but I hadn't thought about you in years until I laid eyes on you just now."

She said, "See you." And she seemed to mean it, as if thirty years hadn't preceded this moment.

It was another one of those times when I felt I'd been sent on that route on that day for reasons beyond delivering the mail. I was sent as an agent for some larger power, to let Rhonda know that the world was still outside waiting for her. That she wasn't yet a ghost. My job that day was to see her and to offer proof of life.

The route will always send you something interesting, if you keep your eyes open. I was out on "big-box" duty again, hauling nothing but a pickup load of parcels. This time there was a sort of jumbo mini fridge, just under seventy pounds. It was the biggest box in the rest of my load for the day: some flat-pack lawn furniture, several boxes of oatmeal and Cheetos, and an assortment of unguessable Amazon boxes. I had a good route where I could hit a number of places on the way down to the river on Price's Fork, then turn up Mount Zion and deliver the big boy.

It was one of those early fall mornings that you can get in Appalachia, where the predawn hours are so clear and cold that you can see spy satellites zooming from north to south and south to north in the sky, as big as a school bus with their high-powered optics, as shiny as a Coors can at the bottom of the river. But as dawn comes on a dense ground fog rolls in from the river, pushing up the valley and into the hollows. A classic temperature inversion, where up on top of Brush Mountain it was Colorado clear, but just five hundred feet down the mountain the fog was so thick you were literally inside a cloud, a light rain falling on you out of the gloom. In these fogs you can hear an owl for miles, but sometimes a truck can come up on you at 60 miles an hour as quiet as a cat, the sound lost in the damp and the trees. Spooky and cold.

The address I was delivering to was down on Mount Zion, just a stone's throw from the New River, and the farther down Prices Fork I went, the thicker the fog got. But I knew where I was going. These folks were just down the road from Amanda Cleveland, the witch. I had delivered to them a number of times. Their mailbox was at a small bend in the road, and I knew their home was a good distance back in their acreage. Like a lot of people who lived way out, they had a parcel box closer to the road, where the letter carrier and the UPS man could leave packages. In this case it was a jumbo-sized Rubbermaid utility tub hidden back behind a honeysuckle thicket, just before the locked gate to their driveway. When I say driveway I don't mean mirror-glaze-smooth blacktop with evenly spaced Malibu landscaping lights running along the shoulder. This was two dirt tracks in the grass threading between the big oaks and cottonwoods down in the Tom's Creek floodplain.

I pulled off the side of the road, got the mini fridge out of the bed of the Tacoma, and walked it down to the parcel locker. I knew how big that locker was, and I was pretty sure the fridge would fit with a little space to spare. I got behind the honeysuckle, put the fridge down, and flipped up the brown plastic top of the parcel box.

The entire interior of the locker was filled with a single box, with a big square UPS dot-matrix MaxiCode slapped on the side.

I cursed the UPS guy's name. You couldn't have slipped a credit card between the sides of that box and the inside walls of that locker. It was that tight.

The black print on the outside of the box said it was a "mini freezer," and the lightbulb clicked on in my head. These folks had their refrigerator-freezer die, and with all the stores closed there was no way to replace it. So they ordered a mini fridge and a mini freezer, because they were stuck at home in the pandemic with no refrigeration. I was worried that with this ground fog, it could start raining, and I had nowhere I could responsibly leave the mini fridge without it becoming porch-pirate bait or drenched. Then I remembered what we were told about parcel delivery at the Academy. As the manual says:

> Parcels are to be taken out for delivery on the first trip after receipt. If a parcel is too large for the box, the supplier is required to attempt delivery to the customer's residence if on the line of travel, or within ½ mile on the line of travel and retrace (total of 1 mile) to transact business, when necessary, to affect delivery. Dismount, if necessary. If the parcel cannot be delivered on the first trip, leave a PS Form 3849 in the customer's box.

I know what most seasoned carriers would have done in this circumstance. They would have closed the lid on that parcel locker, written out a 3849, and smoked a cigarette in the truck. But I was bored, and I had a wild hare up my ass.

I was going to dismount and walk both units up to their house.

Our number one job was the sanctity and security of the mail, and these people needed to replace their dead refrigerator. I could do it!

To get the UPS box out I literally had to turn the parcel locker upside down so it could slide out. Then I went back to the Tacoma and got the nylon load straps I typically use to cinch stuff down in the truck bed. I wrapped the first one around both boxes, pulled the strap tight against the ratchet, gave it a couple of strokes, and the boxes were snug together. I took some nylon rope I kept in the toolbox and wedged it into the gap at the bottom of the two boxes, pulled it up a bit, ran a length up each side, and stabilized the whole thing with a couple of taut-line hitches around the top. Now I could pull the boxes up onto my upper back, and as long as I leaned forward and held a rope in each hand, I could carry the whole thing like a backpack. Feeling very proud of this Boy Scout knots-against-adversity moment, I set off down the trail.

The sound of running water grew louder, until I reached the stream. Of course. Grant, you dumbass, you were walking downhill in a floodplain toward a house that you knew was uphill from your position. It was Tom's Creek, about thirty feet wide or so, and running a little swift, maybe eight to twelve inches deep across a freestone creek bed, the usual Appalachian mix of gravel, embedded rock, and slabs of the living stone from the valley floor.

I had on my good Danner boots. They were Gore-Tex lined, which they will tell you at REI means they are waterproof, but that's bullshit. The water was too deep here, and freestone creeks in Appalachia that get partial sunlight are slicker than snot from the algae.

So I took off my boots, slipped my socks inside, and then tied the laces together in an overhand bow where they could hang around my neck. I jammed my jeans up over my calves. I was ready. Carefully sliding one foot forward at a time, I began to inch my way across the creek, feeling for patches of sand or gravel with my toes. It wasn't snowmelt-cold but it sure as hell wasn't warm. Look at you, Steve, you old river rat. You can still wade a creek barefoot with the best of them. Not bad for an old office jockey.

This lasted for about twenty seconds, until my foot landed on what I thought was sand but was actually a layer of sand on top of a very slick rock. My right foot shot forward, and I started to fall backward. To kill my rearward momentum I had to bend forward from the waist, my feet moving farther apart until I was contorted into something close to what they call Trikonasana or Triangle pose in yoga, except that I had a hundred odd pounds of Chinese refrigeration on my back. Bent over at the waist, staring down into the creek as I watched my boots swinging around like bell clappers in front of me, struggling to keep the two giant parcels balanced on my back, I somehow managed to get upright again, my feet under me and then moving much more slowly. Sliding each foot forward I finally reached the far side of the creek.

This was personal now. I was going to deliver these fucking fridges.

With my boots back on and the load mounted on my back, I got into a rhythm. It was a mild climb through a big pasture, but with the fog I couldn't see the edges of the field. But now I could hear voices ahead, a man and a woman talking.

Then, piercing the fog, I saw the prow of a sailboat.

I'm not talking about a little Hobie Sunfish you might take out on the reservoir. This was an oceangoing thirty-five-foot boat with a gleaming white fiberglass hull, a cabin with portholes, the deck covered in cleats, winches, windlasses, and all the other rigging of a cruising blue-water boat. It was so big it looked like they had built up the wooden hangar around it. How they towed it across the same creek bed I had just forded I do not know. Magic seemed likely.

Past the sail barn, the field opened up and the fog began to blow away, if only for a moment. I could see the farmhouse ahead at the end of the track. Then it was lost in the fog again. Another shift in the wind and I could see downhill across the gold grass of the field. There in the gray light of the morning was an observatory, up on stilts and a couple of stories tall, complete with a white-domed turret, big enough to hold a very serious telescope. The lower level of the observatory had big windows and through them I could see two big monitors with images of the moon on them.

Where am I? What mystic land is this?

It was the land of wizards.

They were sitting on their front porch in long hooded robes, sitting in Adirondack chairs, drinking steaming mugs of coffee so big they had to hold them with two hands. The woman saw me first. In the fog I could now hear every word, despite her stage whisper.

"Jesus, there's a man walking up from the field, Tom." She stood up and spoke at full volume now. Tom was still in his seat. "Good morning? Can I help you?"

"United States Postal Service, ma'am. I've got your freezer and your refrigerator, I believe."

"Did you ford the creek with that on your back?"

"Yes. There wasn't enough room in the parcel locker, and I didn't want you to have to come into town."

"I will be damned. I think you are the first person that's been to the house since March. Would you like a cup of coffee?"

"I would love one. Is that a telescope?"

"Yeah, that's the observatory. We built it ourselves." No further details were provided, and I decided that I would allow the sailboat and the observatory to remain arcane mysteries, in keeping with the vibe of the pocket reality I had waded my way into.

There has never been an America without the Postal Service. The original Post Office was actually formed and operational before the Constitution was ratified. Our young country hadn't figured out how the government would work, but everyone knew we needed a Postal Service. It's written into the Constitution, a perfect example of Alexander

Hamilton's notion of what a people's government should do—the things that the market can't, the things that promote domestic tranquility, that create the mechanisms of wealth and commerce, that bind the country together with roads, correspondence, and the idea of a common destiny.

During the pandemic, the Postal Service held the country together. Most of us think of doctors and nurses and first responders as essential—indeed they are, and they were; they absolutely were. But we postal workers are essential too. Sure, none of my *Boy's Life* fantasies of postal adventure came true. There were no last-minute rescues of farmers trapped under tipped-over tractors on a remote back road. No heroic defense of voters' ballots or any of the other fabulist crap I'd imagined. What was essential was just doing your job.

Sometimes the heroic act is simply showing up. It's like being a parent. It's not about taking your kid to Disneyland or sending them off to their first-choice college without student loans. It's the fact that you went to work every day to keep a roof over their heads, took them to the doctor, read to them, walked with them, talked to them, took them to their grandparents' place, kept them from drinking their weight in soda or playing on screens until their brains were as smooth as kidney beans. The act of being a parent is about the consistent sincere effort to create something larger than yourself, a family in which your child can grow up into a good daughter, good sister, good friend, good citizen. It's the same being an aunt or uncle, related by blood or by love. The US Postal Service has been that uncle to the country for two and a half centuries now. Always there, no matter what. And when something is there long enough, consistently enough, it becomes part of the culture. Part of our nation's collective unconscious.

For generations, back to the American Revolution, to the founding of the republic and through its many struggles to better itself, to communicate with itself, the story—the nation's inner monologue—has been the same: It's not some Great Man who was coming, just a very ordinary man. Somebody from your town, a normal sort of person. But under even the craziest, most extreme conditions—hurricanes, gloom of night, a civil war—that person was coming. No matter how far up the hollow, we were coming. Your refrigerator was coming. The feed for your chickens was coming. The Post Office was coming. You are not alone.

I came to believe that the American people hold a collective memory of a time where news of the outside world was carried on the back of a lone man or woman who was authorized by the people's government to travel on foot up mountains and across creeks to deliver not just the mail but a reality that must be believed in to exist. Reminding us that we are *a people*, that our job is to love and protect each other, that our government at its best is *us*, and that when we are alone, we are still together, joined by ideas, history, correspondence, chicken feed, and refrigerators. Out of many, one.

Chapter Eighteen

HIGH LONESOME

ROUTE 4 COVERED TRAILER PARKS AT THE START OF the route and then snaked its way down into Ellet Valley to Deercroft. Directly across Luster's Gate Road from the Blacksburg Country Club ("your club in the country"), Deercroft was home to doctors, lawyers, car dealership owners (one of whom I knew from high school), university administrators, entrepreneurs, department heads, college football coaches—in short, the moneyed class of a prosperous university town. Route 4 was typically carried by Diana, in her white right-hand-drive Jeep, the bossest ride in the shop.

Route 4, other than a couple of cluster-box units at the start, was basically a mounted route. The old joke with traditional rural carriers that drove long routes is that if their car was on fire, they would try putting it out from inside. Nothing could entice them to get out and walk. You drove from box to box, sitting in your vehicle and doing the old "wax on, wax off" of grabbing DPS, flats, and spurs by reaching across your body, loading up your left hand, then reaching out with your right and stuffing the target mailbox while you slowly drove past, steering with your knee and working the pedals. Repeat several hundred times. Unsurprisingly, this put a lot of stress on your right shoulder, and Diana was out with a torn rotator cuff, a repetitive-stress injury.

This is one of the reasons I actually liked dismounting. My regular route, Route 10, was effectively a dismounted route, more like a city carrier route. But driving Route 4, with its disposable income and parcel volume, was an exercise in hop out, hop in. It meant slinging hundreds of packages along with the mail. It was not unusual for me to get twelve thousand steps on a day while I still spent hours driving. The good news was that since I was carrying the mail and not just parcels, I got to drive an FFV, which made throwing mail into roadside boxes a heck of a lot easier.

One morning, when I was loading up the truck, I reached down into the package cage to pick up the first of four identical packages, each about the size of a large pizza box. Most packages this size are pretty light—framed art or LPs packed in bubble wrap. When I grabbed the first one, it didn't budge. I reached in with both hands. It was heavy as hell, and each one weighed about the same.

"Hey, Dean, what do you think these are?"

"Who knows?"

"Hey, Erica, what do you think these are? They're really heavy."

"Something heavy."

So much for a lively exchange of ideas.

When I got to the address, I drove all the way up the driveway and did a quick two-point turn to point my roll gate at the garage door in order to minimize the distance I had to hump these things to the front porch. I had gotten the back open and had the first one in my hands when a big guy in a Carhartt work jacket and MultiCam utility pants came out of his garage to meet me. He was a few years younger than me and did not look like the banker I expected to come out of this brick Williamsburg-style home with its groomed rhododendron trees evenly spaced along the front walk.

"Good morning! These must be for you—are they rifle plates for body armor? That was all that I could guess." Maybe this wasn't the guy

I should have been playing "guess the parcel" with, but honestly, I had never had a single customer say, "Mind your own goddamned business!" It was habit at this point.

"You're close! They're steel rifle targets. I just got a new Smithfield M1A in 6.5-millimeter Creedmoor." He was helping me unload the truck while we talked.

"Six five? I've heard a lot about it, but never seen anything chambered in it."

"Hey, I'll show you!"

He disappeared into the garage. Not thirty seconds later he was back, with a full-sized battle rifle. It had a beautiful walnut stock and was topped with a big scope that I didn't recognize. The M1A is the civilianized version of the M-14, the grandchild of the M-1 rifle carried by GIs in World War II. The military version is an accurate, hard-hitting .30-caliber rifle that was used by designated marksmen in the US Army during the Global War on Terror.

"I carried one a lot like this in Afghanistan," he said.

"But in .308, right?"

"Yeah, but I didn't want anything that big. So I got the Creedmoor. Flatter shooting, better BC. And I got the new Vertex variable power scope with the integral BDC." You always know you're dealing with an enthusiast when the conversation turns into alphabet soup.

"Here, take a look." He began to hand me the rifle, then stopped himself. "You're not a felon or anything, are you?"

"I'm a sworn federal employee in a position of trust."

"Oh yeah, right! Of course. Yeah, man, check it out."

Of course you just hand a rifle to the mailman in your driveway.

And of course I just took it.

He pulled the magazine and locked the bolt to the rear, then handed it over. I eyeballed the breech myself. Nothing up the pipe; the gun was safe. Then I shouldered the rifle and got my cheek weld on behind the sights. The sight picture through the scope was the clearest optic I've ever looked through. Behind the ocular lens, the world was converted into a hyperreal shooting gallery. I picked out a female cardinal on a slender branch, with her golden-brown feathers. It was nature photography, the image was so clear. The bullet drop compensator was illuminated like a videogame, marked in ranges out to one thousand meters.

"That's a hell of a piece of glass," I said.

"I'm going to use it for pronghorn out in New Mexico. Just take some time by myself."

"That is a beautiful rifle. Thanks for letting me look at it."

"It's nice to show it to someone who might appreciate it. Gosh, I don't think I've actually spoken to anybody other than my folks face-to-face in a few weeks. Still feels like there are too many people here." I knew by "here" he meant this town, this house.

As he stood there talking to me, he cradled the forestock of the rifle in the crook of his left arm, his right hand holding the grip, his trigger finger carefully indexed along the stock. There was nothing forced about it; it wasn't a pose. He was just outside, holding a rifle, talking to another man. His body relaxed into place, rooted like a tree.

"You live here?"

"No. This is my folks' place."

"You grow up here?"

"Yeah. You too?"

"Yeah, grew up. Left. Came back. You ever been to New Mexico?"

"Nope. I'm looking forward to it. I got to get the fuck out of here."

"Sometimes this is a good place to get the fuck out of."

"Thanks. Be safe, brother."

"Good hunting, friend."

Sometimes you wind up back in a place, and it isn't until you get there that you remember how hard you had worked to get out of it. When I was eighteen, I would have done crime to get out of Blacksburg. Yet here I was, standing with another reverse refugee, who dreamed of getting out.

Maybe he missed the feeling of carrying a rifle in high, dry country.

Maybe he couldn't stand the walls being too close, the overheated feeling of being back under his parents' roof. Not when he had been out in all that space and light, the high lonesome near the roof of the world.

I don't know how much I had in common with the man. I had never been to Afghanistan, never served, never even hunted white-tail. But I knew what it felt like being back living under your parents' roof as a grown-ass man. When I first moved back to Blacksburg at the age of forty-one, I was back in my parents' house, sleeping in my dead grandmother's bedroom. I lived the definition of buyer's remorse in those months of staying with my folks. The tiny windows in their brick ranch house would shrink down into pinholes of light. I was living in a camera obscura where the outside world could only be inferred, seen in a pale inverted image that was worse than memory. That is the suffocation of a small town, and I wonder sometimes why it gets so idealized, largely by people who don't have to live in small towns.

There were times in Blacksburg, even living in my own house, when the routine and the fluorescent lights, the overwhelming regularity of it all, a town run by bureaucrats and engineers all synchronized by their Outlook calendars, all of it a hydraulic press for the soul, slowly compressed me into an aluminum ingot. In my memory, Blacksburg was a wild place, God's country. When I was in the city—Los Angeles, London, New York—I would daydream about coming back here. To be wading a small water creek, fishing the pocket water. Or hiking along the ridge, sometimes for hours without seeing another human being. But the reality of moving back had been something very different.

What had drawn me in was a trick of memory, that somehow these mountains were an empty, unoccupied space where I would be free. But the endless grind of work still followed me, and instead of a blank slate, I found myself surrounded on all sides by ghosts, preconceptions, fossil forms of past injury brought back to life, *Jurassic Park*–style. Nothing was empty; every feature of the landscape carried some significance I had to contend with.

I had thought I needed solitude, the right to come and go as I pleased, the room to think. And Blacksburg eventually offered that room. But I also needed to do battle here, in my hometown, to return as an adult, as a man, and discharge this power that these memories had over me. There was no blunt-force solution to dealing with family history—the rages, the blame games, the scorekeeping, the latest version of a multi-generational cascading failure. What I had learned in my time back here in Blacksburg was that the deconstruction had to be done on-site. If you genuinely wanted to fix things, between people, within yourself, then you could not run forever.

Returning home can be a default choice, a place where you wind up out of inertia. But returning home could also be forensic. You can return as a different person, with new tools, tactics, techniques, and strategies. You can return with a promise to yourself that you will slowly unwind the whole mess, unbolt every part from the stock, lifting out the receiver, sliding out the connecting rod, pushing out the pins, and stripping the surfaces down to white metal. The reality of the issue is not as simple as a busted part, or a misadjustment. It's the whole thing that needs rebuilding. Once you've pulled it all to pieces, in context, things can be reassembled with care, part by part. Then you understand how the whole machine is actually supposed to work.

And when it is too much, then you seek out solitude. If you really want to go beyond your job, and your family, and your faith or lack thereof, if you want to get down to the bare metal of who you are, of your soul, then what is required is solitude. And if you need solitude, delivering the mail is a good job, because once that mail is cased up, you are out and on your own. The days when the job clicks into place, when all the parts are machined to precision tolerances, running perfectly—those are the days when the world becomes an exploded diagram and you can start to contemplate how it might be put back together, assembled into something deliberate and new.

That solitude is the high lonesome. There is no substitute. And for the soldier home from the war, that rifle was nothing more than a promise from its owner to himself that someday soon he was going to walk free from this godforsaken place.

Maybe he would return again, the job not yet done.

He might need to return many times.

But one day, the last component would snap into place, the job complete, the machine whole, and he would walk away one last time, forever free.

Chapter Nineteen

THE THINGS I CARRIED

BACK AT THE ACADEMY, THEY TOLD US THAT WE shouldn't carry anything we weren't issued by the Postal Service. But when you're a rural carrier you aren't issued much of anything at all, and by the end of my time I carried around twenty pounds of gear with me, either in my truck or in a backpack.

The first thing I carried was a blue logbook, which I used to write down the days I worked, the routes I ran, the miles I drove, when I put gas in the postal vehicle. I would write down when I took receipt of certified or registered mail because I wanted my own contemporaneous record that I had delivered everything as asked, because from the way registered mail was treated (delivered in a locked bag, stored in a bank-type safe, signed out for delivery, considered safe for classified documents) it felt like I was carrying the nation's nuclear codes. I wrote down when I arrived at the MPO, when I started casing the mail, when I departed the MPO for the road, and how long it took me to carry the route, because I wanted a sense of my performance. I wrote down the weather on days that it was horrible but I never wrote down when it was beautiful, though I sometimes took pictures with my phone, another thing I carried. And when I cut myself and realized I needed to bring a first-aid kit, I wrote down BRING FIRST-AID KIT. I wrote down the things that happened to me, like getting attacked by dogs, and I wrote down the things I felt, like ABSOLUTE HELL, THIS SUCKS, and FEELINGS ARE APOCALYPTIC because those things happened to me too.

Because I sometimes worked 12-hour days and would often walk 15,000 steps a day, 7 miles, which burned around 1,200 calories, I learned to carry PowerBars, beef jerky, peanuts, apples, and thick chocolate bars because, just like when you are backpacking, your lunch will get crushed so you need crush-proof food. I had started out eating organic food prepared by Alicia, but like a real mailman, I ultimately wound up eating shelf-stable garbage because it was just easier. I picked up a Slim Jim habit that I am still carrying with me, because I grew to love their taste, and to this day when I think about my time carrying the mail, I start to crave one, especially the Tabasco-flavored ones; the hotter the better. When it was cold, I burned even more calories, so I would sometimes carry a big sandwich that I would buy from 7-Eleven, their "American Sub," a sandwich improved by being smashed flat in a backpack, an Appalachian muffuletta, because burning up that brick of processed meat in my guts kept me warm. I carried that hate of being cold with me too, and I still carry it to this day. Now, when I see it cold and raining out I cannot help but think *you poor bastards*, and I think about those crummy sandwiches and getting hypothermia.

Because all summer long it was hotter than Satan's house cat, I learned to carry a mini cooler with ice packs in it, frozen bottles of water, and Gatorade, learning in time to love the unofficial favorite flavor of the USPS, Frost Cherry, which was white like snow or skim milk. Just the color of it somehow made you feel cooler. In the winter, when it was bitter cold, I put hand warmers in my pockets. Kathy had handed them out to all the rural carriers as a Christmas present—a very thoughtful one and surprisingly tender from a tough lady.

As a rural carrier I was never required to wear anything—there was no mandatory uniform, other than closed-toe shoes. I wore running shoes in the summer and my Danner boots in the winter because you needed traction, dry feet are a survival skill, and as a carrier you never knew when you might need to run. Despite the fact that I wasn't required to wear a uniform, it was the pandemic, people were home, and I didn't want anybody to think I wasn't a legitimate agent of the federal government, because southwestern Virginia is an armed camp. So I wore my US Mail hat, gray shorts or gray pants, my blue USPS fleece jacket, or my USPS reflective vest. Cash always wore one, and he said it was for the same reason. He wouldn't come out and say it, but he was a Black man in Appalachia, so he needed to carry something that helped him read as "mailman" not "random Black guy on my property unannounced." Because it was reflective, in red, white, and blue, and identified me as a mailman, I am fairly certain that my blue fleece USPS official-issue jacket, which I scrounged out of the extra uniform pile in the storage room, saved my life one dark December night.

Every day, I carried my Streamlight Stylus penlight, because I didn't like reaching into dark mailboxes as a daily act of courage. I carried my Swiss Army knife, the Climber model with the corkscrew, which I never used to uncork anything on the job, but I got a lot of use out of the penknife, screwdrivers, and tiny pair of scissors. I cut tape with the big blade, cut my apples, spread peanut butter with it, and cut the plastic bands that held stacks of mailers together. How the other carriers did their job without a Swiss Army knife is beyond me, but then I've carried a pocketknife since I was eight years old, and like anyone who carries a knife, I am always looking for an excuse to use it.

Because the mail is the battle of order versus disorder, a library that you organize every morning and then deconstruct over space and time, I carried rubber bands, fluorescent index cards, my clipboard with a yellow legal pad, pencils, Sharpies, and plastic grocery bags. I used the fluorescent index cards to note where I had parcels and cased them into my mail. Most days I didn't need them anymore, but I still carried them because there was always the chance of getting thrown onto a new route. On long parcel runs, I would write things down on the yellow legal pad, grouping the deliveries into order. All of that went onto my clipboard, and when I didn't need it I kept it in the laptop compartment of my go-bag. I had scrounged the dayglow cards from a supply case for carriers, the clipboard I found in my garage at home. When it rained, if the customer's mailbox was crummy, I would wrap their mail and parcels in a plastic grocery bag. I kept hundreds of them in the truck, jammed into the seat pockets and in my mail satchel.

Nothing got a customer angrier than wet mail.

Because we would carry in the rain and snow, I always carried my Patagonia rain jacket. It was a tough gray hardshell, not some ultralight backpacker jacket that was thin like Saran Wrap. This was heavy nylon with a Gore-Tex liner, a survivor from a more affluent time in my life. I noticed that the vapor barrier was delaminating from the inside because when I would take the jacket off, I'd be covered with flakes of PTFE dandruff. I couldn't afford a new one, so I covered up those flaking spots with duct tape, and the English major in me couldn't help but feel like this was a metaphor. I was once a premium product, and maybe I still looked like one on the outside, but on the inside everything was provisional, held together with duct tape, just like the USPS: hacked together with Priority Mail tape, rubber bands, and the human capacity for suffering.

Everything in the post office is held together with rubber bands. There are piles of them everywhere because the mail just wouldn't get delivered without them. I carried six or seven on my left wrist, where I could pull them over a bundle of letters in a movement that became as instinctive as reaching for a wallet or tying your shoes. I would fall asleep at night with them still on my wrist, having forgotten they were there. Sometimes I would wake up when Alicia gently pulled them off me, stacking them on the nightstand. A couple of years on at this point, I'm still finding them in the floorboards of the Tacoma, or in my briefcase for work.

I carried Glacier Gloves that Todd gave me for Christmas. He had done research on a website for letter carriers and found that the Alaska River fingerless version was highly recommended. Designed for fishermen, they were a game-changing piece of kit for a mailman. They had a high-grip neoprene liner on the palms and windproof fleece on the back. My fingers were free to sort the mail, use my Arrow Key to open cluster boxes and blue boxes, to use a pen or punch buttons on my scanner, all stuff where you needed fingertip feel. They kept my hands from freezing and let me keep working. Every time I noticed that I could still work in the cold and the wet, I thought about what a thoughtful gift they were, heartfelt and practical like all the Flinchums. The gloves and the love with which they were given should be standard issue for everyone who carries the mail.

To tote all this kit out to my mail truck or to the Toyota I carried a big gray backpack. It had MOLLE nylon loops on the outer surface, perfect for attaching the pouch I used to carry my scanner, water bottle, and Sharpies. I used the thumb-button type that could be operated with a clicker, one-handed, so I could write on the mail as I held it in my left hand. Writing on the mail in that big black ink was one of the great undocumented pleasures of the job. Kat always said, "I hate it when people write on the mail! Stop writing on the mail, Steve!" I still did it. In fact, I made a point of never missing a chance to mark up the mail on Route 11, the route I shared with Kat. Writing IA, UTF, NSN, NMR in stinky Sharpie block letters gave me an extra jolt of pleasure just because it irritated her. Sorry, Kat.

I carried a small spool of baling wire and a pack of zip ties in case I needed to fix a flapping mailbox lid. I carried a Gerber multitool with its handy pliers because you could fix just about anything with one. I carried my Suunto compass, because for land navigation in unfamiliar terrain there is no substitute, especially when there's no cell signal, and as a new letter carrier you almost never know where you are. I carried a *Virginia Atlas & Gazetteer* with its topographic maps and back roads for the whole commonwealth because it worked when Google wouldn't. I carried a first-aid kit because when I started, I had soft information-worker hands and I was always cut and bleeding, and if you think customers don't like wet mail, they *really* don't like mail that you've bled all over. But that blood sacrifice is demanded by the mail gods from all new carriers.

Every carrier I knew carried a headlamp. I carried a Petzel headlamp because when the days started getting shorter and the mail volume got higher, I would still be out delivering the mail in the dark. I needed my hands free to work. Of course, the first time I needed it, the batteries were dead. I cursed myself, cussed myself up one side and down the other. Did I congratulate myself that I had my Streamlight flashlight in my pocket, because had I built redundancy into my load-out? No. Did I remind myself that even my redundancy had redundancy, like the Photon Microlight II that I had attached to the main zipper pull on my go-bag? Somehow that never made me feel better.

I carried so much shit with me. Out of boredom. Out of compulsion. Out of the superstition that it would keep me safe. Out of the conviction that if a situation arose and I wasn't ready for it, it would be my fault, the dark side of an Appalachian upbringing and engineer father, the psychological downside of my youth spent in the Boy Scouts of America, and at times I could hear Lord Baden-Powell laughing at me in the darkness that I had forgotten spare batteries for my headlamp, that when the time had come I had not been prepared. It only happened to me once because after that, I carried spares, carefully ganged together with electrician's tape, which I also carried. In addition to my boo-boo kit of moleskin and Band-Aids, I carried a "blowout kit"—two rapid application tourniquets, pressure dressings, rolls of gauze, and QuikClot. You know, for gunshot wounds, or a motor vehicle accident. Just in case.

I carried everything, and it still wasn't enough.

I involuntarily carried things that were barely physical, only detectable as traces—powders, residues, particulates. There is a smell to the mail, the smell of burnt oil sneaking through the heat exchanger in the FFVs, the smell of ink rubbing off on you. The smell of the paper—newsprint, magazines, the notices and posters that have been hung on almost every available surface telling you to stay alert and stay alive, to look out for suspicious powders, to be aware of the Narcan dispensers available in breakaway boxes hung from the wall in case a bag of illegally mailed fentanyl busts open in the casing room. It's the smell of cigarette smoke that floats in through the loading docks and the wintergreen smell of chewing tobacco. All of that fused into a kind of incense that would get into your clothing, under your nails, into your hair, so you would carry it with you out on the route or when you headed home. Alicia hated the smell of it—everything had to go into the washing machine when I got home, and I had to go into the shower. The inside of my truck carried that smell for a year. But other post offices—in Philadelphia; in New York; in Blue Jay, California; in Waimea, Kauai, Hawaii—they all had that same smell. It is the smell of the mail.

When I was driving my truck (never my official USPS vehicle, because that's a federal crime) I carried my 1911A1 .45 ACP pistol. I carried it in a leather holster in the center console of my truck. I never wore it on my person because that was against regulations. I carried the sidearm in my personal vehicle because while the place where I live and work is incredibly safe, that is just a number in a chart, and I carried in my guts the knowledge that while civilization means you can meet a stranger on the road and not kill him, things aren't always civilized, and it was my preference to be prepared for those temporary outages in the rule of law. Part of the reason I carried the pistol was that other people were carrying them. A lot of other people.

But I also carried it because come September I carried people's ballots and I carried an intuition that those ballots would become fraught, freighted with meaning and controversy. Time would prove me right on this, but I was thinking too small. I thought some lone nut would try to get the ballots from me on an isolated road in Bad Luck Hollow. I was wrong about this. Nobody ever came for the ballots. Why grab a few ballots when you can just grab the whole US Capitol?

I carried with me the feeling that I was probably crazy for lugging that dangerous hunk of metal around. That it could get me fired. Maybe thrown in jail. But I couldn't stop carrying the feeling that there were people out there a lot crazier than me, despite all the assurances of universal love from the good people at the Postal Academy and what I typically felt in my own lived experience. Threatened with violence, I had already made up my mind that the bandits were welcome to my truck, and to whatever mail they wanted. There was always more mail where that came from. The sole exception to this were the ballots for the general election. Those were irreplaceable. The air around the election had become so charged that it seemed like anything was possible. So I made up my mind that if they came for them, I was going to respond with whatever means necessary to deliver those ballots to be counted. Dog spray, fists, a forty-five, or simple expedient of running them over with the truck.

I had a recurring daydream of delivering the mail with Barack Obama. We would talk books and history and economics. But mostly we would talk about the fate of the nation.

"I just don't know how we make it through this, Mr. President."

"It's just you and me and the mail, Steve. Please just call me Barack."

"Barack, you've got to see it too. How is a democracy supposed to work when a huge portion of the electorate is so divorced from reality?"

"We've been in worse spots than this."

"Like what?"

"The Civil War?"

"You've got a point."

I saw us rolling up on a makeshift "Citizen's Checkpoint," announced by the sign they had spray-painted on a four-by-eight-foot sheet of plywood, looking to make a posse comitatus confiscation of the ballots I carried. The barricade was an old church bus parked across a narrow bend of the road.

"Barack, you take the ballots and slip out the back of the truck."

"I don't know this area like you, Steve. Hand me the rifle." We had been issued an old, clapped-out M-16 from the National Guard armory in Christiansburg. I charged the rifle for him, but before I handed it over, I had to ask him something.

"You even know how to use this thing?"

"I was commander in chief for eight years. We killed bin Laden."

"All due respect, you weren't pulling the trigger. I can't let you do this. You've got kids."

"We both do. We swore an oath, Steve." And in my vision I would watch him drive away, accelerating as he went. By the time I had slipped into the creek with the ballots, Johnny Escape-and-Evasion, all I could hear was gunfire, hundreds of rounds, good old boys dumping their magazines into the truck in a mad minute, like the Fourth of July.

Yes, I thought this up and then kept thinking it. Over and over. Elaborating it, thinking through conversations and action sequences. It was fucking insane. I got to carry that stupid scene in my head for months, unable to stop myself from watching it loop in the YouTube of my mind. And now you get to carry it too, along with the knowledge that someone capable of thinking this up was legally authorized by the federal government to carry your mail.

I know I wasn't the only person thinking these things. I carried the understanding that while Obama and I delivering the mail was a fantasy, and the backwoods citizen's checkpoint was imaginary, the cosplay militia members were real. In my daydream, I was a latter-day Paul Revere. But while I was never issued an M-16 from the National Guard armory in Christiansburg, I know those militia members were real, because I saw them storm the US Capitol as they brought their dream to life. Because we were men in small jobs that needed to feel like we were players in some world-historical event. Because while we were willing to bear any burden, meet any hardship, and spend a lot of time shopping online and chatting in forums, the one burden we could not bear was our powerlessness. That's when the cosplay patriots would all board the dream train to Failed State fantasyland. When I would catch myself thinking this crap, these eruptions of self-awareness would burn me up from the inside out. I got to carry my main character fallacy, my own fabulist absurdity around with me the rest of the day, until it would blissfully sink back into a hidden compartment in my consciousness for a time. I could return to deluding myself again, the only real mercy in this waking life. At least I tried to escape my meaninglessness solo, as opposed to acting it out live at the US Capitol Building. At the very least, I did my fantasizing inside the privacy of my own skull.

I carried the US flag on my sleeve. I was never able to forget that I represented the US government for most folks during that dark time. I was the one person from the federal government who came to their home, who showed up with bills and pills and hair gel and ballots, the guy who embodied everything wrong and everything right with a constitutional republic.

That wasn't fantasy, or delusion, or compensation. When I carried the mail I was never just me, but something much larger. That's what I carried all summer and into the fall. When it all felt like a pointless performance, when people yelled at me, when I was accosted by the naked and insane, when I was greeted with indifference, or delight and kindness—it wasn't me. It was the things I carried for them.

Chapter Twenty

A PEACEFUL TRANSFER OF POWER

"NAKED BALLOT! NAKED BALLOT!"

Marge was one of the city carriers. A powerfully built woman, tall with a muscular voice and energy, energy that might not have been entirely natural as one morning she entered the sorting area shouting "LORD I SHOULDN'T HAVE HAD RED BULL FOR BREAKFAST!" She had a calendar of Ronald Reagan on the side of her case, though it was hard to say what year it was from, as the month never changed. It was always of the Gipper on horseback, somewhere in a Republican California that no longer existed. She brought her own radio with her in her FFV so she could listen to Rush Limbaugh at maximum volume. Now she was standing near the outgoing-mail area, waving a piece of paper over her head.

"Naked ballot! This is a naked ballot! Somebody opened this up and tampered with it!"

"Marge, look, the envelope it came in is right there, next to where you picked it up." This was Cash, his voice as soothing as a hostage negotiator.

"Somebody needs to call the cops! This is election interference."

Cash picked up the envelope that the ballot had slipped out of from the concrete floor. Tall as Marge was, Cash had wingspan. He reached over her head, plucked the ballot from her fingers, slipped it into the envelope, and then said, "See, the person didn't lick the glue. It wasn't sealed. Everyone saw that nobody tampered with the ballot, right?" A number of other carriers, all doing their forwards at the end of the day and eager for this piece of political performance art to be over, agreed.

Cash slid the ballot back into its outer envelope. The mail-in ballots in Virginia actually sealed against themselves, and then that sealed ballot went into a security envelope for mailing. The ballot itself had been sealed all along, its vote never exposed to the outside world. All Cash was doing was putting it back in its security envelope. A vote for Trump, Biden, Jill Stein, or Britney Spears: none of us knew because the privacy of the vote had never been compromised. Cash sealed it in with a piece of tape, then dropped the envelope into the special box for ballots.

"You can't do that! That's election interference!" hollered Marge.

"Not if nobody tampered with the ballot, and nobody did."

"This is how they are stealing the election!" Marge stormed off, followed by a number of female carriers. It wasn't as if they agreed with her. They were worried about her having a very public, political meltdown at work. Nobody needed to get fired over a Hatch Act violation.

That ballot and all the rest we collected would be delivered directly to the Office of Elections at the Montgomery County Government Building in Christiansburg. This was called "local delivery" and it meant that, with just days to go in the election, these ballots would be taken the same day they were collected directly to the election officers down the road. The ballots would not need to take the trip down to Greensboro and back. I can't speak for any other office; I can only tell you what I saw with my own eyes: everyone in the Blacksburg MPO was taking the election very seriously. If you put your ballot in your mailbox, in one of our blue boxes, or handed it to your mailman directly, I can tell you that in Montgomery County, Virginia, your vote got counted.

Later, I could hear Marge apologize to Cash. "Cash, I don't agree with a single bit of your politics, but I love you. We all love you." And then they hugged. It took a big person to apologize and another big person to accept that apology. I don't even think Cash voted for Biden. I remember when I was training with him, he said he planned to vote for Tulsi Gabbard.

Why can't our politics operate like this? And why can't people see the reality of a system that operates with airtight integrity, at least at the local level?

The second question isn't easy to answer. The American people overwhelmingly trust the Postal Service, or at least they did before the 2020 election. We know they trust and for the most part love "their" letter carriers. But all of the hard work to keep the mail safe, all the training and vigilance, the Postal Service's own federal law enforcement, all of the invisible effort to keep the mail secure happens offstage. Just like aviation safety, we only think about it if there is a problem. The safety of the mails is critical for business, national security, our legal system, and our elections. That is why calling into question the security of the mail without any real cause is so toxic to our democracy. If there is doubt in the integrity of the system, then the institutional trust that powers that integrity begins to erode. Why is your food safe to eat? Why are planes safe to fly in? Why is your college degree from an accredited state university worth something? Because all of these systems operate in institutional trust. There is nothing realistically stopping your letter carrier from taking your mail-in ballot and throwing it in the trash.

But they don't, because the sanctity and security of the mail is the most important job of every letter carrier, and we all took it as a matter of personal integrity and vital national security. The trust that has been placed in us, the oaths we swore to the Constitution, the USPS's ability to facilitate a fair election, all are well placed. We have earned the trust of the American people over more than two centuries of faithful service to this republic. The trust we have been given by the citizenry we serve strengthens the efforts to maintain that trust. It's the endowment effect—as postal workers we've been given something invaluable, so we work to protect it. There is a great danger in insulting the integrity of a group of hardworking people who are motivated by more than a just a paycheck. It is corrosive to the machinery of democracy.

Sixty-five million votes were cast by mail in the 2020 general election. There were fewer than five hundred cases of voter fraud nationally, mostly consisting of people attempting to vote with a dead relative's mail-in ballot or double dippers attempting to vote with a mail-in ballot and then vote again in person. There was one letter carrier in New Jersey who was caught dumping ballots before they were delivered to voters for use, a pro-Trump carrier who wanted to prevent ballots he saw as likely Biden votes from being counted. One carrier, out of more than 330,000 letter carriers.

Politics were always out in the open at the USPS. At the post office I worked with all sorts of people—militant leftists, MAGA Republicans, general hillbilly government rejectionists, the politically uninformed and uninterested, garden-variety labor Democrats and standard-issue rock-rib Republicans. Yes, the politics were there, but there was no hate. Republican red, Democrat blue—at the end of the day we were all postal blue. The mail always came first. When you work with people, when you get to know them *as people*, it becomes much harder to hate them, at least for 99 percent of folks. And that remaining 1 percent is hateable entirely on their own human merits.

So why can't we vote our consciences and then go back to being citizens and neighbors? I don't have a good answer here. But to suggest that holding an ice cream social would somehow neutralize a culture war that goes back to Reagan, or the 1960s, or the American Civil War, or the fundamental division between Jeffersonian yeoman democracy and Hamiltonian capitalist centrality, is an exercise in absurdity. What I do know is that the way our country is becoming more segmented across class and education isn't helping. How are we all supposed to work together when our labor force has never been more specialized? When blue-collar folks are by definition working in the physical world, while the knowledge workers and professional managerial class are all working remotely over fiber-optic cable? Work has always been at the center of American life. We are an industrious and enterprising nation. We either work together or we will wind up working ourselves further and further apart.

Distance means we don't know these people that we hate. When you have never been to California, it is easy to imagine the Golden State as some pansexual, politically correct dystopia run by feral packs of homeless people and chardonnay-sipping elites. It is just as easy, if you've never been there, to imagine West Virginia as a sort of living-history reservation for poor whites, with some white-water rafting and performative coal mining thrown in, a place where birth control is illegal and carrying a concealed weapon is mandatory. Both of these statements have some kernel of fact, but I can tell you from firsthand knowledge that California is still the cutting edge of what America can be, and that the toughness of the American character flows from a wellspring in the mountains of West Virginia.

What I saw at the post office wasn't regional caricature but in fact people from all over, not just southwestern Virginia, working together. That's why Cash and Marge knew each other not as political figures, but as brother and sister carriers. We don't have to agree with each other. We just have to agree to work and live together.

I wish the rest of the country operated along similar principles. It was just days before the election. A warm October morning, before I set out on my route, and I was pumping gas into my FFV. I liked to leave Cash a full tank at the end of my shift, and our trusty truck was getting low.

There was an Exxon station with a nice convenience store right behind the MPO. We were issued USPS credit cards to gas up wherever we chose. For a bureaucratic organization, there was zero paperwork associated with this. Pick your gas station, get the credit card for your vehicle, gas up your rig, and go. It struck me as a high-trust, gentleman's-rules way of handling it, which was consistent with the autonomy we had as rural carriers.

Usually, I never bothered locking the truck while I was pumping gas. After all, I was standing right next to it. This time, a big fat guy in a worn-out T-shirt was over by the C store and talking to a civilian getting ice, who clearly wanted nothing to do with the guy. There were waves of agitation coming off this dude. I stepped down out of the right-hand side of the cab, locked the door, then walked around to the left-hand side and locked it too. The normie with his bag of ice had managed to flee the scene, which left me with the three-hundred-pound lurker with a buzz cut. The fuel tank on the FFV isn't huge, just thirteen gallons or so, but now it felt like it was taking forever to fill up. Yep, he was now beelining toward me across the parking lot.

"Hey, buddy, do you work for the post office?" asked Buzz Cut. *No, pal, I've actually stolen this official USPS vehicle fully loaded with mail while wearing a USPS hat and shirt.*

Typically, I would say "How can I help you?" but the vibes already had me looking forward to this interaction being over, so all I said was, "Yes, sir, I do."

"I've got to get into my PO box. I'm between apartments and I've got to get into my mail."

"The main post office is right down there, next to the Kroger. I'm sure one of the clerks can help you."

"I got thrown out of my apartment, and now I've got to get my mail."

"Like I said, buddy. One of the clerks can help you get your mail if you're having trouble with your key."

"I haven't paid the bill on it for a few months, and now they won't let me in!"

"Well, that is what happens when you don't pay for the box."

"I'm a taxpaying citizen!"

"The USPS doesn't take a dime of taxpayer money. Just pay your bill and they'll let you right in."

"My concealed-carry permit is in there! I've got to get it, with the election coming up. Biden is going to send the ATF down here, to take our guns. But the sheriff is a constitutionalist. He's going to deputize all the armed citizens. The ATF won't be able to take shit!"

"Will you need a CCW if you're deputized?"

"Man, I need you to get me into my PO box!" He was red from the neck up with rage and the way his face was twisted up would have been funny if he hadn't had two inches on me and fifty pounds. The guy had been creeping closer to me this whole time. I was now blocked in between the pump, the FFV, and the open door to the cab. I was officially no longer in control of this situation. If I was wearing a sidearm, it would have been in my hand.

"Sir! It is a federal crime to interfere with the delivery of the mail or the official business of a letter carrier. You want a visit from the postal inspectors? What I need you to do is step back over there by the store. If you want your permit, try paying the Postal Service what you owe them."

He slunk off toward the ice cooler, his chance to confront tyranny face-to-face now over. Maybe he was imagining standing silhouetted against the sky as the black helicopters from the New World Order arrived, with him and his CCW-permitted pistol as the last best hope of the free world. Or maybe he was going to shuffle off to whatever couch he was sleeping on, to end the evening eating cold Kroger macaroni and cheese out of a Tupperware tub, while he felt the cold steel of his handgun warming in his lap while he tried to find something on Netflix.

Real hate requires either psychological distance or inescapable intimacy. In the worst of all cases, it combines both. Here we are, all of us stuck in the same country, inescapably intimate with the fellow citizens of our shared republic. Here we are, all of us sorted into groups where we hold each other at arm's length, naked with uninformed disgust. I've always found hate alarmingly easy to access, a physical experience that comes from inside us. Hate justifies violence and inspires violent action. Hate immediately divides people into the hater and the hated. Hate does not recognize institutions, except to hate them too. Hate sees only groups and individuals, never systems; history only has value as a pretext for more hate. Hate is hot, while the peaceful transfer of power is so reasonable and boring. Hate never bothers to recognize the waiting envelope, right there, asking to be picked up and put to use, the fundamental vehicle of a system that had worked for 231 years and was once the envy of the world.

Chapter Twenty-One

SANTA CLAUS AND SAM COLT FISTFIGHT IN HEAVEN

IN THE CHRISTMAS CRUNCH, I WAS OUT IN THE BOOgie woods again, the sticks. Even after all the talk of "Christmas volumes" in the summer, even after the Amazon Wars, Christmas was still bonkers. I delivered a couple of loads a day, and with the shorter days, these trips would go on long after the sun went down. I was delivering a popcorn machine to some folks out on Catawba Road, one of the very last parcels of the day. I don't know why but it seemed like the high weirdness always saved itself for those last packages. The address was on the hairy fringe of the Blacksburg MPO. Any farther and I'd be closer to Roanoke than home. I turned off the main road. The secondary road snaked through heavy woods until I came on a farmhouse with just one streetlight on, and one light on in the house. Even with my flashlight, I couldn't see the house numbers, but Google Girl suggested that the address was farther up the road.

It gets dark early in December, of course, but there's town dark, and then there's country dark. High trees, narrow roads, few homes, a moonless night. Past that one utility light it was as black as the insides of a black cat at midnight. The pavement stopped and it was just gravel, then dirt.

There were a couple of trailers, one with a light on, but when I dismounted with my flashlight, I could see they were abandoned, full of trash, just a naked bulb burning inside an empty kitchenette. Something about that empty space gave me the creeps. And when they set in, they didn't stop.

I got back in the truck, kept driving. I was bone-tired. Somehow it was even darker, the way that trees absorb light at night.

The road ended. There was nothing there but an old log smokehouse, a place where people once butchered and smoked meat. In a horror movie, this is where the scary piano music would start in.

I will admit it. I got the whim-whams. The woods don't scare me and the dark doesn't scare me. I'm a six-foot-three man, in my hometown. I grew up in the woods. But tonight, for whatever reason, maybe it was the sight of that smokehouse in my dim incandescent headlights that cued visual memories of *The Blair Witch Project*. However I got there mentally, I was electrified by animal fear.

It had been a long time since I felt fear like that. When my dad was shot in 2007, that was the last time I had felt mortal fear—even though the actual shooting was over by the time I learned about it. Seung-Hui Cho woke on the morning of April 16, armed himself with a Walther .22 LR pistol and a 9mm Glock 19, dozens of magazines, pistols he never should have been able to buy because he had been legally adjudicated as mentally incompetent, and attempted to kill my father. He was loose on the Virginia Tech campus for two hours after he had killed two people in a dorm, free to kill many other people, and wound Dad.

I had been shot myself by that point in my life. I got shot on Guadalupe Street in Austin, Texas, in 1998, while I was at the South by Southwest film festival. A random dude in a Chevy Blazer shot me in the hip with a .22, and five other people. The bullet skipped off my hip, cutting a hole in my jeans, scooping a furrow of meat out of my flank. I had a bruise on my hip the size of a tortilla the next morning, but it didn't faze me. I was young and stupid. I thought I had guardian angels. Two other people wound up in the hospital, one with a spinal injury. In the years since, I've felt guilty over turning the kind of thing that leaves people feeling unsafe the rest of their lives into a story I would tell at a bar.

But when Cho tried to kill my father, it didn't feel like a mass shooting. It did not feel like random violence. It felt very personal, nothing random about it at all. And I have carried that fear and anger with me ever since.

Part of what made the Virginia Tech shooting so scary was that the violence exploded in a space that was so deliberately benign. Norris Hall, where the bulk of the killing happened, was also where Dad's office was. I would walk there after middle school, struggle through my math homework, and stare at the bones of the inner ear. My father had a small display of the hammer, the anvil, and the stirrup mounted on a little wooden pedestal that sat on his desk. I used to wonder about whose head they once rode around in. My father was one of the world's leading experts on the vestibular system, the way the human body orients itself in space, finds gravity, tells up from down. The tiny space described by those three delicate bones were the focus of Dad's life's work. Norris Hall is the place where my father's colleague was killed in front of him and my father was shot in the arm. This was supposed to be as safe as a place can be. Virginia Tech, all universities really, are temples to human rationality and striving, at least when they are at their best. And now I cannot orient myself in space because that sense of place, of safety, is gone.

During the cleanup after the shootings, somebody stole Dad's inner-ear display. It only lives on in my memory. Like that sense of safety that comes from living in a middle-class college town, in a country with a functioning democracy and the rule of law. A bubble of safety, and just as ephemeral as a bubble. One perturbation and in a blink it's gone.

That's what guns turn the world into, a bubble about to burst, a place that's always thirty seconds from violent, permanent transformation. They bestow this power on anyone, regardless of who they are. We weren't supposed to have a weapon with us as postal workers. Never on federal property, never in a government-owned vehicle. Having one in your personal vehicle was a gray area. But even if it was legal and you had a permit, you were not allowed to carry a firearm, even if you could maybe keep one in your car. I never carried one on Route 10, my main route early on—because that's nuts. I was driving an official Government-Owned Vehicle, and the route was basically an office park and apartment complexes. It was high-density suburban, totally vanilla. But out in the sticks? That's bandit country. I think you'd have to be crazy to be out on one of the long routes and not have something other than harsh language at your disposal if things got hairy. It did not seem crazy to me under those circumstances. I felt within my natural rights.

And so, that night two or three weeks before Christmas, I gave in to my fear. I did what four previous generations of Americans have done when they get the whim-whams at close range. I unlocked my center console and reached for John Browning's masterpiece, an M1911 pistol, chambered in .45 ACP. The 1911 is a handgun so good they haven't changed the design in a century. I racked the slide and jacked a big 230-grain Speer Gold Dot JHP round into the chamber, flipped on the safety, and stuffed the pistol down the front of my pants, cocked and locked. And I felt better. That's what guns do. They don't make you safer. They make you feel better. Until they don't.

It was all hindbrain, caveman stuff. The totem of that big American hunk of steel made me feel safe. I wasn't just my squishy flesh-and-blood body anymore. When the tweakers I now imagined were hiding in those trailers, nested like racoons in piles of rags, decided to rush me, I was going to be ready. This is the mental tape that I think plays in the mind of mostly white American men. Before I was a victim waiting to happen. But armed, I was ready.

I slowly drove back down the road.

No tweakers springing from ambush. No cannibals. No militia. No mothmen.

No bugbears of any kind. Just my stupid, primitive fear.

When I pulled up to the farmhouse I had passed before, with its one big orange sodium vapor utility light, I figured this had to be it. There were a couple well-maintained trucks parked in the driveway, and the whole place looked cared for. I stepped out of the truck, took a couple of steps toward the front of the house. In the quiet mountain night, the sky as clear as a bell and cold, I could hear the faint sounds of a television from inside. Tiny black address numbers unreadable from anywhere but the driveway showed me this had been the right place all along.

And I cursed myself. *Grant, you dumb son of a bitch. Stop being a pussy and get your head on straight.* Not only was having a gun on me against regulations, it was stupid. This was a great way to lose my job and maybe spend a few years in prison. I walked back to my truck and pulled my idiotic pistol out of my waistband, careful to keep it out of sight in the passenger-side footwell. I dropped the magazine, shucked the round out of the chamber, and dropped the stray bullet into my hip pocket. It was dark, so I teased the slide back and checked the breech with my finger. Totally clear. I dropped the slide, put the pistol and the magazine back in the center console, and locked it back up.

I have never felt more naked and more stupid in my whole life. Time to deliver this accursed parcel and go home.

I carried the big popcorn popper to the front porch—it was one of those red metal carts like you'd see at a fair or a corporate event, just disassembled for shipping. I left it at the front door, knocked, waited a bit, then turned to get back to the truck. I could hear the TV inside but couldn't make out the program. From the front porch I could see the lights on in the kitchen, but not the occupants.

Waiting for me in the driveway, under the orange glare of the driveway light, were two very solid, very bearded men. One was wearing a pistol and the other carried a pump shotgun at port arms. Their wives were in the background behind them.

If you've ever been trained in the defensive use of a handgun, they teach you to look at the threat's hands. Brother No. 1 had his pistol in a holster on his belt; his hands were loose at his sides. Brother No. 2 had both hands on his shotgun, and his finger was inside the trigger guard. Not good. All I had was the bullet in my left pocket. Two minutes earlier I had been armed. Fucking figures.

"Hey! Who the hell are you?" the one with the shotgun shouted.

I was now presented with a very limited menu of options, for which I thanked God and the wisdom of my two-minute-ago self.

I did the only thing left to me. I threw up my hands and said, "United States Postal Service! I'm a rural letter carrier. I was just delivering a popcorn popper to the folks that live here."

Silence. Then someone blasted me in the face with a flashlight. Thank God I was wearing my USPS reflective vest and the blue uniform fleece I had lifted from the supply room.

"I hope I didn't spoil anybody's Christmas." That was all I could think to say.

"Oh hell! Man, I'm sorry. We didn't know you were the mailman. We were getting calls from every little old lady up and down this valley about the flashing lights that were up at Daddy's house."

I had an LED flashing light on top of my truck's cab, and USPS "Mail Carrier" magnets. But the magnets weren't reflective. You couldn't see them at night.

"I'm really sorry. Didn't mean to get anybody wound up. Just didn't want anybody to have to go into town to pick this thing up. It's big," I said.

We all shook hands and I went on my way. But my heart was like a jackhammer in my chest as I drove off.

Twenty seconds from a one-way gunfight in the middle of a dark driveway. Because I'm too dumb to just orange-slip the customer. The moment I couldn't find the place, I should have just taken the popcorn machine back to the MPO and cited "route interference." What I should not have done was confront my fear by arming myself. I'm not saying it's never right to do this. On the contrary. But what I am saying is that by doing this, by using a gun as prosthetic courage, I fundamentally changed the reality of the situation I was in. Because while guns absolutely function as an emotional prop, it doesn't change the fact that the holes they blow in people are very physically real. And the machines that make these real holes in people are carried by other people, who can be scared or enraged or insane. They are carried by people who have incomplete knowledge of a situation, who can't see in the dark, who can't discern the difference between a teenager with a bag of Skittles or a hardened criminal with a handgun. Right or wrong, natural right or historical accident, when you introduce a gun, you instantly go from a zero percent chance of someone having a hole in their guts, their lungs, their brain pan to a nonzero chance. From nothing to something is about the biggest leap there is.

That is life in rural America now, the continuous nonzero chance of someone shooting you. This does not feel like resistance to tyranny. It feels like turning the world into the Wild West, and everyone seems to forget that in Dodge City, Kansas, guns were banned inside the town limits in 1878, by American hero Wyatt Earp, because too many people were getting killed. It is a miracle every day that more people aren't shot, but plenty are. Around forty-five thousand each year, nearly as many as the entire roster of US combat dead from twenty-plus years of war in Vietnam. Tens of thousands more than the 7,700 soldiers killed in our twenty-year global counterinsurgency after 9/11. But given the option, with all those guns out there, it will always be my preference to be armed in the presence of my countrymen. Not because I want to be armed, but because they are and I do not trust them.

The right to bear arms and the post office are both enshrined in the US Constitution, a document that is difficult to alter, by design. For better or worse, both are resistant to the changing currents of history, built to last, even as many citizens wonder why we have either of them. Except that the US Postal Service only kills a couple of carriers a year, and the Second Amendment kills forty-five thousand Americans. Do we still need them both? The question is immaterial, because by the Founders' design, one hundred years from now there will still be a Postal Service, and there will still be guns in American hands.

Chapter Twenty-Two

FEAST OF THE EPIPHANY

IT WAS CHRISTMAS EVE, A THURSDAY, SO WE WERE DElivering. I was carrying what had to be a Christmas present, a small box addressed by hand and wrapped in what looked like a paper grocery bag to an address down a back road off a backroad off Mount Tabor Road, which for many folks would already qualify as a country lane. It was the Christmas crush, hours after sundown, and this package was my very last for the day. I was overdue back at the MPO, and I knew my phone would be blowing up with calls wondering where I was, but there was no cell signal to receive them.

This was one of those roads I had seen from Mount Tabor when I was a kid and always wondered what was down it. In the dark woods there wasn't much to see, just the quiet light absorbing the black of the trees in the December cold. I could hear water running along the side of the road, hollows emptying into bigger runs as I drove up toward the low ridgeline that ran between the foot of Brush Mountain and the Catawba road.

I had been shooting my flashlight onto the house numbers, feeling my way toward this parcel's home. After a bend in the road, there was a broad yard and a two-story brick house lit as brilliantly as a winter wonderland. Twinkling candy-colored lights along the eaves, around the windows, and glowing peppermint sticks marking out the driveway. Ten-foot-tall inflatable snowmen and yeti illuminated white from within, elves in their curve-toed boots, soaring fake pine trees of green lights. The centerpiece was a full-size Santa in his sleigh with this reindeer, with a prancing Dancer and dancing Prancer, motorized into animatronic motion, right down to the red navigation light on Rudolf's nose. If you'd seen this in town, it would have won the award for best-decorated house in Blacksburg. Instead it was hidden in this dark valley, visible only from this bend in the road and at night from low earth orbit, everything framed by the blackness of the woods.

In all the glare, I couldn't see the house number, but figured this had to be it. I parked, with my flashers drowned out in the electric brightness. It was late to be out, pushing eight at night, bitterly cold. People were not expecting the mailman at that time, especially on Christmas Eve. But I had on my reflective "Don't shoot me" USPS vest and my blue fake-fur USPS Ushanka. I looked about as official as a rural carrier gets.

At the front door, the woman of the house greeted me, already dressed in sweats for a night at home. I could smell dinner from inside, something hot with gravy.

"Merry Christmas, I've got a package for you, ma'am. Looks like a Christmas present to me." I couldn't help myself. "Wow, how long does it take to set all that up?"

"My husband starts setting things up before Thanksgiving, and leaves it up all twelve days of Christmas."

"Oh! Until the Feast of the Epiphany."

"What?"

"When the wise men show up at the manger, with the gifts for baby Jesus. That's when my mom's family used to open their presents."

"Really? Who does that?"

"Louisiana Catholics."

Her reply was a raised eyebrow. She took a look at the box. "This here is for Mrs. Slusher, over there, honey." She pointed across the main road. "You can leave it with me. I'll take it over to her tomorrow. You should get on home. I can't believe they've got you out here on Christmas Eve."

"I should leave it for her," I said. "Came all the way out here. Don't bother yourself."

"Let me call over for you. Don't drive your truck over that bridge of hers. It won't take the weight."

I pulled out of the driveway and drove over to the bridge. I had seen it on the way in, hand-built from railroad ties, stove-bolted together, a solid job. It led to an honest-to-God clapboard cabin, in the classic deep mountain style. When there was so little flat land you tucked your house into the foot of the mountain on one side of the creek, built a bridge, and parked your car on the other. The swollen creek was up. The creosoted planks were icy, and the only light was the pale blue-white from my headlamp. I could see the cold water and rocks ten feet below, the water strobe-dancing the way it does in the subliminal flicker of LED light. The porch on the far side was stacked with firewood, to keep it out of the rain and snow. There was a single window, with a dim incandescent lamp inside.

Mrs. Slusher, a tiny white-haired woman, opened the door.

"Cindy called me. You didn't need to bring that all the way over here to me, son."

"How else were you going to get it, ma'am? Didn't want you to have to drive into town."

She went back inside and returned with one chocolate chip cookie. "Merry Christmas," she said.

"Merry Christmas, ma'am."

Chips Ahoy, as near as I could tell.

Back in the truck and almost done for the night, I headed toward town along the tiny dirt road. Behind me I could see the light of Santaland in the dark, the old woman's home already lost in the effulgence from across the creek.

A single bend around the trees and the lights were reduced to an indiscriminate glow.

Just the silhouettes of treetops, then even the fading lights were lost.

December sound and temperature. The only evidence now of the calendar was the planet's tilt away from the sun's light.

All that was left was the cold, dark woods and the wind moving through.

Then just nothing.

Chapter Twenty-Three

UNDER COLOR OF AUTHORITY

IT IS TRUE WHAT THEY SAY ABOUT DOGS AND POSTmen. I am a dog person. I love dogs, and the feeling has been mutual most of my life. But I have never had a dog hate me the way they did when I was a mailman. These are mortal enemies to the mailman, rural or city. Enemies at the level of the Batman and the Joker. Sherlock Holmes and Professor Moriarty. Magic Johnson and Larry Bird.

It was an aura thing. As a civilian, I could carry a box to a stranger's house and the dog might not even bark. But carry the same box under the aegis of the United States Postal Service and that Yorkie would be possessed by a demon only released from hell in the presence of a mailman.

At the Academy we were given a whole unit of instruction on dogs and dog safety. We were taught by Hank, the Iraq War vet. Hank was a great trainer, because he was funny. And because he was funny, and a great storyteller, you remembered what he taught you. Hank was the letter carrier I wanted to be when I grew up.

Our instruction started with a video. We open on a cute, hot sort of Betty Page indie rock city carrier who is just diddy-bopping along, listening to her hot-pink earbuds in the Southern California sunshine. The music sounded like a Funkadelic knockoff, but from the looks of this woman I knew she was really listening to the Pixies. Looking back, this woman was not tan enough to be a city carrier in LA. Her skin was too Goth pallor, not the deep bronze of a real park and loop carrier, the uniformed sort who walks from house-to-house.

An old woman up the street loses control of her two brindled pit bulls, who crash free from her small front yard and immediately begin charging up the sidewalk in pursuit of Betty Page. But Betty can't hear them coming because of the Pixies. She must sense something, because she pulls out an earbud and the soundtrack becomes tinny, diegetic. This whole industrial was shot by somebody who went to film school.

She starts to run, drops her bag. But dogs are pursuit predators! They get her on the ground, one viciously clamped on to a leg. The other jumps up and grabs her on the arm and in realistic fashion she is mauled to death in a long sequence that feels like Tarantino forcing you to watch a torture scene.

There were groans from the trainees.

Then the room went silent and the lights came up.

Hank was back at the lectern.

"Okay, Listen up. Dogs are serious business. Over five thousand carriers are attacked by dogs a year, and the dogs always manage to kill a carrier every year or two. Usually it's city carriers, but dismounted rural carriers need to look out too, because out in the country those dogs are crazy. A dog will ruin your whole day. They hate letter carriers. It's not a joke."

A guy in a baseball hat raised his hand.

"If a dog attacks us, can we shoot the dog?" These were the only words I ever heard him speak during our two weeks in the Academy.

"We already covered that you cannot bring a gun to the post office. You cannot carry your gun out on your route. You cannot carry a gun on your person. So no, you can't shoot a dog on your route."

"What about bears?" This was from another guy in the room. He had formerly worked at Best Buy.

"Seriously? No. You cannot shoot a bear on your route! Because you cannot have a gun on your route."

"What if you feel like you're in danger?" This was from Jackie. She was wondering about being safe out there in the sticks.

"Guys. One more time. You cannot carry a gun on your route. Like I said, I wouldn't carry anything that wasn't issued to you by the Postal Service."

"If somebody messes with you, all you got to do is grab their ear and pull down real hard. You'll peel their face off like a goddamned banana." This was from Claire, who was about six feet tall and always had on a tie-dyed T-shirt with an animal on it—seals, Saint Bernards, zebras, koalas. In the two weeks we were together, there was never a repeat T-shirt. "That's what my daddy taught me and that shit works," she continued. "I did it to a guy when I was tending bar down in Jacksonville and he needed the plastic surgeon to put that ear back on."

"Okay, for real this time. Pay attention to me." Hank was not joking around now. "On your route, you will meet a dog. He will be *that dog*, the dog that is not your friend. I don't care if you're Saint Francis or Doctor Dolittle. Your number will be up and that dog will be there to punch your ticket."

Jackie leaned over. "Who is Saint Francis?"

"Patron saint of animals."

All that got out of Jackie was a wince.

Hank could hear us talking. "Hey, are we going to talk about the saints or how to stay alive on your route?"

"Sorry, Hank," I said.

"Let's talk about situational awareness. This isn't a nature hike. When you are on the route, no earbuds. You need to be alert. Head on a swivel. You rural carriers, most of the time you're in your cars. But when you dismount to carry a parcel up to a customer's porch or front door, that's when you need to be frosty. Keep your scanner in your right hand; those old Honeywell units are indestructible. You can beat the tar out of a dog with one of those. If you are carrying a satchel, keep it up on your left arm, like Captain America. You guys are all going to be rural, so you probably won't have a bag. But let me show you all my load-out."

Hank put his carrier's satchel up on the table at the front of the room. I could already see he had a can clipped off to the leather strap.

"This is Halt! dog spray. Unlike a lot of gear that's issued here, this stuff really works. Just make sure you've got a fresh can, and give it a test shot before you take it into the field. After you test it, wipe the nozzle down with some rubbing alcohol. Be careful with this stuff, it's essentially pepper spray, so know which way the wind is blowing before you cut loose with it.

"I keep one can right here, where I can grab it, on my bag. If I see a dog and he's giving me bad vibes, I'll go ahead and get it in my hand. Then I've got a double unit that I keep in my left-hand pocket. I've got those jungle taped together, with this paracord dongle so I can fish it out fast if I need it." Jungle tape, paracord—this was all infantryman talk.

"The ones in my pocket are in case my primary goes down, or there is more than one dog. These things will jam on you when you need them most, because Murphy always gets a vote. So have a backup. Two is one and one is none. That's why I've got three cans on me when I roll out. I had this one dog launch at me off the porch, and it must have been eighty feet back to my ride. That's always the safest bet, just get back in your rig. If you run them over on the way out, that's their problem. So I hear the door bang open behind me, see the dog, and start moving faster to my rig. But it was too far, way too far. So I figure I've got to stand my ground. I get my satchel into shield mode and get my spray deployed. The dog is closing in on me, so I line up on his face and trigger the can and . . . nothing! The spray went out on me, crud in the nozzle. By the time I was reaching for my backup in my pocket he was on top of me. So I gave him the old two-piece and a biscuit."

I raised my hand.

"That's a fake with your left, a real swing with your right, and a kick. The kick connected, I punted that dog between the uprights and bought myself enough time to deploy my backup. Then I let him have it. Guys, if it has come to spraying a dog, empty the can. Spray it till the can goes dry. Get them in the T zone: eyes and nose, eyes and nose. If you don't remember anything else I tell you, remember to spray them in the T zone till the can runs dry. And remember, if there was one dog, there might be two. They are pack animals AND THEY WANT TO KILL YOU! So don't celebrate until you're off the X."

Claire was shaking her head. But I believed it.

When I was in kindergarten, I had a half a mile or so walk back from the bus stop. It was the 1970s and we used to let our kids do stuff like this. About a third of the way up the street there was a house whose dogs were always out loose. These two big dogs would charge me, knock me down, and I would start to cry. I am pretty sure they were just trying to play with me, but it was no fun.

Mom had grown up in Baton Rouge, Louisiana. She'd never had a dog. So she gave me dog treats in a plastic sandwich bag. "Give these to the dogs and they won't attack you." A nice idea, but one that flew in the face of canine nature. Now I was not just a bite-size toy, but one that came with hors d'oeuvres. I would throw the treats as far behind me as possible, while I ran in the opposite direction. This just made it into more of a game, for the dogs at least. On a day after it had rained, the dogs knocked me into a ditch. I was covered in mud, and doing my best not to cry when I got home. Dad had gotten home from work early.

"Your mother doesn't know a thing about dogs," he said when I explained what had happened. "Come on, we're going to fix this." We went in the basement and filled a plastic spray bottle with ammonia. "Go get some of those dog treats." I grabbed a handful and then Dad loaded me in his car, where he let me ride in the front seat. We drove down to where the dogs were.

"Call them over," Dad said.

I was in the passenger seat, on the dogs' side of the street. So I called out, waving a treat in my hands. And the dogs came charging. I remember being really scared, despite being inside the massive Chevy station wagon. As the dogs jumped up to get at me in the window, Dad pushed me back into the bench seat and sprayed them right in face with the ammonia. They howled and then ran off.

When I told Dad this story, years later on a fishing trip, he didn't remember.

"We did that?"

"Yeah, Dad."

"Well, when in doubt, try brute force."

So maybe that's what I had been thinking on when I kept asking about getting some Halt! dog repellent, USPS issue. They never gave the rural carriers shit, but one day when I was back in the office, the new city supervisor called out to me. I had been asking after it for months, along with Narcan training.

"Hey, Red! I got your dog spray." At different points in my life I've been called Red, Big Red, or You Redheaded Son of a Bitch. But that's always stuck with me, that she called me Red, because I think it's the only time she spoke to me.

I grabbed two cans and carried them with me for the rest of my tour: one in my left pocket next to my penlight, and one clipped off inside my jacket. Gear queer that I am, they were just another piece of kit that I felt I "needed" to deliver the mail. Until I actually needed it.

It was spring of 2021. I was on six-day-a-week parcel duty, down toward the river, delivering packages out in the roads off Prices Fork. This one house was someone's retirement dream—a big brick McMansion with a huge expanse of lawn, at the end of a long gravel driveway. I was generally zoned-out. I had been on the job long enough at this point that I could go into a sort of autopilot. I had been listening to an economics podcast, so I wasn't thinking about where I was. I was thinking about supply shocks. My head was not on a swivel. Had I maintained the correct level of situational awareness, I would have noticed the dog door in the garage door. The large dog door. I would have noticed the dogshit in the yard on my long walk to the front door.

I rang the doorbell. Old-school, just an illuminated white plastic button. No answer. I scanned the parcels, left them by the door, and turned to head back to the truck. This was when I saw the dogs. Brutes, long-legged like a coon dog, but with the blocky, bone-crushing alligator head of a pit bull. Two of them, a big guy and a smaller one. They had hidden around back, behind the house, waited for me to get all the way to the front porch. They came at me in a pincer movement, cutting off my access to my truck. It was very clear to me this was a number they had run before. These big boys knew what they were doing.

I kept eye contact with them as I got my heavy blue Honeywell scanner into my left hand and a can of Halt! in my right. I thought that if I just walked right at them, no fear, they would get the picture. But nothing doing. I was the most entertainment these dogs had gotten in a good long while.

When they came at me, it was fast. It's always the small dogs that start shit. The smaller of the two was snarling and snapping, then in a flash he was coming at me, trying to get inside the guard of my scanner.

They say that under stress, you revert to your training, and I am here to tell you that's a fact. In that moment I heard Hank: "Get them in the head with that scanner! Keep them off you!" So I swung at him but didn't connect. And that's what the big guy was waiting for. He came in low, striking for my ankle. This is how dogs take down game in the wild: grab a leg, get the prey on the ground, let the other dogs in the pack go to work. And in my mind, Hank said, "T zone! Spray them in the T zone! Eyes and nose!" I didn't even think about it, just mashed down on the trigger and let the big one have it. The sticky red spray smelled like Tabasco—just the backscatter alone was eye-watering—but I caught him right in the eyes. Time slowed down, the way it does when there's real danger. I had a moment to think. Then I walked the red snake of spray down to his nose and sent a long burst right up his snout.

I would like to take a moment to thank the manufacturers of Halt!, because that stuff works exactly as advertised. The big guy dropped to the ground like a log and I spun on the little guy and cut loose. Hank had said in training, "Spray it till the can is empty!" and that is just what I did. The can ran dry. I only connected with smaller dog's left eye, but with his still-functioning right eye he could see the big dog making for the garage, slunk low with his tail between his legs. The little guy looked at me as I switched the scanner to my good hand and unlimbered my backup can of Halt! with my left.

Suddenly I heard myself yelling "Go on! Get!" and it sounded like my father in full redneck mode inhabiting my body. The little one dropped tail and disappeared into the woods.

I stood there feeling exhilarated. Then slightly stupid. Then scared, as it occurred to me that if the owners were home, I was about sixty seconds from catching a chest full of buckshot.

Do you know what happens in the Postal Service when you have to pepper-spray a customer's dog? Nothing. You're a federal agent! Interfering with the delivery of the mail is a federal crime! If you want, as the carrier, you can file an Animal Interference card and stop their mail. You can shut down the mail to the whole neighborhood until the dogs are properly secured. It happens all the time.

But I didn't tell anybody when I got back to the office, because I wasn't sure what the fallout would be. I just got a replacement can of Halt! When I told my supervisor about it a few days later, he asked me if I wanted to stop their mail. "We'll stop their damn mail!" I told them there wasn't any need for that, but I did file an orange Dangerous Dog card and slipped it in the case. The next time Kathy, the carrier whose regular route I had delivered on, saw me, she told me that she knew all about those dogs and I didn't need to file the card.

When I told her I had pepper-sprayed them, all she said was "Good."

I didn't have much power as a mailman. Once, I was delivering mail to a massive trailer park down by the hospital. I had no idea it was there until I carried the mail to it. It was hidden behind a thick wall of woods on a bluff, but there must have been a couple hundred trailer homes in there. They had a bank of cluster-box units under a wooden pavilion. I had seen maybe two letters from state and federal prisons in my year of carrying the mail, but at this trailer park there were dozens in just one day.

I started opening up the box units with my Arrow key, and like a dinner bell, the folks in that trailer park started wandering over. First one, then another, but then they started to form a ragged sort of crowd, milling around *Walking Dead*–style. Some of them started asking me for their mail, and the bolder ones began trying to walk around back to just grab it out of the open units.

"Back up!" I said. There were shocked expressions from the crowd.

"I'm just tying to get my mail," said the first guy, clearly unhappy.

"You can get it when I'm done."

While I was talking to him, another guy was trying to get to his mail behind me. It was turning into a free-for-all, and I was losing control of the mail, the one thing we were never to allow to happen.

"You too! Back up!" I walked back down all the units, locking them shut. I was pissed. I felt like the substitute teacher, being taken advantage of.

"I want you all to listen up! It is a federal crime to interfere with the delivery of the mail, or with a letter carrier. Stand in the gravel and wait till I'm done, or I'll just take the mail back to the post office. All of it."

And then I stood there. Waiting. The crowd wandered off.

Just like when I pepper-sprayed the dogs, under my anger was exhilaration. Pepper spray, threats of federal crime, and withholding the mail from a bunch of people waiting on letters from incarcerated loved ones—these were the thunderbolts I wielded as the pitiful Jupiter of the Postal Service. And after months without control of my schedule, of at times being looked down on—ignored, I'll admit it, it felt good. Dangerously good.

Was I the lawbringer? An authorized agent acting under the color of authority, protecting the security of the mail?

Was I an innocent civil servant, forced to act in self-defense when an irresponsible homeowner left his dogs loose to attack me?

Maybe I was the government, out in the field, operating without any real restraint. With feeble powers, high ideals, the self-importance of postal necessity. No accountability, a living example of the corrupting influence of power.

Or maybe I was just scared.

Chapter Twenty-Four

BOOK OF THE MONTH

IT IS PART OF THE ORIGINAL MISSION OF THE USPS TO encourage the shipment of books, magazines, trade journals, and professional publications. Philadelphia's Ben Franklin became postmaster for the British Crown in 1748, seeking out the role after a rival printer who was the previous postmaster refused to carry *Franklin's Gazette*. Along with William Hunter, a Virginian, they overhauled the system and established post offices and the Dead Letter Office. Delivery time for letters and newspapers from Philadelphia to Boston dropped from three weeks to two days. US Route 1, still in service on the eastern seaboard, was established by Franklin as the backbone of the postal road system. When the Department of the Post Office was removed from the president's cabinet by Nixon, it became quasi-independent, but its mission was the same. As the Postal Reorganization Act of 1970 reads, the USPS has "the obligation to provide postal services to bind the Nation together through the personal, educational, literary, and business correspondence of the people." I was born in 1970, and while that may have been the dawn of the information age, we lived in a decidedly analog world. The USPS was and still is our national physical internet, the way we move information encoded on paper, atoms instead of bits.

One morning I was sorting out my parcels onto the float when I came upon a group of identically sized packages, each labeled Book of the Month Club. If someone had pulled up outside in a horse-drawn carriage I couldn't have been any more surprised. "I can't believe this is still a thing," I said, holding up the blue box.

"What?" asked Diana, whose case was right across from my parcel cage.

"The Book of the Month Club. Is there room in the market for this? I can't believe a single-negative-option business model is still in operation."

"Lord, you are always thinking," said Diana, shaking her head. "Do you ever shut it off, all that thinking?"

"I don't even see how somebody can read through a whole book. I get through one page and I'm asleep." This was from Erica, who lived in a trailer out in Giles County, with five pit bulls that she had rescued from the trailer next to her when the owner took off and abandoned them.

"I'll tell you who gets a shit ton of books! It's Steve," said Dean, the sub for Terri on Route 8, where I lived. "But I don't care, man, because you've got the best goddamned mailbox in the neighborhood. It's just beautiful." A couple of months into carrying the mail, I had replaced our plastic piece-of-shit mailbox out of shame. Our house had come with a garbage Rubbermaid box with its brown speckled polyvinyl and ugly-ass fake Ionic column base. Its tiny capacity, propensity to attract hornets and spiders, and lack of address numbers had become intolerable. I replaced it with the rural letter carrier's favorite, the Gibraltar Elite Large galvanized steel mailbox, set on a cedar post that I sank two and a half feet into the ground and set in concrete. Perfect height for delivery, zero wobble. Big reflective numbers and a card listing the last names of the occupants made it rookie carrier-friendly. This was the mailbox that carriers dream about.

"How many books does he get?" asked George, who carried my parents' mail.

"Oh, Steve gets a couple a week," said Dean.

"Heck, Steve. And I thought your daddy got a lot of books."

"Dad reads a lot, but he's not as fast as me."

Erica looked at me and shook her head.

For me, during my time as a letter carrier, other than ballots, books were the most important thing I delivered.

I remember one day I delivered a book with a French return address. The postmark was from La Poste, the French postal service. Their first-class mail is delivered anywhere in France in one day and second-class in two. During Napoleon's reign, he instituted twice-a-day delivery in Paris, with the thought that a higher speed of correspondence was needed to support the country's global ambitions. Napoleon, an artillerist and engineer, was the original technocrat, obsessed with the flow of information. This was the man who wrote the metric system into the Napoleonic Code, after all.

The address was down on Route 3, past the head of Lick Run and up the southern slope of Gap Mountain. I had never been up to any of the homes on that road, since all of the mailboxes were down on Norris Run, a pretty common architecture for rural mail route design—build a long rail for multiple mailboxes up a spur road, down along the main service road in the valley. I was running parcels in the Tacoma, so getting up the mountain wasn't going to be an issue, and they had given me the book because it needed to be hand-delivered. It was signature required.

The whole way there, I practiced my French. "Bonjour! C'est le courrier Américain. J'ai une livraison de livre." The climb up the mountain was paved, then gravel, then a narrow dirt track. None of that prepared me for the house at the end of the road—a two-story Victorian, covered in architectural gingerbread, brightly painted in purple, yellow, white. Mardi Gras colors. A perfectly maintained white picket fence surrounded the manicured yard, with planters of flowers. Classical music was floating out of the windows. There was nothing around it but trees. It was like that scene from the Director's Cut of *Apocalypse Now*, where a picture-book French country estate looms out of the fog along the upper reaches of the river. Perfect and utterly out of place.

As I walked toward the door, a woman came out to greet me, all four foot eleven of her. Her hair was in a bob, a scarf around her neck. I had arrived at a French elf's home on the mountain.

"Uh, bonjour! C'est le courrier Américain. J'ai une livraison de livre." I sounded significantly less confident than I had in the privacy of the truck.

What followed was a joyful explosion of French, a fountain of Gallic vowels and growled consonants. I caught snippets about a pleasant surprise, and maybe something about receiving visitors. But the fact is that I didn't really speak French, only sort of read it, and this *confection parfait* of what sounded like high-diction, exuberant French was very far beyond my command of the language, which extended to "D'accord!" *I agree.* And "Le chat est noir." *The cat is black.*

"I'm sorry, ma'am. I don't really speak French. I'm just excited that this book was from Paris and I thought I'd try."

"You said it with such verve! I was so delighted to receive this book from a close friend of mine, and from a French-speaking mailman, no less. I thought, *Does the US Post Office have francophone mailmen now?*"

"Sorry to disappoint."

"Not at all. It was a delight."

"I'm still going to need your signature, s'il vous plaît, madame."

"D'accord! Bien sûr."

People during the pandemic were selling books and sharing books, and so I picked up more than my share of them for delivery. One morning, the super grabbed me on my way out the door and said, "Don't forget, there's a pickup on Winchester Road. Kat was supposed to get it yesterday but she missed it."

Winchester Road was on Route 11, the half route that Kat held down while supporting other routes. I was still her sub on it, in part because

I had figured out how to deliver it in my pickup truck without the girls' help. One of the tricks to delivering solo in the Tacoma was driving Winchester Road backward. It was a dead-end road, so I would pull my DPS out, reverse-sort it, and then drive up the left-hand side and deliver it out the window. There was a neighborhood that was laid out in a loop and another dead-end road that made up the whole back third of the route, so I could also deliver that stretch with the same trick. At the end of Winchester there was a small family-run body shop that was also a farm. Once, early on, I saw a man driving a Caterpillar excavator with a skinned hog hanging from a chain. There he was, trundling across the property with eight hundred pounds of pork hanging from the end of his backhoe. I'd known that just beyond the university bubble, Blacksburg was about as rural as it gets. But the space between that concept and the reality of a hog hanging from heavy equipment is a big one.

I was driving back up Winchester when I got to the brick bungalow where I was supposed to do the pickup. An older white-haired man in hickory-stripe bib overalls was already in the driveway as I pulled up.

"I saw you go past, so I didn't want to miss you."

"Yeah, I was told you had a pickup for me. Some books?"

"Yeah. The lady that came through said she couldn't take it but that you could."

"Okay. Happy to pick it up."

"I'm going to need you to load this. My old back can't take it."

"Happy to load it for you. Just show me where it is."

The man turned around, grabbed the garage door handle, and rolled the door up. Covering the entire floor of the garage were bankers' boxes, two deep in places.

"Which of these do you need picked up?"

"All of them. It's a law library. I got the whole thing for just a song down at an estate sale in Hillsville. I had them load my flatbed, and I paid the boys down the street to unload it." As I stared at box after box of books, I wondered if I could pay those boys again to help me load my truck.

"My daughter is a lawyer, can you believe it? Here I am, worked my whole life as a welder, and there's my Jenny and she's a lawyer. She was always smart, but I just wouldn't have believed it if I hadn't seen her graduate with my own eyes. Well, I saw this library and I called her on my phone and she said she wanted them for her new office."

He was shipping every one of these books, hundreds of them, by Media Mail. But that's what Media Mail is for, to bind together the nation through professional and legal correspondence.

Each box had a printed label and bar code. "I weighed each of these on my shop scale. I can show you the scale if you need to see it. I paid everything like I was supposed to."

I scanned the first box with the Honeywell. The code was good.

"No need, sir. Scanner says they're good."

The man stood there, talking about all the studying his daughter had to do to become a lawyer, and how he couldn't believe any job needed all these books, but that she said she needed them. That was how the law worked. The man talked the whole time I loaded the couple dozen bankers' boxes into my truck, gave me the entire narrative of a father raising an upwardly mobile daughter. His daughter was going to help working people who got injured on the job.

The law library filled the entire bed of the truck and by the time I was done, the back end of the Tacoma was sagging onto its springs, the nose halfway pointed to the sky. I was looking up into the forest canopy on my drive back to the post office.

I made sure Kat knew that I had picked up those boxes, next time I saw her. Every last one of them.

"Yeah, I figured you'd like that. You like books!"

"I like reading them. Not moving them by the truckload."

"Steve, that one had you written all over it."

Maybe libraries of paper books are obsolete, but I have a hard time believing books are obsolete any more than knives are. Unlike a knife, which wears with use, a book grows more valuable with each reading. Each reading spreads the ideas it contains further, to new minds where, if read with care, they will unlock new thoughts. But a book is also fragile. Leave it in the rain, let the dog chew on it, and the information in it becomes lost. That's always why I treated book deliveries with such care. The obsolete book, printed on paper, is both immortal and perishable at the same time.

Maybe the post office is an obsolete idea too, like the Book of the Month Club. A great number of people don't read, not to study or for pleasure. Anything beyond functional literacy is unnecessary, the definition of a luxury. But the book, as an organized form of human thought and knowledge, is one of the most powerful design patterns we have ever created. It allows one person to share their thinking and their spirit with potentially millions of people. It was just the tool for a nation of self-improving farmers and craftsmen to bootstrap themselves into shade-tree mechanics, scientific agriculturalists, engineers, and yes, artists. With the help of the US Post Office, the homestead was no longer some isolated island of humanity. Instead, by a coal oil lamp and later electricity, it became a node in a network, connected to a larger universe of ideas. Public institutions that provide universal service, like the Federal Aviation Administration or the Food and Drug Administration, are never perfect. They can be inefficient, fragile, and difficult to update. But they also provide the kind of access and infrastructure that creates safety, the rule of law, freedom of travel, freedom of enterprise, and the freedom to speak and think as individuals in a civil society.

These networks are also fragile. If there is a breakdown of trust in an institution, the people can't see its value. They start wondering what their taxes are paying for. If you wanted to destroy the USPS, this is how you do it: Slow down its service, mistreat its workers, refuse to capitalize it appropriately, and the post office, an institution as old as America, an institution that built America, becomes sclerotic and antiquated. A TV show punch line for inefficiency. This is always the plan with the institution-hating anarchist wing of the right: Cut the budget of an institution until it is struggling to operate. Block the legislation that would allow it to modernize. And then, once it's small enough, weak enough, wounded enough, that's when you can "drown it in a bathtub," to quote the reliably crazy Grover Norquist. But once you break a beautiful analog thing, you may not be able to fix it again.

This country is full of people who would love to get rid of books and get rid of the Postal Service. Illiberalism—and I'm not just talking about from one side of the political spectrum—operates from the notion that ideas are dangerous. No shit. So are antibiotics, electricity, jet engines, chain saws, and the internet. Government is not here to shut down ideas. The government is here to do the things that the market can't do, like promote freedom of speech and of thought. Freedom of navigation, of space and of ideas, is written right into the Constitution, along with the US Post Office, right there in Article I, Section 8, Clause 7: "The Congress shall have Power . . . To establish Post Offices and post Roads." It is the same section that grants the government the right to establish a currency, borrow money, declare war, punish pirates, promote science and art, and protect intellectual property. Book bans and attacks on the Postal Service are nothing less than direct attacks on the founding documents of our constitutional republic, no different than the storming of the Capitol by an illiberal mob of cosplay fascist "patriots." It's just that attacking the post office doesn't look as exciting on TV.

I remember a research course I had to take as an undergrad. The librarian kept talking about linear feet of books, which seemed like such a strange way to talk about blocks of language. I saw ideas, the minds behind those words. But I guess if you work with them every day, the books become something else. Something more like cordwood, another unit of linear feet and volumes.

That's the way I looked at people as a marketer. A commodity sorted into different grades of value. Hardwood for furniture, white pine for dimensional lumber. The rest as cordwood. To be hewn, carted to market, seasoned into flammability and then consumed for its utility. But human beings are something much larger than economic units of preference and demand. I feel like garbage even admitting it, but I had lost that sense of humanity in my twenty-five years of pushing people's buttons to sell them stuff. Stuff that maybe they needed and maybe they didn't.

Commerce is vital, but it is only one of the freedoms this country promises. Commerce is the easy part.

The Postal Service has never seen the American people as consumers, but as citizens. They saw a people who had been schooled to nearly universal literacy, and who, when given the chance, would be able to teach themselves how to grow better food, fix machines, mend broken bones, and with their new wealth perhaps begin to cultivate the life of the mind. To become an informed citizenry, the sort of people who would expand democracy and maybe even share it with the world. The US Post Office saw the American people as good waiting to happen, saw that there was a better version of America inside itself. All the nation needed was a few books.

The Jesuits believe that it's the Lord's work to clothe the naked, feed the hungry, and, perhaps most importantly, break the bondage of ignorance through education. They believe that every word you write is a blow that strikes the devil.

Every book I delivered did the same.

Chapter Twenty-Five

RESCUE PARTY

IN A LATE SNOW, I WAS OUT RUNNING PARCELS IN THE Tacoma when Chuck, the new rural super, called to tell me that Kat had slid off the road out toward Christiansburg. The USPS tow truck was out in Roanoke and couldn't come to get her for over ninety minutes.

"You've got your truck, can you go help her?"

Look, from a union perspective, I should have told him to piss up a rope. I wasn't a USPS mechanic. But it was Kat. I couldn't stand the thought of her stuck out there in the snow. Plus, I had a tow strap and had waited years for a chance to use it.

When I got there, there was a group of men with their full-sized diesel pickup trucks up at the top of the hill. Smoking. Just standing around looking at Kat, stuck in a ditch. A lack of chivalry and common decency that must have had my granny spinning in her grave.

"I don't guess any of you all were going to help her?" I asked. I was pissed.

"Ain't that your job?"

In an office setting, I'll be honest, I had learned to be cold-blooded. When it comes to the bottomless pit of white-collar work, a hard heart is an asset. But there's struggling with a PowerPoint presentation, and there's being stuck out in the snow on some distant back road. Here at the post office, it was us against the mail. Always overmatched and underresourced. If we carriers didn't look out for each other, nobody would.

I hooked up to the front bumper tow point on the FFV. Kat pressed in on the throttle while I pulled in four-wheel high and she was back on the road. I was finally the one rescuing Kat for a change.

Another rescue. I had finished carrying Route 11 on a bluejay-perfect spring day when Chuck asked me to go find "the Kid" out on Route 4. The Kid was fresh out of the Academy, and according to Chuck his scanner hadn't moved in about half an hour and he wasn't answering his phone. I felt a momentary swell of pride. I was enough of a carrier now that I was part of the rescue party. I took a quick look at the map on Chuck's computer and hit the road.

I found the FFV out on Luster's Gate Road and pulled off onto the shoulder. It wasn't even a third of the way along the route. I parked behind the Kid with my flashers going and felt like a state trooper as I approached the right-hand side of the vehicle. The Kid was sitting there, just staring ahead, engine off. He looked so young.

"Hey, buddy, how's it going?" Nothing. Nonresponsive. "Hey, man? You okay?"

"Yeah. I'm okay."

"What's going on?"

"Just . . . Just . . . yeah." He was shell-shocked. In some kind of dissociative state.

"When's the last time you had any water?"

"I don't know."

"If I went and got you a Gatorade, would you drink it?"

"Sure." I got the impression if I had asked him to accept Jesus Christ as his personal Lord and savior, he would have said "sure" to that too.

I walked back to my truck and got the Kid a Gatorade. Erica and Dean pulled up.

"What's up with him?" asked Erica.

"Not sure. He seems overwhelmed?"

"That kid was in the Academy with me. I don't know why he's just starting to deliver the mail now," said Erica. "He said his favorite thing to do was videogames."

"This might not be the job for him."

"You think?"

"What are we going to do?" asked Dean. Somehow I was now in charge of this clusterfuck.

"I'll take all the parcels. You guys split up the DPS, flats, and spurs three ways, and we get this done."

"Let me smoke a cigarette first," said Erica.

We got it done. But it was the kid's last day on the job. We never saw him again.

When I was casing mail the next morning, I mentioned how hard it was starting out as a carrier and Kathy said, "Honey, I think I cried every day for three months." It was hard for me to imagine her crying over anything. But the truth was, even once you graduated to the rescue party, you still had days you cried. It was the sticking around that mattered.

I was delivering a full route in a high-rent neighborhood of lawyers, car dealership owners, football coaches, and university administrators—what passes for money and power in a big university town. I was just finishing a row of mailboxes when I heard a woman's voice, as piercing as an angry mockingbird.

"Excuse me! Excuse me!" The voice was coming from a small, lean woman in yoga clothing, her feet inside yellow Crocs big enough to be clown shoes. She was huffing toward me in an almost comic-opera level of agitation, elbows swinging, arms pumping. Right behind her was her husband, another lanky yoga body with a sullen bearded face.

"Yes, ma'am. Can I help you?"

"Do you have my package? Where's my package?" She had the gaunt look of a militant vegan who was professionally miserable.

"I don't have packages for this address today, ma'am."

"Ma'am. Ma'am. Don't *ma'am* me—my package was supposed to be here five days ago! That's what the computer says. It still hasn't been delivered."

"I can't do anything without a tracking number. But if you give me the tracking number, I can look it up for you."

"*I* can look it up. I *have* a computer. What I want to know is where is it?"

"If you give me the tracking number, I'll do my best to find it for you. It's probably just hung up at the processing center."

"You're useless! Oh, it couldn't be *your* fault. It's the *processing* center. Nobody ever takes responsibility!"

"Ma'am. I'm just the substitute. I'm doing the best I can. I really am."

"This is intolerable! I won't be treated this way! Don't patronize me! 'I'm just the substitute.'" That last part was said in a mocking singsong tone. She stormed off, up her driveway, her husband following her back toward their big glass house. About fifty yards away she turned to shout, "TAKE RESPONSIBILITY!"

The tone, that was the thing. The high-hat classist talking-down-to, as though I was stupid. Not a human, but a mailman. Something for a dog to bite, a punch line. And so she spat out words that tore into me, pulling me down to the ground. Words to make me hurt. To make me small.

What I would have liked to do is take my pepper spray and give it to her right in the eyes. I've thought many times over the years since about how good it would have felt to send a long jet of caustic chemicals into the mucosa of her nose and listen to her howl.

But instead, like my mother's rages, I just took it. Which is what happens to a dog when you beat it long enough.

Once, as a boy, my father and I were in the basement, getting ready for a backpacking trip. I had just joined the Scouts, and I was a still a little guy, twelve years old, maybe just five foot or so. I was supposed to be working my way down the checklist out of the Boy Scout Handbook, methodically. But I was dreamy, the way ADHD people are, already thinking about the old log cabin that was near our first night's campsite. I was a “space cadet”; that was the old man’s favorite insult. “Out to lunch!” “Just not taking things seriously.” My father never suffered fools. It wasn’t a question of tolerance. It was hatred, maybe fueled by self-hatred. In truth, he was just as dreamy and ADHD as me.

“What are you going to do, huh?” he asked. “When you get out there in the woods and you’ve got no lighter? Sit there in the dark and shiver?”

“I’ll have my patrol with me. If I forgot my lighter, someone else will have one.” Dad’s reaction was immediate. He had to bend at the waist to get all six foot three of himself down to my level, down in my face.

“One of these days, you’re going to be out there, alone. Nobody’s going to help you. What are you going to do then? All you’ll have is what’s in your pack, what’s between your ears, and what you can do with your own two hands. Nobody is coming to help you. So get ready.”

My dad was never a great dispenser of advice about what to feel when faced with moral conundrums, how to deal with dark midnights of the soul. His interior life was a mystery he took to his grave. His advice was always for navigating the physical world: recharging the air-conditioning in your car or fault-isolating the load that was tripping a breaker. He was a man who believed in triple redundancy, in overengineering a margin of safety so large that there were margins for his margins.

Dad was almost superhumanly right about many things, but when he was wrong, he was very wrong. His prediction that one day I would find myself alone, that no help was coming . . . it was wrong.

He was even wrong about his own fate. Whatever had happened to him as a child, what happened at the end of his life was one long effort by the people who loved him to save his life. I drove him to the ER many times, stayed with him when he was in pain. My brother John drove him three hours up to the University of Virginia in Charlottesville to see a specialist. My other brother Dave came down to help around the house and take him to the oncologist. Once, while he was as openly scared as I’ve ever seen him, I carried my father out to my truck like a child. I drove him to the ER in Pulaski, held his hand when I could see the fear that gripped him, but I never drew attention to it. Never made him feel small, or stupid, or that it was his fault. Even if it was, even if he was too goddamned stubborn to get the help that likely could have given him a few more years of life. To whatever degree he was alone, it was self-exile. And even then his sons never gave up on the hope of rescue. Because despite all his talk, he had always come to rescue us.

In my mind, the madwoman's words became septic. After months of a resilience that surprised even myself, I was slipping. One morning, as I cased the mail for what felt like the umpteen thousandth time, every letter felt like it weighed ten pounds, and I could feel a lead snake wrapped around my heart. I knew this feeling, and I hadn't felt it for a long time. This was the big D, a deep adult depressive episode. After bubbling below the surface for a few weeks, now it was here.

Alicia texted me, just a love check, to see how I was doing. What I sent back was a power surge of negative emotion.

I CAN'T DO THIS ANYMORE.

You're just having a tough morning, love.

I CANNOT WORK IN THIS GODFORSAKEN PLACE ANOTHER FUCKING MINUTE.

Sweetheart, see if you can get through the day. When you get home, things will be better.

THIS ISN'T GOING TO GET BETTER. THIS IS FUCK CITY. HOW HAS THIS BECOME MY LIFE?

This was the full Grant playbook. When you're miserable and hurting, share your misery with the people you love, so they can be just as miserable as you are. Negative deviance, haul everyone down into the shit.

That bleak power burned through me all day. Somehow, the woman on Route 4's poison soul had jumped like a current discharge and gone to ground right through my body. When I got home that night, I was still Mr. Bad Times. Alicia and the girls tiptoed around me. They had a snack waiting, but I just stomped upstairs. I could see what an asshole I was being, but I felt powerless to stop myself. I lay on the bed and stared at the ceiling, cataloging my manifold failures as a father, husband, and man.

I was a fifty-year-old loser. I had worked at the most celebrated creative agency on the planet. Been the strategist for superstar brands. Been a vice president at a Fortune 50 company, starting their behavioral economics lab. I had a master's degree for fuck's sake, and what had I done with all of that? Pissed it all away. I had never managed to build any job security. I was a tap dancer, a bullshit artist, and the thing about bullshit is that it works until it doesn't. The lady screaming for her package was right. *Take responsibility*. Take responsibility for throwing your life away. Mom and Dad were right too. I hadn't amounted to a hill of beans.

Alicia came into the room.

"How about you take a bath? It might make you feel better."

"Sure. Okay." I was The Kid now, catatonic at the wheel on the side of the road.

When I slipped into the tub, Alicia came to talk to me.

"Babe. Those texts you sent me today . . ."

"Yeah?" It came out angrily, because I was angry.

"You can't do that to me. I know you are hurting right now, but you can't just blast me like that. It hurt me. It hurt the girls too. Everyone is worried about you."

"Everyone is worried about me because I'm a goddamned loser."

That's when the tears started. Whatever it was that had been carrying me to this point—stoic resolve, a white knuckle grip on my selfhood, a sense of adventure, grit, mania, fantasy, prayer—it was gone. What was left was grief. And fear. The precarity of life, my ability to take care of my family. The wild card of my cancer. The terror of recognizing how fragile my sanity was, that it was something so easily broken. Under everything, madness.

While I sobbed, naked in the bathtub, Alicia didn't leave me. She didn't stand there, gawking at the spectacle of it like those jackasses in their pickup trucks while Kat was stuck in the ditch. She just waited with me. She did not leave me alone.

In psychologist Viktor Frankl's *Man's Search for Meaning*, Frankl says that even when everything has been taken from you, you can choose your attitude: "Between stimulus and response there is a space. In that space is our power to choose our response. In our response lies our growth and our freedom." I had always thought this idea was bullshit. But nude in the bathtub, a grown man crying, I felt that space. Thanks to my wife's love, her patience, her endurance, I had that moment to decide.

I was done feeling angry. I was done feeling like a loser, done thinking that way about myself. People needed me. Inside me, instead of the depression's usual swamp of rotting plant matter and tar, I found something else: a door. All I had to do was step through it. Maybe it had been there the whole time, but this time I could see it, and I stepped through it.

It wasn't complete transformation. It wasn't perfection. But I changed. People who knew me noticed. They said I was different, that it was even visible in how I carried myself. I never told anyone why. It just seemed too woo-woo for public consumption, too out of alignment with the idea of me as a practical, serious person.

But it is the truth.

When I was lost, Alicia came to save me, the way that people who love you will always form a rescue party and come looking for you.

When we are in trouble, the people who love us will come for us in the dark. They will come with flashlights and tow straps and whatever else it takes, if we just call out for their help.

Chapter Twenty-Six

THE THOUSAND NATURAL SHOCKS

CARRYING THE MAIL IS A PROFOUNDLY PHYSICAL job. White-collar work just isn't. Your body is a vehicle for your brain and mouth. You think, you talk, you type. And while you can imagine what it is like to carry the mail, to case it up, to load it, to drive a route, what is almost impossible to imagine is that just like *The Matrix*, you cannot be told what it is like to inhabit a human body in all its frailty while you deliver the mail. You have to experience it for yourself.

Take a look down the carriers' area, starting with the city carriers. They all have fantastic calf development. But it goes deeper than that—with a few notable exceptions, they all have very similar body types. Broad-shouldered, stocky. Strong legs. Some of this had to be physical adaptation to the job, but part of it must have been survivorship bias: only the carriers built this way survived long enough to become career carriers. There were a couple of exceptions: the wiry tough and the just plain big and strong. But there were no willowy ballerina types, no moody bird-chested emo guys. In middle age, hell, in their thirties city carriers looked like NFL players at the end of their career—and I'm not talking Tom Brady, supple from yoga, a zillion-dollar anti-inflammatory diet, and a deal with Satan. These bodies looked more like the shambling Frankenstein wreckage of Peyton Manning in his final Super Bowl.

Stiff-necked, leg dragging, shot full of corticosteroids, held together with braces, Ace bandages, and an iron desire to persist to that golden day when they would ride off into the sunset of one of the few remaining pensions available in the US labor market. To this there were no exceptions, for under the sun of the US Postal Service the race is not to the swift, nor the battle to the strong, no favor to men and women of skill; time, chance, and orthopedic injuries happeneth to them all.

The job just grinds you down. According to OSHA, the average American on-the-job injury rate is 2.8 per 100 full-time employees annually. For Postal Service employees, it is 7.0 for every 100 workers, although what I saw at the Blacksburg MPO looked far higher than that. If you're wondering, this injury rate is higher than for coal mining, construction, and being a police officer. Loggers, oil-drilling workers, garbage collectors, and roofers have us beat, but that's it. And none of those statistics factor in working during a pandemic.

Rural carriers didn't avoid injury, they just got different ones. Blown-out lower backs from sitting splay-legged in privately owned cars. Torn rotator cuffs and neck injuries from driving with your left hand and then reaching across your body and behind you, over and over. The rural carriers weren't as lean as the city carriers, in part because they simply didn't get the walking. My soft information-worker hands got rougher. My grip got strong enough that I could pinch large parcels by their edge and carry them that way.

To every physical test there is a season. The heat of summer stops being a conversation point and becomes something to survive. Forget hot yoga. Until you've spent a ten-hour day in an aluminum box being heated by the sun, you have not been hot. If I saw a hose in a customer's yard, I would sometimes just hold my head under it. The way my blood would cool would give a whole-body high, the relief was so great. I learned to keep a mini cooler with me in the mail truck, loaded with ice. I'd keep frozen bottles of water and Gatorade in there too. I'd cut the Gatorade fifty-fifty with water, because it's actually too salty right out of the bottle—you'll lose water drinking it.

There were customers, beloved customers, who would leave coolers on their porch for us. Coach Fuentes did not distinguish himself as the football coach at Virginia Tech, but his wife had built an aid station for us on her front porch—a big cooler full of all sorts of drinks, particularly the letter carrier favorite, Frost Cherry Gatorade. She also left out Nabs, candy, gum, even Chapsticks. I never met her in person, but I would have crawled under machine-gun fire to deliver her mail, simply for that thoughtful act of human kindness. Her packages were laid on the ground like each and every one of them contained a million-dollar Ming vase. I did my damnedest to be gentle with all my customers' packages, but I'd be lying if I said I treated her the same as all the rest.

I had some customers on my Aux route down near Merrimac who, in the winter, would put out hot coffee in a thermos and donuts. I ran into them one morning, drinking coffee and taking in the sun on a warm day in a cold season. They were a young, good-looking couple, with toddlers. And they still took the time to leave something out for us carriers, to notice our humanity.

"Hey Mr. Mailman, can we pour you a cup of coffee?"

"I will never turn down coffee," I said. "I just don't have a cup."

"Oh don't worry about that. Take a mug and just leave it in the mailbox next time you come through."

Kat was the career carrier on the route, and when I mentioned the couple, her face lit up. A cup of coffee goes a long way in a cold world.

To those folks down on Merrimac Road, to Mrs. Fuentes, and all the others who took care of us that long, overloaded pandemic year, I want you to know that Saint Gabriel, the patron saint of letter carriers, is waiting to wave you through the pearly gates to your special place in heaven. We took notice of your kindness and we loved you for it.

Winter and the cold. Jesus wept it was cold. There is a special kind of cold in the winter in Appalachia, what I've called Appalachian Misery

Training (AMT), when we would take Scouts out camping in it. I would prefer the zero-degree dry-prairie cold of the upper Midwest any day over the harsh winter weather of the Blue Ridge. In the full-freight version of AMT, the leaves are gone from the trees, because the wind has stripped them off and now those polar winds could run free. The sky is gray, and it is raining, a cold rain continuously threatening to turn to ice, but never getting down to it. The wind runs the show, moaning through the trees and gusting up the valley. I would look up the road and watch the raindrops maintain level flight, suspended in air, water swirling in vortices around trees, rocks, mountains. It was like being the test body in a wind tunnel. You could see the slipstream play out as it chilled every living thing in its grip. I've been scuba diving in a rock quarry in the dead of the North Carolina winter, and I was never as cold as I was delivering the mail.

In time, I learned to dress for the weather. In the summer I wore fly-fishing shirts I could unbutton to ventilate a bit. I wore a buff, to keep the sun off my neck, and shorts, worn commando. For the cold, it wasn't just "dress in layers." You needed layers that would insulate even if they got wet—synthetic long johns and wool. I would wear a beater Patagonia base layer, an old Merino wool sweater over that, and then my blue USPS fleece with the reflective tape sewn into it. If it was really windy, I had an old Gore-Tex raincoat that was tough. The jacket had pit zips and those were critical, because if you got too hot you would start to sweat, and in windy wet weather a degree above freezing, sweating into your clothing was the shortcut to hypothermia. I had a wool neck gaiter and knit cap and both of those were incredible because soaking wet they still kept you warm. Finally, I had a pair of fingerless Glacier Gloves. My fingertips would go numb, but that's why jackets have pockets, so toughen up, buttercup.

All of the above gear was my personal equipment. All of it should be standard issue for rural carriers. None of it is. I inherited a bunch of top-flight gear from backcountry fly-fishing and backpacking, and that's because I had the time and means to accumulate it before I started carrying the mail. What most rural carriers wear is whatever they can afford. As insane as it is that we are expected to buy our own vehicles to deliver the mail, the fact that our government sends rural carriers out into the heat and the cold with nothing but warnings to drink water and stay warm is criminal. I don't mean this rhetorically. Carriers die every summer from the heat. What the USPS needs is a sponsorship from Patagonia and Carhartt. Carriers deserve tough, technical gear that is right for the job, made in America.

If you think this instructional unit in cold-weather mailwear indicates I invested a lot of time and effort into dressing for the job, you are right. I spent a lot of time designing a modular clothing system for letter carriers, in my mind. I engaged in this rage ideation because I learned about dressing the wrong way the hard way. In the Blue Ridge, it wasn't the heat but the cold that almost got me.

I was carrying Route 10. It wasn't even winter yet. It was November, and we were having a cold snap. Cash had called in sick, so I got called in late. By the time I got into the MPO, someone had taken Cash's FFV, Old Faithful. Instead I got a leftover FFV from the motor pool. I soon found out why the FFV was available. The heater didn't work.

I had left home in a rush, dressed in jeans, running shoes, a cotton T-shirt, a gray fly-fishing shirt, and my US Mail baseball hat. And I didn't realize how cold I was getting until I was finished with the Corporate Research Center. Still, this was Route 10. I only had another hour to go. How bad could it be?

The rest of the route turned into Zeno's Footrace. The first half an hour took thirty minutes. The next fifteen minutes took thirty minutes. The next seven and a half minutes took thirty minutes. Each slice of time seemed to take longer and longer as I got slower and slower. I felt like my body was a robot that I was programming by voice command. I watched my hands working like they were distant bionic prostheses operating on the ocean floor. As I finished the daycare center, the fraternity, and finally the cancer center at the tail end of my route, I realized something was really wrong. As has happened whenever I've found myself in serious physical danger, I fell back on my training from the Boy Scouts.

Long exposure to the cold and the elements? Check.

No longer feel cold? Check.

Slow mentation, confusion? Check.

Skin pale or even bluish in tint? A quick look in the side-view mirror confirmed that I had a light blue tint like the belly of a small-mouth bass. Check.

A bubble of a thought rose into my mind, as from a great depth. I had been shivering a while ago. Now I was no longer shivering. My movements driving the FFV were clumsy and uncoordinated.

I was a case study for a First Aid merit badge. I had a moderate case of hypothermia.

When I got back to the MPO, I parked the truck, carried all my outgoing mail back to my case, and dropped it onto the workbench. It felt like it took half an hour just to zombie-walk the distance from the loading dock to the rural carriers' area. In the men's bathroom, my skin felt like the room was furnace-hot, but my insides felt like the ice cream in a Baked Alaska. I got into one of the stalls and just sat there, wracked with shivering so powerful that I thought I might be going into convulsions. I could feel my organs shaking inside me, my arms so tensed that they felt strained for days afterward. This feeling went on for several minutes, and I had warmed up enough to start feeling cold all over. My whole body felt refrigerated.

I grabbed my outbound mail, sorted out the forwards, logged in my scanner and the keys to the white frozen eagle death machine, and got the fuck out of there. During my drive home I ran the heat in the Tacoma flat out and I still felt cold, down in my guts. My liver felt like a lump of congealed bacon grease. I drew a hot bath and got in and stayed in. I was in there for an hour until like old Sam McGee sitting in his cremation fire, I finally felt warm.

If you are wondering, yes, I should have gone to the hospital.

Our training had covered very little on hypothermia. The danger they were fixated on was open-toed footwear. We were told every day at the Academy that we were required to wear close toed shoes. I always wanted the protection for my feet, and wicking socks at least kept things tolerable in the heat. There were rural carriers who would change into flip-flops once they were in their POVs, which I get from a temperature control perspective, but I saw it as taking my life in my hands. I couldn't risk gumming up my brake pedals, and I worried about stubbing my toes. I managed to run my foot over once with a parcel float, and that was bad enough in a pair of boots. Plus, traction may not seem like a big deal walking on sidewalks on a dry day. But when you are in the sticks, traction becomes something you think about all the time. Mud, wet leaves, wet grass, black ice, broken glass. In the real world you need real shoes—Danner boots or Brooks running sneakers.

While it is the official position of the USPS that all accidents are preventable, I would argue that even with the right footwear they are not. Not when you are racing the clock, not when the world is an unplanned obstacle course. Out on Big Falls Road one pleasant fall day, I pulled up to an old farmhouse. Big Falls runs along the floodplain of the New River, so almost all of the homes are below you, downhill from the roadbed. This house had two parcels that day, one big and cubical, one smaller, about the size of a Kleenex box. I already had this one mentally rehearsed: turn, grab the big box off the floor, the little one out of the stack next to it, set the emergency brake, leave the door open, cross in front of my truck, and then bound down the sloping, grassy berm to the front porch.

It had rained the night before.

The first two steps went as planned. The third step came down on some wet leaves on wet grass, on a slope. My feet went out from under me. I was looking directly up into the bright gray sky above. Then darkness.

It is the only time in my life that I've actually been knocked unconscious. Choked unconscious? Yes. Blackout drunk? Of course. Nearly blacked out from an accident involving homemade diving equipment? Absolutely. But I had never been knocked unconscious—until then.

When I came to, I was still holding the big package on my chest, like the sarcophageal statue of a medieval king holding a sword. I looked at my G-Shock. I'd been lying there for just under twenty minutes. Big Falls is in one of the radio holes on Route 3. Nobody knew where I was. I wondered how long I would have lain there before someone came to look for me. If I had been cold like I had been on that day when I had hypothermia, that could have been it. Lights-out. It's not even terrifying to think that the space between delivering the mail and death could be a half an hour in someone's front yard. The thought is more existential. The pointlessness of it. What a fucking way to go.

But there were also days the job was exhilarating, like the day I was assigned to assist the Hollins office, nearly sixty miles away in Roanoke. As I was running parcels in and out of apartment buildings, a middle-aged woman with stringy blond hair began working her way toward me, walking right down the middle of the parking lot.

"I SEE YOU." Her voice was deep and operatic. She made eye contact, and like one of the weird sisters from *Macbeth*, pointed an accusing hand at me.

"YOU AREN'T A REAL MAILMAN! I CAN SEE YOU!"

She moved pretty fast for a big lady. Suddenly she was pounding on my driver's-side window, spit flying. We were right there, face-to-face, just separated by the safety glass of my window.

It occurred to me that I should be scared. But I actually started to laugh. Here it was, the zombie apocalypse! This was *fun*.

I slammed the Tacoma into Reverse, goosed the throttle, and put about twenty yards between me and her. All this did was activate her prey drive. But I was in the Tacoma, and there was plenty of room between two oaks on the landscaping strip between the parking lot and the main road. I threw the truck down into Drive, cut the wheel 90 degrees right, and gave the engine the spurs. In a bounding sprint I was over the grass like a rally driver and back into traffic. The lady chased me into the street, but for all her crazy, I had 235 horsepower howling under the hood, and I was behind the wheel of the best goddamned truck on the planet. My friend and companion, a man and his horse.

Joy! I was a Viking! I could take everything that the mail could throw at me and come out laughing. I had a great truck and we were a great team. It was great to be alive! Despite heat and cold and heartache and the thousand natural shocks that insult these frail bodies of ours, I felt more alive than I ever had before. White-collar work never offered physical thrills. I had worked in a climate-controlled environment for almost thirty years, a sensory-deprivation chamber. Working outside with the mail, I felt close to the land, the weather, to my own material person. I wasn't just a brain in a jar. I could scramble hills, dodge dogs, deliver the mail in the dark of night and the noonday sun. My body could do it all. Sometimes, looking out over the valley and eating a 7-Eleven sandwich, I would be struck with how fucking good it was, to be outside eating a sandwich. To be hungry, have something to eat, and then feel full. To be in the rain and have a really good set of raingear, to just laugh at the weather and be part of it. It was so good to be flesh and blood, and know it.

I was also sane, my mind and body and spirit all one thing—and yet I never had a deeper sense that that link could be broken. When Dad was dying just two years later, his body shutting down, eaten up with cancer, his mind was still intact. In the immediate aftermath of his passing, I remember sitting at his desk in what had been my childhood bedroom. Sitting at Dad's desk was always something of a transgression; he was a man jealous of his space. I sat looking over an engineer's pad half full of equations, his Pentel P 205 mechanical pencil resting there, waiting for his return. He was working on new science down to the last minute, brilliant to the end. Mom was the picture of physical health, but by the time Dad died her mind was gone, her body carrying a consciousness that was lost in time and place. Sometimes she was with us; at other points I was her brother, or even her father, decades ago and half a continent away.

To be present in time, in your own body, your spirit intact, your selfhood whole, it is a gift—and it will not last.

Chapter Twenty-Seven

THANK YOU FOR YOUR SERVICE

I HAD A CUSTOMER ON ROUTE 11 WHO HAD MY DREAM subscription list. *New York Review of Books. London Review of Books.* The *Atlantic. Harper's.* The *Economist.* All of the expensive, humanities-major, culture-class publications that even in a more flush time would have felt like a luxury to me. All printed on beautiful paper, so you could imagine sitting in a coffee shop with a big tabloid spread, drinking a coffee and reading about all the books that you were never going to read. It felt good just thinking about books, that people were still out there writing them and reading them and talking about them. When I would reorganize parcels in the truck, sometimes I would read an article or two before I delivered, and it felt like a gift, a lifeline. *Anybody who gets all these magazines is a fellow pilgrim,* I thought. They won't mind if I ask for a favor. So I wrote them a note: *Hello, I am Steve, your mailman on Route 11. If you recycle these magazines, I would be happy to pick them up and recycle them later for you. You have a great selection here.* Jenni, the subscriber, sent me a text saying how happy it would make her for all these periodicals to get a second life, and she left me a grocery bag full of them, with of course the majority by volume being the *Economist.* When the universe arrives at its heat death, there will be nothing left but unread issues of the *Economist.*

When Jenni was ready to recycle again, she would text me and I'd come to pick them up from her front porch. I was driving over to pick up my latest installment when I saw Kat and Jenni talking in her driveway.

"Hey guys, what's up?"

"Jenni can't get her van started, and we can't even figure out how to jump it. I don't even have cables," said Kat. "What are you doing here? Don't you have today off?"

"I do, I was just picking some stuff up from Jenni. What's up with the van?"

"She got the battery charged at the shop, drove it home, now it won't even start."

"How old is the battery?"

It was seven years old. I told Jenni I figured she needed a new battery.

"That's what I was thinking," said Kat. If you are a rural carrier, you know cars the way a cowboy knows his horse.

"Hey, I've got cables and tools, I'll help her out, you go finish your route," I told Kat.

Kat took off and Jenni and I went to look at her Honda minivan. This was a classic computer-designed Japanese engine—everything clicked together like three-dimensional *Tetris*. The two of us weren't even sure where the battery was, but YouTube told us how to get to it. We removed the cold-air intake and got the battery disconnected, then I pulled it out of the engine compartment.

All Jenni needed was for her daughter to drive her to Advance Auto Parts to buy a replacement.

One of the things I loved most about being a mailman was the chance to do a good turn daily. Customers always thanked you when you did something extra, which kept me looking for other chances to help my customers, except for the assholes. If you think your letter carrier isn't keeping a list of who's naughty and nice, you are not living in reality. And letter carriers talk. If you are mean to one of them, we're all going to know. So saying thank you is in your enlightened self-interest. But it's more than that, because while getting thanked feels good, saying it is vital. Transacting makes you a consumer. Saying "thank you" makes you human.

Sometimes I would be thanked just for being a mailman.

On cold mornings, I would load up my truck and then zip across the street to the Starbucks that had been installed in a building that was once a Western Sizzler. If you're driving a postal vehicle, drive-thrus don't work, because the window is on the opposite side of the vehicle from you. I would try to guzzle as much caffeine as I could at home because it was so much cheaper. But on a day of freezing rain, the extended dance remix of the Appalachian misery experience, it was hard to resist the idea of having that just-below-boiling send-you-to-the-burn-clinic hot coffee from Starbucks.

The woman at the register was the manager, midtwenties. She had the look about her of someone who had gone out and worked in the world, then came back to get a college degree.

"You're a mailman?"

How did she know? Oh, right—I was wearing my blue USPS polar fleece.

"What kind?" That's an interesting question because most folks don't know about the city-rural craft split.

"Rural carrier. But the route I'm on is a lot like a city route, down by Smith's Landing, so they give me a postal vehicle."

"Lots of CBUs."

"You were a carrier?"

"Rural carrier. It was brutal, especially when it was cold. I don't know how you do it."

"I don't either some days."

"The coffee is on us today. Stay warm out there, brother."

As long as she worked at that Starbucks, I never paid for my coffee. She wouldn't let me. One time when I was driving the Tacoma, the guy at the window said, "Manager said that mail carriers don't pay for coffee here. Have a nice day!" Through the drive-thru window I could see her, and she threw me a quick wave. Through that window she saw a past version of herself on a cold day—but she also saw me, about to head out into the weather and do a cold job.

I'd like to thank her, for the coffee, for carrying the mail, and for her kindness.

I drank a lot of coffee that year. I had been a coffee drinker for a long time. I started drinking it as a treat when my granny would make it for me as a boy—Community Coffee, roasted in Baton Rouge, where Granny was from. She made it for me with a lot of milk and sugar. By the time I was in college I drank it black, the terminal state for all hardcore coffee drinkers. When I was cold and wet, it felt like there was a missing organ in my body that needed filling up with the hottest coffee I could lay my hands on. If I was near a McDonald's or a 7-Eleven, I'd kill off twenty ounces of that garbage-grade stuff as soon as look at you, because it was black and made out of coffee. On a cold day, if you had boiled an old sock filled up with Folgers in a hubcap I would drink it and thank you for it.

Which is how I found myself another day in the drive-thru line at the McDonald's in downtown Blacksburg. I ordered a large, black coffee and when I pulled up to the window a young Black woman at the pass took one look at me and said, "You're a mailman?"

"Yeah, got a truck full of packages to deliver. Felt like my coffee tank was empty."

"This coffee is free for mailmen. My uncle and my granddaddy were both mailmen."

"Wow. Thank you!" I don't know if the coffee was donated to me by the McDonald's Corporation or if this young woman bought it for me. What I do know is that this simple act of kindness elevated things above a simple transaction and into something more humane.

And then she said something surprising.

"Thank you for your service."

"You're welcome," I said reflexively. "It's my pleasure."

But driving away, I went from the warm mailman glow of free coffee to a feeling of fraud, guilt, even shame. I had never put my life on the line for anyone, much less for an ideal. I wasn't a soldier or a front-line worker in a hospital during a global health crisis. I was a guy who needed health care for his family, who at times felt like he was cosplaying a mailman. I didn't deserve to be thanked this way. But I took it. Because when you are given something valuable that you don't deserve, that's called grace.

I'd like to thank all the people at the USPS for everything they gave me. For all of their help as I learned to do their difficult job as best I could. For the humility I was taught. For the chance to test myself. For the opportunity to be a part of something so much larger than myself, a national story, the long route the US Postal Service has carried through this country from its creation to the present day.

To all the grandfathers and grandmothers, moms and dads, aunts and uncles who carried the mail, and who made the USPS the most beloved service provided to the American people, thank you. To all the mail handlers, the clerks, the city carriers, and most of all my brother and sister rural carriers, I want to thank you for every day you do your vital job. It does not go unseen. We see you and we love you.

Thank you for your service.

Chapter Twenty-Eight

PANCAKES

AS A MAILMAN, YOU ARE A FEDERAL AGENT ON THE people's business. You never set the route. You go where the mail takes you.

One weekday morning, the geographic roulette wheel gave me a parcel for a family friend: Kathy Rohr, the widow of John Rohr, a public policy professor and former Jesuit priest. Their younger son Mark had been in our Scout troop with David, John, and me. According to Mark, sometimes his dad's old Jesuit buddies would stop by, get drunk on wine together, and talk Latin. The most impressive part of that story is not the speaking of Latin. It is speaking conversational Latin while drunk.

I got excited at the chance to talk to Kathy. It had been years since I'd seen her. But when I rang the bell, nothing.

I looked at my G-Shock. It was still early morning. I had the whole day ahead of me. Mom and Dad were maybe a half mile down the road.

So I did something I never did. I popped in. I wanted coffee.

I had a Faraday bag I kept in the truck for just such occasions, something to block the cellular radio signal from my scanner. If you turned it off, I figured it sent a transmission that you were turning it off. But if you blocked the signal, that was just bad cell coverage, right? I figured that would buy me at least half an hour.

I rang the doorbell and Dad came to the door, dressed head to toe in Patagonia fleece.

"Hey, man! What are you doing here?"

"Just delivered to Kathy Rohr, so I reckoned I'd stop by."

"Come on in, your mother is making pancakes."

As a hard rule, my parents and I did not pop over to each other's houses. It was always preceded by a phone call. Could I bring the girls by? Could you bring the truck over and help me move a tree I just sawed down? The last time I had pancakes over at Mom and Dad's had been years ago, picking up the girls in the morning after a sleepover. They had been little, elementary school age. Having our own families changed the dynamics of things. I had my house and they had theirs. At least that was the story I told myself.

Mom was at the kitchen island in her robe. The electric griddle was out, its cast-iron surface so seasoned it looked varnished. It was old. I had memories of this same unit being operated by my grandmother, who had been gone for over thirty years.

"Can I get you some coffee, Steve?" asked Mom.

"I'd love some."

"Get him the K-Cup," said Dad. "Don't make another pot."

"I'll make a fresh pot."

"Joy! Just do the K-Cup!"

Mom made a new pot.

"That coffee we make is Seattle's Best," Dad said. "That's the best there is. Way better than Starbucks."

"Dad, Seattle's Best is a Starbucks brand. It's how they market the coffee that doesn't pass QC to carry the Starbucks mark."

Dad just kept looking at the TV. "Seattle's Best is the best there is."

Mom caught Trump on the news as she looked out over the griddle. They had remodeled the kitchen. Instead of the old yellow Formica countertop, she was working on a white marblelike surface, the whole room painted white and lit like a surgical theater.

"I hate that man," she said. "I can't stand him. I can't stand the look of him." Looking back, I can see that she was already losing her proper nouns. A few years later, when we were checking her into a memory care facility, she told the evaluator that the president was "Not Trump," which is a pretty solid description of Biden.

"Christ, he's an asshole," said Dad.

"His dumb face. Just the sight of him."

"Maybe you should just turn the TV off?" I said.

"Your father likes the TV."

We got to talking about work, which I said was good. I told them about the Faraday bag, which got a laugh out of Dad.

"You still looking for work?" he asked.

"Yeah, I'm talking to a couple of outfits. I think the economy is warming back up."

The truth was that I was talking to one person, and every time we spoke it seemed like the possibility of a job moved out another month, and then another.

Mom looked up from the griddle.

"The Post Office is a good job," said Mom.

"He's not going to keep doing this, Joy. He's an executive."

"The Post Office is a good job." This from a woman who repeatedly told me that I should look into being a plumber. That they made good money.

"It is, Mom. But I need to get back into my career." My career. The fact was, I needed to get into better-paying money. I really enjoyed delivering the mail, better than most of the jobs I'd worked. But I had a mortgage to pay, and girls that were going to need tuition. The post office just flat-out didn't pay enough, and every passing day our emergency savings got a little closer to zero. As Joseph Conrad said, it's a bad world for poor people. So I was desperately looking for a job I didn't really want to work.

That's when I caught myself. Did I dare to have a real conversation over pancakes in my folks' living room about what I wanted from my work and life? No. Here I was, a grown man of fifty, still trying to impress my parents. I wanted Dad to be proud of me. I wanted Mom to not worry, because if she was worrying about me, she was thinking about me, and if she did that long enough, she would eventually be disappointed with the results.

Standing there in the living room, I was disgusted with myself. That I was still so hungry for something from them.

Those were the last pancakes of my mother's that I would ever eat. Pancakes made the same way for as long as I could remember. The buttermilk powder that came in a round cardboard canister, tan-colored, with a cartoon chef on the label. The same old stainless-steel measuring cups. The scientifically precise way Mom measured everything out, to the gram, lab technician to the last.

In a couple of years, Dad would be dead and Mom's dementia would have progressed to the point where she lacked the procedural memory to follow a recipe, even one she had made hundreds of times. I came over one morning in Dad's last weeks and saw Mom trying to make pancakes for my brother Dave, and the sight of it enraged me. That Dave would ask Mom to make them. That Mom would still try to make them for him. I wasn't mad at Dave. It was my old self-protective anger, masking a deep sadness. Over fucking pancakes.

Because the fact was, I'd never once asked her to make me pancakes, when Dave asked so freely. There was some strange economy of mutual withholding between Mom and me that kept us apart.

It was the randomness of my stopping over, that's why I remember that morning. It would have just been another couple of pancakes out of the thousands I'd eaten in that same kitchen, from the same buttermilk mix, buttered with the same tub of margarine, the same Aunt Jemima syrup. A meal that I could re-create anytime if it pleased me. It would take ten minutes of shopping in any supermarket in America.

I remember eating them, and was there to eat them, because I was a fifty-year-old mailman in my hometown and had delivered a package to an old neighbor and then decided to swing by my parents' place.

I wanted something, and what I got was pancakes.

Those pancakes are no longer available.

Chapter Twenty-Nine

THE VARIETIES OF RELIGIOUS EXPERIENCE IN THE RURAL LETTER CARRIER

I HAD MY FIRST RELIGIOUS EXPERIENCE WHEN I WAS twenty-one years old.

I had been alone, mountain biking out on North Carolina State's Centennial Campus, several hundred acres of rolling hills, bottomland, and newly constructed, completely empty laboratory and classroom buildings, all built in red brick. I loved heading out there alone. Someplace deep inside me, my internal environmental registers were set for Appalachia—deep silent woods, high windswept mountaintops, long empty stretches without any people. The place reminded me of home.

I had spent the day out riding, early May and unusually hot. I was probably dehydrated. I had lost track of time, riding in a long loop through the undeveloped pine woods of Dorothea Dix Hospital, the state mental institution, then down toward campus through the power cut for the high-tension lines that marched into the city from the nuclear plant to the west. If you were going to imagine a perfect spring day in Carolina, this was it. There was a softness to the sky here that Virginia never seemed to have. Everything was flatter, hotter, more pastel to Virginia's hard copperplate edges and cooler palette of colors.

I rolled down a long grade into the built-up area of the new campus, an effortless coast down a red dirt track, then the sudden change in sound of dirt tires rolling over the new blacktop. The new buildings on Centennial Campus were typically unlocked, and I thought I would go in and see if I could get a drink of water from the water fountain before riding back up home.

The window glass around the entrance to one looked green, and I could see into the atrium. The curved aluminum handle of the doors was hot from the sun. Inside, from internal balconies, banners hung from the railings. It was the College of Textiles. Textiles were everywhere.

When I opened the door, I managed one step inside before I was dropped to one knee. Not a voluntary movement, just settling, like kneeling in a pew. Pressed down by something unseen.

I could feel cold air flowing over every inch of my skin, could see the evaporative cooling in real time, see each molecule change state from water to vapor, absorbing heat in the phase change, the fundamental heat exchange of life on earth, the engine that drives the planet's weather happening right there on my skin.

Light flooded in through my eyes. I heard music. Not individual notes so much as chords, some on a geologic time scale, some phasing in and out with the systole of my heart, others at the high piccolo pitch of molecular heat and in a harmonic above that quantum noise. I felt as if this instant was nearly frozen, but at the same moment I could perceive the hugeness of time.

It was a whole-body euphoria, and I felt a oneness with everything. I could see the fractal improvisation of the world organizing itself. Then only moments later came the terror of the sublime. The universe was not only vast, it was indifferent. I was just a single mind afloat in it, a piece of sentient, terrified flotsam in a cosmic foam of white water, reality nothing more than a computer that was calculating itself, from quantum moment to quantum moment.

The feeling passed.

I rode my bike home, shaken. I didn't tell anybody about it right away.

For the following week I had intrusive thoughts that maybe I was suffering the onset of schizophrenia.

I spoke to my roommate Jamie about it. He was a psych major and said that as near as he could tell, I wasn't schizophrenic. I wasn't having any sort of persistent auditory or visual hallucinations.

I told Alicia about it. We had just started going out, and I suppose it was a trial balloon of sorts. *Hey babe, I might be deeply mentally ill*? I guess I wanted her to know that whatever the value proposition she had bought into, part of the cost basis might be a somewhat elastic grasp of reality on my part.

Then I returned to being a relatively normal English major fuckhead for a couple of years.

I had another episode on Urraca Mesa in New Mexico when I was twenty-three. No, there were no drugs involved. I was there as an adult leader with my old Boy Scout troop. We had been out on the trail for two weeks. It was incredibly dry, 2 percent humidity. Just handling water is strange when the air is that dry, the way it almost explosively evaporates. It's New Mexico; high weirdness abounded.

Urraca Mesa was supposedly haunted. The Zuni Indians believed that it held gateways to other worlds. Our last day out, I woke up at dawn, before everyone else, and went to the mesa's edge to see the sunrise. On my way to the outlook, I could see ball lightning floating through the trees, hovering about four feet above ground level. I followed these electric ghosts right to the edge of the mesa as the twilight lifted and the morning stars sang together as they faded before the sun. As the sun rose, red and perfect, I felt it again—that oceanic feeling of oneness, the disaggregation of time and perception down into their component parts. This time I let it just roll through me, my brain a lightning rod to let this transcendent overcharge ground out against the earth.

Then I went and ate a breakfast of dehydrated eggs with my brother John.

Over the years I had a few more. Once on a mountaintop overlooking Los Angeles. Another in the Mojave desert, just me and a great blue heron. These episodes were more than just awe. They were whole-body altered states of consciousness. But by the time I was thirty, they were gone. The union between me the whole of creation became estranged. I didn't have another vision for twenty years, until that day delivering on Anthracite Road, overlooking the New River.

After a twenty-year drought, the raptures kept coming.

In a field along the biggest bank of honeysuckle I'd ever seen, springtime bees were hard at work in their invisible order. A cold December morning, the physics of refraction as the sun cascaded through ice on the trees. In the cold rain, walking a package up a long driveway, feeling individual drops fall from all the way up in the troposphere, the phase change playing out directly against my skin.

I've never been a seeker. I am a student of the profane, not the sacred.

Why me? Why now?

The fact is that religion has always oscillated between terrifying and ridiculous for me. One day, headed into work, as I looked north over Brush Mountain, a Hawaii-grade double rainbow hung over the mountain where I grew up and now lived. The inner rainbow was Technicolor, the outer arc strong and translucent. As a meteorology major dropout, my heart leapt with joy, then fell with the sense that my day was likely to be all downhill from here. I took a picture.

When I started casing up my mail for Route 11, Maggie, one of the regulars, was already casing up Route 2. She said good morning to me. "How are you doing, Steve?"

"Great! There was an awesome double rainbow outside. Look, I took a picture." Proud of my *National Geographic* moment, I showed her my phone.

She exploded into tears. "That's my sister and my niece, crashing on through to heaven!" And with that she rushed off to the women's bathroom.

I stood there, frozen. Cash came over.

"What did I do?" I asked.

"You didn't do anything wrong, nothing at all. It's just her niece died of Covid, and her sister is in the ICU, on a respirator."

When Maggie came back out, Cash came over and talked to her, his voice calm and strong. I felt like an interloper, and I will admit that I was too chickenshit to deal with her raw feelings. I was also scared by the simple certainty with which she spoke about the afterlife, and the idea that the physical world spoke to us about the metaphysical. Rainbows not as refracted white light, but coded information.

Religion was not something that you experienced emotionally in my household growing up. My mother and my grandmother were hard-core Louisiana Roman Catholics. Granny prayed the rosary every day, went to mass multiple times a week, observed holy days of obligation. When I was younger we didn't eat meat on Fridays, until the policy was abandoned at my father's insistence because he was not Catholic and wanted a hamburger on Friday night. My granny thought that if you were in trouble, you should pray to the Virgin Mary. My father was convinced to his last day here on earth that we are all pretty much on our own. Later, as an adult, when I asked him about going to church, all he would volunteer was "What a waste of a perfectly good Sunday morning."

Rainbows, visions, personal revelation, received wisdom—none of that was modeled for me. In my house it was the catechism or the scientific method, take your pick. This was the spiritual as the procedural. I didn't even know someone who had what I would recognize as a personal relationship with the divine until I was in college. While I was working as a nature counselor at the City of Raleigh's day camp, I became friends with a fellow counselor named Sarah. Among a camp staff that seemed long on shotgunning beers and short on debating the nature of free will, she was a fellow traveler, even if I was a hardened materialist and she was some flavor of Pentecostal, something more personal and do-it-yourself than the Catholicism in which she was raised. I guess that was something we both shared, our lapsed Catholicism. Sarah has been a classic Catholic good girl, until she and her best friend were walking along the earthen dam at the recreational lake where they were counselors at another summer camp, this one for Catholics. A summer thunderstorm had blown in, and they had been sent to make sure all the kids were back at the main hall. A lightning strike killed her friend, right in front of her. She said that this was the beginning of her new relationship with God. I told her that if God killed my best friend, it might change my relationship with him too. She said, in her gentle way, "I pray for you, Steve. I want you to know that. I pray for you all the time."

The idea of people praying for me always freaked me out a bit. Either they were talking into a dead telephone, a well-intentioned waste of time, or they were actually doing something, in which case I was making a real mistake by not getting on the phone myself. This is a preposterously literal way of thinking about prayer, but you have to remember, I am the son of an engineer.

When I told Sarah about my religious experience mountain biking on Centennial Campus, she punched me in the arm.

"You drive me crazy! Can't you see? God is talking right to you! You're like a prophet. I wish he'd talk to me like that."

I can tell you thirty years on, Sarah, that he can talk to you too. Just deliver the US Mail.

After being exiled to the mundane for over twenty years, my religious experiences became a regular occurrence. With practice and exposure, it got to where I could sense I was going to have one. I could see it coming, like a wave I simply needed to paddle out for. It became less like a divine mystery and more like lifting weights, feeling good as you walked up to the bar knowing that today was the day you would deadlift four hundred pounds. I could deliver the mail for ten or twelve hours, put in a hard day's work, and be rewarded with a few minutes of religious ecstasy. Enjoy it, like a cold beer at the end of a long day.

These days always featured an early start, waking with the sun.

Long stretches of solitude. Being far enough out in the sticks that there was no cell service helped.

The wind and the weather played a part.

They seemed more likely to happen at golden hour, the world transformed into a Terrance Malick film. That interplay between light and clouds and the land gave things scale.

The last piece was the vista, being small in a vast world. Typically there was a quick transition from the close woods into a wide-open view, a cinematic reveal, a wide horizon and unexpected explosion of space. When I would see everything laid at my feet like that, if everything else aligned, the moment of existential awe dropped into place like someone flipped a switch.

When I was twenty-one and it happened that first time, it seemed to come from nowhere. But at fifty I understood that to have these experiences, my mind needed to be free. Free to weave its own thoughts on its own timetable. I guess I never realized how much I'd given up of myself, renting my brain out to the highest bidder. Delivering the mail was hard, but it wasn't cognitively intense. Now my brain was free to set out into the wilderness. The listening station was back online, the big antennae ready to receive the signals zooming through space. Those signals are always there, but now after a long hiatus I could hear them again.

During my time delivering the mail, I would listen to music on Spotify. There were moments when the music would slow down, like an old reel-to-reel tape recorder flipped to half speed. This slo-mo sound was probably some kind of graceful degradation built into the app, to keep the music from just dropping out if the data stream got slow. Intellectually, I knew this. All I was hearing was the effect of moving in and out of poor cell reception. But as the year wore on, I couldn't shake a superstitious, magical-thinking thought: that in those moments when the music slowed down, it was reality playing musical chairs. If I concentrated, if I manifested it, I could choose the timeline I wanted to inhabit. In physicist Hugh Everett's many-worlds hypothesis, multiple worlds were always proliferating from any given moment in time. The question was, which one was I going to inhabit with my family? What wave of the present would I ride into the future, out of the multiverse of coexistent possibilities? When my Spotify would slow down, I would try to visualize a world where Trump lost, where I could pay my mortgage and afford to send the girls to college, where I got back to my career, where Alicia wouldn't have to worry so much, where my daughters grew up strong and happy, where humanity began to capture atmospheric carbon to sequester it under the earth. I would meditate on these things, offer up my work to them.

On the road, with a truck full of mail, I was praying.

When I had my final vision, it felt different. I knew it would be my last as a letter carrier. I had been applying for jobs. One of them, with a media company, had moved to interviews. I knew that I was on the cusp of change, that my time as a mailman was coming to an end. I didn't know how, but I knew it.

It was a gray day, the undersides of the clouds forming a very visible boundary between clear air and the heavens above, a ceiling over the world. I could see all the way down the valley where I had grown up. South to the familiar spine of Paris Mountain, Ellet Valley, the bottomland with Blacksburg down there like a model in someone's electric train set. My family down there, the gray stone of Virginia Tech, all of it down there, rolled out in front of me. In that moment, reality felt like a game board, like I could reach down and make the next move with perfect, transparent intention. A weight that I had carried with me for a year changed states and evaporated. It wasn't just that my mind felt unburdened, but my body too. To be whole and alive, the goodness of it.

And I thought, for the first time in my life, *Thank you, God.*

What I felt wasn't just oneness—eminent and transcendent—but also gratitude. Gratitude that brought tears to my eyes. My thanks were spontaneous and sincere. Thank you, God, for providing for my family. Thank you for sparing them real hardship. I gave myself over and you used me. If I was created for this moment, and this is how you wanted to use me, thank you for the opportunity. Thank you for the fact that, despite everything, I'm in the right timeline. Because this was where I was supposed to be. If it wasn't the best of all possible worlds, it was pretty damn good, and I knew it right down to the roots of the mountain.

That's what received wisdom feels like, and I hope you get to feel it at some point in your life.

Right now, I have the ordinary work of life to attend to. But one day I will return to the mountaintop.

I'll be asked back.

But not yet, Lord.

Not yet.

Chapter Thirty

THE LAST MILE

I HAD BROUGHT A DRESS SHIRT WITH ME ON MY ROUTE and hung it from the security door rail, where I usually kept my go-bag. My final job interview was this morning, this one with the CEO of the media company where I had been trying to get hired for three months now. There had been no way to move my mail schedule, and CEOs are always hard to get time with. This interview was critical, the last way station between me and a new job, a return to doing market research. So I hatched a plan.

At the appointed time, I pulled over on Walnut Creek, a quiet stretch of dirt road. I changed into my good white shirt, then propped up my phone against my pack so the camera looked out on the pasture behind me. There were horses in the background. This would work. I would simply think office thoughts.

The CEO was charismatic. He liked my big ideas—creating new alternative data for the capital markets, using AI to simulate consumer behavior. He knew I was down in Virginia.

"I love that view from your office. I've been down to horse country down there; my daughter is an equestrian."

"Thank you, yeah. Lots of horse farms down in the valley. Virginia Tech has a big equine veterinary program."

"Are those yours?"

"Mine?"

"Are those your horses?"

"Oh, no. Those are the neighbors'. We've got a black bear that lives down behind our house, though."

"Really!" He was fascinated. People who live in big cities are always thrilled about the idea of wild bears, so I never passed on an opportunity to play up the idea that I lived in a wilderness. From then on, he would always ask about the bear and the horses.

I clicked off the phone with a nervous feeling. For months I had felt like a phony delivering the mail. Now, talking about working as a strategist felt like an act, a pose I had to fake. Maybe this was the future I was headed toward, where everything I did felt fake forever.

It didn't help that I was giving the interview from inside an FFV full of other people's mail.

The vaccine was coming. At an all-hands meeting, the postmaster read a letter that said taking the vaccine was a personal choice. The vaccine was generating plenty of talk on the loading dock.

One morning I was loading up next to Kevin and Diana, who were smoking, Kevin in his soldierly way, hand cupped to protect the cherry from the wind. Diana's Virginia Slim just hung from her lip.

Kevin was talking about the coronavirus. About how people kept saying it wasn't real. "Not real?" Kevin laughed when Diana brought it up. "That virus is as real as a bullet, and will kill you just as dead."

"All I know is that they knocked that vaccine together in five months. There's no way it's safe," said Diana.

"Hey! People need to take this virus seriously!" said Kevin. I thought to myself, *This is good!* Kevin was respected. People listened to him.

"It's germ warfare!" Kevin continued. "In China, the Chinese Communist Party controls the internet. They control the news. They control everything. Think about it, they got a population problem. After that one-child policy, they got way too many men. What does coronavirus do? It kills more men than women. They knew they could kill off a bunch of extra men and hurt America at the same time. China, they play the long game. That was no accident. Germ warfare. The CCP don't give a shit about anybody else, they don't even give a shit about their people. They don't give a shit about human rights."

Three people on a loading dock, three different opinions about the pandemic. Safe, unsafe, what I knew in that moment was that things were never going back to the way they'd been before. But I wanted that vaccine, because it worked, and I wanted what the vaccine meant. I was ready to move forward into whatever came next.

A week later I got an email from the Virginia Department of Health saying that vaccinations were going to be held at the Radford University basketball arena, just one town over. All letter carriers and folks from the other delivery services were eligible. I printed out a few copies of the email and gave them to Cash. People would listen to him. Cash was the one who went carrier to carrier, letting people know. Beyond the stand-up meeting with the postmaster there was never any official communication about the vaccine to the USPS workforce.

I was given the day off to get vaccinated and drove to Radford. The basketball stadium was full of letter carriers, UPS people, FedEx people, hundreds of us. I saw my UPS guy from the CRC and waved hello. I wondered how anything was getting delivered in our part of the state. I hadn't been around this many people in one place since the whole pandemic started. It was shocking, all the people, all the energy in a big public space.

Then I recognized my old therapist, Jane, even with her mask on. I was suddenly like one of my customers, overwhelmed with seeing someone from the outside world, from the Before Time. She was there volunteering. When she hugged me, it felt like things really were changing.

It was an incredibly well-run operation, and in thirty minutes I was done. I was vaccinated.

Things were not going to go back to "normal." But they were changing into whatever came next, a timeline in which I would no longer be a mailman.

In the stadium parking lot, I saw I'd gotten an email from HR at the media agency.

I got the job.

When I told Alicia, she said we had two hundred dollars left in our emergency savings.

We'd made it.

It wouldn't start for a month, so I looked into health care options to see if I could get a couple weeks off of work before I had to start my new job. I had delivered a lot of flyers about Medicaid, so I thought I would see if I qualified. After a few minutes on the website it was clear that from my current income, I qualified.

Jesus, I had qualified all along.

The story I had told myself, that I needed this job for the health care, the story that led to me delivering the mail for a year, it wasn't true.

You have got to be fucking kidding me. I couldn't believe it. I could have simply applied at the start of everything, when I got laid off. I hadn't needed to do any of this.

Once, I would have cursed myself for being so stupid. Instead I sat in silence.

What was it all for then?

It was so I could be a mailman.

It was time to go. I had a new job, I had made up my mind. I'd give my supervisor Chuck my two-weeks' notice at the end of my shift.

I was carrying Route 11 that day and had a package for Mabel, one of my favorite clerks, who had retired just a couple of months before. I hadn't gotten to say goodbye. Kat told me to stop pulling out Mabel's mail from the case. That's how I learned she had retired.

It was raining that day, a heavy spring rain. The package looked like a box of candy, and even wrapped in a Kroger bag and slipped inside her mailbox, I was worried that it would be ruined. To be honest, I would have done this for any customer, but especially Mabel. She had been part of a couple of rescue parties for me, and whenever I had a question and Kat wasn't around, Mabel could always give me an answer.

I had never been down her road before. She lived on a spur road off Merrimac, where all the mailboxes were mounted on a rail along the hardball road. I looked up her house and set off. About a mile down, the road crossed a creek. It was nothing small, as we weren't far from the New River. The flow was about fifteen yards across, and angry from days of rain. It was up at full flood stage, the water frothing a chocolate brown. Mabel's house was on the other side of that creek. I gave the water an eyeball, checked in with old Cabrito, dropped the transmission into four-wheel drive, and eased him in.

I could feel the rocks shifting around under the wheels. The force of the current started to push the truck downstream, even though I had nosed in pointing upstream to avoid going in broadsided. About halfway across, the water came up to my windowsill. I was about to turn into a submarine with a truck full of mail. For the only time driving the Tacoma, I wished I had one of those aftermarket snorkels mounted on the air intake. I feathered in the throttle, giving it the power slowly, to keep from breaking traction and we climbed out the other side. A close-run thing.

I got out of the truck and was checking the sidewalls of my tires when a kid on a quad runner came blasting up the road I had just driven down, throwing up rooster tails of mud behind him.

"Hey, man! You got to cross down there, at the low-water bridge. I don't even know how you just did that!" He was shouting over the roar of the water.

"Dumb luck?"

"Guardian angel, more like! Let me show you how to do it."

He coached me back over the low-water bridge, which I couldn't even see because the water was so turbid. On the other side, he pulled up to my window.

"You know Mabel Summers?" I asked.

"She's my aunt."

"I got this candy for her. I didn't want it to get wet in the mailbox."

"I'll get it to her."

"Tell her Steve says hello. Get it to her, okay?"

"I promise, mister. I'll get it to her."

I didn't know it, but I had just done my last stupid thing as a letter carrier.

When I got back to the office, Chuck was at his desk. I had always liked the guy. He was a city carrier who had stepped up into the rural supervisor role.

"Hey man, I've got to give my two-weeks' notice."

"Got a new job?"

"Yeah."

"Is it a good one?"

"A real good one. More like what I was doing before."

"We always wondered how long you were going to be here."

"I really enjoyed it. It was hard. Really hard, but I enjoyed it."

"Listen, you don't have to give me any notice. Heck, most of the time, people just stop coming in, so I appreciate you telling me. If you want to be done today, you're done. We've got things covered. It's okay."

"That's it?" I guess I was expecting some hand-off of duties, something with more ceremony to it.

"That's it. You were a good carrier. You can come back any time. We'd love to have you."

We shook hands.

I handed in my badge, walked out, got in my truck and sat there. I hadn't really had the chance to say goodbye to anybody. But I wasn't a mailman anymore. I was just an ordinary person again.

Just another white-collar ghost with a job that nobody understands.

So I went back to ideas work, knowledge work. I went back to it grateful for the salary and the benefits. But I returned without the sense that it was everything. Without the sense that my job was me.

Like my granny would often say, a man earns his keep by the sweat of his brow. But work does not define us as humans. What I had missed in my decades of corporate life, the fundamental confusion I had labored under, was that work was reality. All those years I had been working, the world went on. The sun on the clouds in the morning. The goodness of a decent lunch. The privacy of your own thoughts. The love of your children, the great gift of being a father in a loving family. I had been prodigal with the abundance of life. Being a mailman gave all of that back to me. I cannot imagine a more precious gift.

By accident, I took a government job, a service job, midway through the journey of my life. After decades of quietly feeling less useful than other people, feeling like I wasn't doing any good in the world, being part of something—even something as mundane as the Postal Service—made me feel whole. I think the distinction between white-collar work and blue-collar work is a false one. Both forms of labor want all of your time and both exact a toll. One form is no more or less noble than the other. The real distinction is between work and service, and I think it's one of the great dividing lines in American life. I wonder if part of how we've become so atomized is that while we all work, few of us serve. It is service that gives life meaning, and it is service to our community and our nation that gives the ideas of "community" and "nation" meaning as well. I think sometimes that if it were possible for everyone in their late forties and early fifties to do a year or two of service—a sort of AmeriCorps for the middle-aged—the country would be a more unified and civil place. Voting every four years does not create a common love of country. Service does.

So while I went back to my PowerPoints and Zoom calls, I'm trying to carry forward with me this sense that I am part of the fabric of my town and of this nation's collective story. One of my favorite things to do, still, wherever I travel, is to stop and talk to the people carrying the mail. We are brothers and sisters. But service is more than just treating letter carriers and postal clerks with kindness. Service is why I started volunteering to help with the polls on election days. Service is why I became part of the adult leadership of my daughter Walker's Scout troop. Because my father was a Scoutmaster, and doing this service makes me feel closer to him. But being a Scout leader means volunteering your time to raise other people's children to be good people and good citizens. "Community" feels like a word that is often abused. But a good Scout troop is like an extended family, where the kids have fellowship beyond sports and school, and the adults have friendships beyond work. It is service that makes community real. I found it in Scouts. Other people find it at the Interfaith Food Pantry, or helping rescue dogs. Without service, all that's left of a town is real estate, parking lots for human souls and excess capital. Service creates belonging, and belonging makes us human.

The thing I carried with me, after thousands of parcel boxes and hundreds of thousands of letters, was this sense of belonging in the world. If I learned anything in my year carrying the mail, it is that I *am* Appalachian. Not the bullshit Hollywood version of ramshackle trailers and rusted Chevys up on cinderblocks. The strangeness of these mountains, the way that the spooky and the sublime seem to be lurking in every fold of these hills . . . I was put here to see these things. This green place is my home, and while I sometimes feel like a stranger in my own country, I grew from these creeks, sprang from the same stones that have carried the Grants for more than two centuries. If my scientist father had not been born in these hills, I don't think he would have had his almost cellular feel for fluid dynamics, the turbulence of water, his instinctive grasp of how the physical world works. In its high grades and rain, its rocky freestone creeks, that tumbling complexity is everywhere here.

My father always seemed like an inalienable part of the landscape, sprung from the living limestone. On our last fishing trip together, Dad and I floated the New River in fall, fog on the wide water. Together. Not father and son, just men fishing on the water. We were laughing. Ripping strikes from the bass. Bald eagles and osprey. Blue Herons wading, feathers and lightning with golden eyes. Dad and I close, like the way we'd been when I was a boy and we would go canoeing together. No history for either of us, just fishing. Dad caught a massive catfish. I caught an adolescent bass, then a Musky—a dinosaur fish from outside time—swallowed it whole, and now I had the great beast on my line, my rod bent into an upside-down U. We laughed at it—the randomness, the glory of it, that we were part of it. That we were together when it happened. I get to keep that, Dad and I together in that moment forever. I was in the place I was meant to be, deposited there by the same forces that shaped the river.

I've learned to recognize that my home is in this timeline, this moment, in this slice of space. Alive with my family, with Alicia and the girls. To keep our home and stay here on the mountain for now. To abandon torturing myself with counterfactuals, to end the ceaseless *might-have-beens*. To simply see the things in front of me, what was actually there all along. The holy fire that drives the world. How it burns inside the people that I love.

That year on the road, carrying the mail, I was working my way home.

I didn't set out to deliver the mail to figure out who I was or where I belong. I joined up to get health care for my family, and maybe have an adventure in the bargain. But working for something bigger than myself reconnected me with my family, with my town. With the mountains and, yes, America. The job was not an endless banquet of beauty. It was work. There were days I prayed for the job to end. For an end to feeling like my family's livelihood hung in the balance. For the uncertainty of the future to resolve. Yet, when it was all over, I missed being a mailman. I still do.

I miss the feeling of being a pilgrim on the people's business. The cool expansive feeling of being a solitary man, alone on the road. Driving a truck full of mail with the mountains out in front. Seeing folks at home with their families, working, eating together, being together. The sense that they're waiting for me. Waiting for letters and magazines and drugs, swords, seeds, tools, and machine parts. The stuff they don't want, garbage and unsolicited junk, disappointments or just the avalanche of the mundane, another day where it feels like nothing special is happening. But it is, it's happening every single day.

The people are waiting.

The whole world is coming with all its inevitability—promises made and broken, cookbooks, novels, instruction manuals, histories of the distant and recent past. Live chicks and live crickets. Scientifically formulated dog food in fifty-pound bags. Photos of loved ones, yearbooks, letters of admission and rejection. Prayers for intercession and pleas for money. Birthday cards, Christmas cards, love letters. Ballots, newspapers, notices. The whole of life in all its fullness is coming whether you want it or not. It's there, waiting to be picked up from that black metal box at the end of the driveway.

And what's in it? Knowing, not knowing. The hope that things will change, or that they will stay the same. Devoted words from family, children, friends, and lovers. Words that carry weight, confessions, business, love, anger, and then just junk, all the trivialities of life. All of it carried in hope and determination, carried up and down a million highways, roads, sidewalks, and footpaths. In the heat and the snow, at daybreak and heartbreak, in the light and in the dark.

We carry it for you. That is the letter carrier's work. Since this nation's birth, we have carried the mail for you—your endowment, yours just for having the good luck to be born American or having the heart to become one.

We carry it. And then we head home to our families and brace ourselves. We pray for strength and then get up and do it all again. To the last mile. Every letter, every parcel, every day.

Every day a miracle.

Blacksburg, Virginia, USA

November 2024

ACKNOWLEDGMENTS

YOU WOULD NOT BE HOLDING THIS BOOK IN YOUR hands if it were not for my agent, David Granger, at Aevitas Creative Management. He saw my initial notes and convinced me it could be a book. He led me through the proposal process and has been a friend and mentor. That a titan of the industry thought this should be a book, and believed that I could write it gave me "exogenous confidence" when my own internal instruments said otherwise. Granger, thanks for your belief in me, for your partnership and friendship.

Priscilla Painton is the editor in chief at Simon & Schuster, and it was her vision that brought this book to that storied publishing house. It was her decision that turned me from an agency guy with an MFA into a published writer. Priscilla, thank you for bringing *Mailman* to the preeminent nonfiction imprint in the world. It's been an honor.

It was Priscilla who paired me up with my editor, Megan Hogan—a brilliant polyglot with the professional calm of an astronaut—and that was a chess master move, because Megan is the one who pulled this book out of me. As a first-time writer, working with Megan felt like I was flying left seat with a gifted instructor pilot. Megan's care and precision brought the best out of me. Editing is a weird job, part technician, part therapist. Megan was a fantastic partner, and I was blessed to work with her. Megan, thanks for your patience, your intelligence, and your insight. I loved working with you, and hope I get the chance to do it again.

Andrew Essex is the only reason any of this happened. When I got hired at Droga5 over a decade ago, Andrew didn't want to talk advertising. He wanted to talk about books and writing. His friendship has been a form of grace in my life. He's given me three jobs at this point, helping me provide for my family. Andrew, thank you for all your support over the years, but most of all thank you for your friendship. If a guy from the Blue Ridge and a guy from Queens can be friends, there is hope yet for this republic.

Elena Dussaq Cash has been my closest colleague and friend at work, across many years and many different firms. Writing a memoir while working full-time, standing up a new business unit inside a massive global juggernaut is maybe the most challenging thing I've ever done professionally. This was all happening during my father's passing and all the transitions that brought along with it. I would never have been able to get either job done, much less maintain my sanity without Elena's love and support. She was my rock, and another person without whom this book would not exist. Elena, I don't even know where to start, but your friendship has been one of the great blessings of my life. Thank you for everything.

Adam Nelson has been my unofficial ambassador to the British people, a fantastic tennis partner in the world of ideas, and the best of friends. It was Adam who read some of the first rough drafts of what would become this book, and who told me that I *had* to write it. It was another one of those signals from the universe that maybe people really did want to read a book about delivering the mail. Adam, thanks for never giving up on the world of ideas, and for the precious gift of your intellect, enthusiasm, and the occasional shipment of Crunchie bars.

Dustin and Sam and all the carriers at the Blacksburg MPO are the reason I was able to learn to carry the mail and actually do the job of letter carrier for my time at the USPS. Dustin, you were a great teacher, and as the new shop steward I am sure the rural carriers are in good hands.

Sam, I wouldn't have made it without your support and kindness. To all the crafts, to the letter carriers, clerks, mail handlers, and maintenance people that keep the USPS running for the American people, thank you for your service.

Todd and the whole Flinchum family are the "relatives we chose." Todd has been the third parent to our girls, and a hell of a reader and editor. Thanks, Todd, for being part of our family, and for your steadfast love and support. We are blessed to have you in our family and to be part of yours.

Dante Harper has been my friend since I was nineteen years old. His generosity over the year it took me to write this book was fundamental to finishing it. Without the farm up in Guerneville, and the magic of the cabin in Blue Jay Canyon, I never would have had the headspace and time to get this done. Dante, thank you for being there, for reading some very rough drafts of this book, and for keeping me focused on what it took to get this book done. I've been blessed to be your friend for over thirty years.

Mathilda and Walker Grant did not volunteer to be my daughters, but they did volunteer to work with me carrying the mail during our short postal partnership. As they have applied for college and different programs, I've read in their essays how the loss of my job at the start of the pandemic shattered a feeling of economic security that I've been working to repair ever since. But you never would have known it at the time. They carried that for me, a burden far beyond their years. It was their resilience and good spirits that inspired me to keep going in that difficult time. Girls, being your father has been the single most important job of my life, and getting to work with you, even briefly, is one of my most treasured experiences. Thank you for all your love, your indestructible joy, and the great blessing of being your dad.

In the predawn of a crisp October morning, in 2024, northbound on 460, El Cabrito, my beloved 2012 Tacoma, gave the last full measure of his devotion. A string of deer leapt in front of us, hidden in the brush along the median strip of a four-lane highway. If you know deer, once one crosses, the rest will go to suicidal lengths to stay together. I dodged three, but the fourth was unavoidable. The Tacoma took it hard in the front bumper, just left of the centerline. I pulled to the shoulder and surveyed the damage. The old boy's heart had been punched in: radiator folded like a tortilla, transmission cooler trashed, the entire front end crushed. The airbags didn't even deploy. The truck was totaled. I had imagined we'd be together through my retirement, maybe a couple of decades left in the powertrain. But it wasn't meant to be. I was heartbroken. The Tacoma and I shared the deep bond that sometimes develops between a man and his machine, and he will always be my mail truck. I'm glad he at least had a hero's role to play in this book. Thank you, old friend.

Dad was always going to be a big part of this book, just as he was a big part of my life, particularly in our decade together in the mountains. His passing as I wrote this book was both a tremendous blow but also a gift. Just after he died, he came to me in a dream, dressed as he would be for winter backpacking in his Patagonia silks and a knit cap. He told me I had to use all my tools, and his too. It being Dad, he then proceeded to list all of his tools and fly-fishing gear: socket sets (both metric and SAE), screwdrivers, electrical and plumbing tools, power tools, rods of every weight, his reels and line, his waders, and an exhaustive cataloging of all his fly-tying equipment, including the instructions for the Cream Sulphur fly pattern he had invented for the eastern waters of West Virginia. He was a big man, and he left a big hole in my life. Dad, I am sorry you were not here to see this book. You were always excited to hear about my latest project. But in addition to your tools, literal and metaphorical, the biggest gifts you gave me were an insatiable curiosity about the world, and an appetite for taking on the big jobs of life. Thank you, Dad, for our time together, and for a lifetime of hard work for all of us. I know what that means now. Thank you.

If there is truly one person without whom this book would not exist, it is Alicia. For thirty years, since we were kids really, she's been there for every crazy idea, for every elusive dream and scheme. It was Alicia who agreed to let a grown man change careers at fifty, even if it was under extraordinary global circumstances. It was Alicia who told me to write this book, as I shared my latest stories from carrying the mail. It was Alicia who turned everything upside down so I could work a full-time job in marketing strategy, while also working to bring this book in on deadline, helping me deal with the aftermath of Dad's death. It was Alicia who kept the lights on while her moody and occasionally deranged partner brought this story to life. Alicia, there is too much to thank you for here. Thank you for your love.

ABOUT THE AUTHOR

STEVE GRANT has worked professionally as a management and marketing consultant for over twenty-five years. His career has spanned consumer psychology, behavioral economics, brand strategy, and product development. Steve has worked as a strategist for Omnicom, Havas, Droga5, and TCS. He helped lead the behavioral economics team at Prudential and was the founder of their Behavioral Science Lab. He has worked as an adjunct professor at Virginia Tech teaching consumer behavior and was an instructor in Tech's startup curriculum. He is part of the film collective who made the 1998 indie film *The Delicate Art of the Rifle*, and holds a Master of Fine Arts in Poetry and Fiction from the Iowa Writers' Workshop. Recently, he worked as a strategist for the Boy Scouts of America, leading the effort to rebrand that organization as Scouting America.

He now speaks on midlife learning and resilience to both private industry and academia.

Born New Orleans, Louisiana. Raised in the Blue Ridge Mountains of Virginia. Eagle Scout.

If you'd like to consider Mailman *for your next book club pick, you can find a reader's guide along with photos, maps, and interviews on Steve's website: stevegrantworks.com.*